MADAM WAR CRIMINAL

OLIVERA SIMIĆ

Madam War Criminal

Biljana Plavšić, Serbia's Iron Lady

HURST & COMPANY, LONDON

First published in the United Kingdom in 2025 by
C. Hurst & Co. (Publishers) Ltd.,
New Wing, Somerset House, Strand, London, WC2R 1LA

© Olivera Simić, 2025
All rights reserved.

Distributed in the United States, Canada and Latin America by
Oxford University Press, 198 Madison Avenue, New York, NY 10016,
United States of America.

The right of Olivera Simić to be identified
as the author of this publication is asserted by her in accordance
with the Copyright, Designs and Patents Act, 1988.

A Cataloguing-in-Publication data record for this book
is available from the British Library.

ISBN: 9781805262862

EU GPSR Authorised Representative
Easy Access System Europe Oü, 16879218
Address: Mustamäe tee 50, 10621, Tallinn, Estonia
Contact Details: gpsr.requests@easproject.com, +358 40 500 3575

www.hurstpublishers.com

Printed and bound in Great Britain by Bell and Bain Ltd, Glasgow

This book is based on the author's extensive interviews with former Bosnian Serb president, Biljana Plavšić—to date, the only high-ranking female politician ever to be prosecuted and sentenced by an international criminal court for crimes against humanity.

I would prefer to completely cleanse eastern Bosnia of Muslims. When I say cleanse, I don't want anyone to take me literally and think that I am insinuating ethnic cleansing. But they've attached this label 'ethnic cleansing' to a perfectly natural phenomenon and characterised it as some kind of crime.

Biljana Plavšić, magazine *Svet* [The World],
6 September 1993

Some things happened during the [Bosnian] war ... for example, ethnic cleansing. They [the ICTY] think that it is something terrible. I can freely say I did not pay attention to that at all. Simply, I did not care much about it. I had been ethnically cleansed together with my family. So what? I was happy that we were all alive.

Biljana Plavšić, personal communication,
15 August 2023

CONTENTS

Acknowledgments   xi
Chronology   xiii
Characters and Places   xvii

Introduction   1
1. Meeting Biljana Plavšić   19
2. Personal and Professional Life   45
3. Indictment and Detention   91
4. In Jail   131
5. Out of Jail   159
Epilogue   175
Annex I: Judicial Documents   193
Annex II: Correspondence on and from Plavšić   201

Notes   215
Index   243

ACKNOWLEDGMENTS

My work draws from the invaluable studies others have undertaken into mass atrocities. I am deeply grateful to those who have laid these foundations. This book has been a long time in the making, and many people have supported and nourished me throughout the years of writing it. There were times when I did not believe I could do justice to this project and questioned whether it would ever come to an end. I am grateful, in particular, to Professor Susanne Karstedt who has always believed in its significance, and provided ongoing encouragement and advice. My thanks also to Professor Barbora Hola and Professor Vladimir Petrović for reading and commenting on earlier drafts of the manuscript. I am grateful for their support over the years and for the hours of collaborative thinking and conversing about many issues that are raised in this book. Their work has been inspirational, and their expertise and friendship greatly appreciated. I have also benefited greatly from conversations with Professor Alette Smeulers and Professor James Gow. I am deeply grateful for their input and collegiality.

Professor, lawyer, and acclaimed writer Philippe Sands has been a wonderful mentor and a gentle supporter from the beginning, pointing out the importance of this monograph to the burgeoning scholarship on war criminals, a field to which he has made immeasurable contributions. Many colleagues around the world have shared their enthusiasm for what I have undertaken, and I thank them all for their encouragement and the questions they have asked, including: 'When will you finish the book?'

I am grateful to the team at Hurst Publishers, particularly my publisher, Michael Dwyer for believing in my vision and bringing this book to life. I would like to thank my editor, Denise Taylor, for her invaluable feedback and support throughout the writing process. I have appreciated her comments and engagement with this project, which significantly improved the manuscript as a whole. I would also like to extend my sincere thanks to the two anonymous peer reviewers for their thorough review of my manuscript. Their insightful suggestions have significantly enhanced the clarity and rigor of my work. If any errors or omissions have crept in, they are my responsibility alone.

Last, but not least, I am grateful to Goran, Andrej, Elise, Ugi, and Iggy for reminding me what life is all about.

CHRONOLOGY

1990

Biljana Plavšić enters politics. From late 1990 until the outbreak of the Bosnian War in 1992, she served as a member of Bosnia's collective presidency.

1992

1 March—Bosnia's Muslims and Croats vote for independence in a referendum boycotted by the Serbs.

5 April—The European Union recognises Bosnia's independence. War breaks out. Serbs, led by Radovan Karadžić, besiege the capital of Sarajevo, the start of the longest siege in history.

8 April—Biljana Plavšić resigns from Bosnia's collective presidency.

22 May—Plavšić leaves Sarajevo under death threats and joins other party members in proclaiming the Serbian Republic of Bosnia. She serves as vice-president under the president and Serbian Democratic Party (SDS) leader, Radovan Karadžić.

1993

January—Bosnia's peace effort fails, and war breaks out between Muslims and Croats, previously allied against Serbs.

CHRONOLOGY

1994

March—US-brokered agreement ends the Muslim-Croat war and creates a Muslim-Croat federation.

1995

11 July—Bosnian Serb troops, under the command of General Ratko Mladić, capture the eastern enclave and UN 'safe area' of Srebrenica, killing about 8,000 Muslim males in the following week. The UN war crimes tribunal in The Hague indicts Karadžić and Mladić for genocide and the siege of Sarajevo.

August—NATO starts air strikes against Bosnian Serb troops.

14 December—The three leaders sign the Dayton Peace Accords which end the fighting and recognises the Bosnian Serb Republic (Republika Srpska) with minority power in the country's joint presidency.

1996

July—The West forces Karadžić to quit as the Bosnian Serb president. Plavšić breaks with the SDS in 1997 after publicly accusing Karadžić of amassing a fortune through an illegal smuggling ring.

September—Nationalist parties win the first post-war election, confirming Bosnia's ethnic division. Plavšić becomes president of the Bosnian Serb Republic (Republika Srpska).

1997

Having being indicted, Karadžić and Mladić go underground.

1998

Plavšić is defeated by a Serb ultranationalist in her re-election bid.

CHRONOLOGY

2000

December—Plavšić receives her indictment.

2001

10 January—Plavšić voluntarily surrenders and is transferred to The Hague.

2002

12 February—Former Yugoslav president, Slobodan Milošević, goes on trial charged with sixty-six counts of genocide and war crimes in Bosnia, Croatia and Kosovo.

2 October—Plavšić admits guilt and is sentenced to eleven years imprisonment. She is transferred to Hinseberg Prison for Women in Sweden to serve her sentence.

2004

11 June—the Bosnian Serb government makes a landmark admission—that Serbs did indeed massacre thousands of Muslims at Srebrenica on Karadžić's orders.

2006

11 March—Milošević is found dead in his cell in The Hague before the end of his trial.

2008

21 July—Radovan Karadžić, one of the world's most wanted men for planning and ordering genocide, is arrested.

2009

26 October—Plavšić is released early from prison after serving nine years of her eleven-year sentence.

CHARACTERS AND PLACES

Local Characters

Alija Izetbegović was a Bosnian politician, lawyer, Islamic philosopher and author, who in 1992 became the first president of the newly independent Republic of Bosnia and Herzegovina. He was the founder and first president of the Party of Democratic Action. An ICTY investigation of Izetbegović ended with his death from heart disease in 2003.

Radovan Karadžić, a psychiatrist and poet, is the former Bosnian Serb leader and president of Republika Srpska convicted of genocide, war crimes and crimes against humanity. He is serving a life sentence in a British prison.

Nikola Koljević was a Serbian politician, university professor, translator and essayist, one of the foremost Yugoslavian Shakespeare scholars. Koljević served as the Serb member of the presidency of Bosnia and Herzegovina alongside Biljana Plavšić, and was the vice-president of Republika Srpska during the Bosnian War. On 16 January 1997, he tried to commit suicide by shooting himself in the head and died a week later in a Belgrade hospital.

Momčilo Krajišnik was a Bosnian Serb politician, and the right-hand man of Radovan Karadžić. They co-founded the Bosnian

CHARACTERS AND PLACES

Serb Democratic Party (SDS). In 2006, the ICTY found Krajišnik guilty of the deportation, persecution, murder, extermination and forced transfer of Bosnian Muslims and Croats. He was sentenced to twenty-seven years in prison. He died in 2020.

Slobodan Milošević was the president of Serbia from 1989 to 1997 and president of the Federal Republic of Yugoslavia from 1997 to 2000. Milošević was indicted by the ICTY in May 1999 during the Kosovo War for crimes against humanity in Kosovo. Charges of violating the laws or customs of war, grave breaches of the Geneva Conventions in Croatia and Bosnia and genocide in Bosnia were added a year and a half later. Milošević died before the trial could be concluded.

Ratko Mladić is a Bosnian Serb who led the Republika Srpska army as a general during the Yugoslav wars. He was later found guilty of committing war crimes, crimes against humanity and genocide by the ICTY. He is serving life in prison.

Franjo Tuđman became the first president of Croatia and served from 1990 until his death in 1999 following the country's independence from Yugoslavia. During Tuđman's life, neither of the ICTY's first chief prosecutors reportedly considered indicting him. In 2002, the new ICTY prosecutor, Carla del Ponte, said in an interview that she would have indicted Tuđman had he not died in 1999.

International Characters

Madeleine Albright was an American diplomat and political scientist who served as the 64th US secretary of state from 1997 to 2001. During her tenure, Albright considerably influenced American foreign policy in Bosnia and Herzegovina. She died in 2022.

CHARACTERS AND PLACES

Carl Bildt is a Swedish politician and diplomat who was prime minister of Sweden from 1991 to 1994. Bildt was a mediator in the Yugoslav wars, serving as the European Union's special envoy to the former Yugoslavia from June 1995, co-chairman of the Dayton Peace Conference in November 1995 and High Representative for Bosnia and Herzegovina from December 1995 to June 1997. From 1999 to 2001, he served as the United Nations' secretary-general's special envoy for the Balkans.

Bill Clinton is a retired American politician who served as the 42nd president of the US from 1993 to 2001.

Carla Del Ponte is a former chief prosecutor of two United Nations international criminal law tribunals. In 1999, she was appointed prosecutor for the ICTY. Del Ponte remained the prosecutor for the ICTY until 1 January 2008, when she was succeeded by Serge Brammertz.

International Criminal Tribunal for the former Yugoslavia (ICTY) was a United Nations court of law that dealt with war crimes, including crimes against humanity and genocide that took place during the conflicts in the Balkans in the 1990s. It finished its work in 2017.

Jacques Paul Klein is a retired American diplomat who served as head of the United Nations Mission in Bosnia and Herzegovina (UNMIBH) from 16 July 1999 to 31 December 2002.

Thomas Miller is an American diplomat and three-time US ambassador. He was ambassador to Bosnia and Herzegovina from 1999 to 2001.

Stabilisation Force in Bosnia and Herzegovina (SFOR) was a NATO-led multinational peacekeeping force deployed to Bosnia and Herzegovina after the Bosnian War. Although SFOR was led by NATO, several non-NATO countries contributed troops.

It was replaced by the European Union Force (EUFOR) in December 2004.

Carlos Westendrop is a Spanish diplomat and politician who was the second High Representative for Bosnia and Herzegovina, from 1997 to 1999. The Office of the High Representative (OHR) in BiH was created in 1995 immediately after the signing of the Dayton Agreement, which ended the 1992–5 BiH war. The purpose of the High Representative and the OHR is to oversee the civilian implementation of the Dayton Agreement.

Places

The Kingdom of Yugoslavia was a country in southeast and central Europe that existed from 1918 until 1941 when it was invaded by the Axis powers. The Kingdom of Serbs, Croats and Slovenes was its official name from 1918 to 1929, but Yugoslavia [Land of South Slavs] was its colloquial name due to its origins. The official name of the state was changed to Kingdom of Yugoslavia on 3 October 1929.

Federal People's Republic of Yugoslavia (FRY) was established in 1945 when a communist government was installed.

Socialist Federative Republic of Yugoslavia (SFRY) was established (renamed) in 1963 and became a federation of six republics: Croatia, Montenegro, Serbia, Slovenia, Bosnia and Herzegovina and Macedonia. It lasted until 1992 with the break-up of Yugoslavia occurring as a consequence of the Yugoslav wars.

Bosnia and Herzegovina (BiH)—Following the breakup of Yugoslavia in 1992, the republic proclaimed independence. This was followed by the Bosnian War, which lasted until late 1995 and ended with the signing of the Dayton Peace Agreement. The

CHARACTERS AND PLACES

country is home to three major ethnic groups: Bosniaks, Serbs and Croats.

Republika Srpska is one of the two entities within Bosnia and Herzegovina. It covers 49% of the country's territory, largely inhabited by Serbs.

Federation of Bosnia and Herzegovina is an entity comprising 51% of the land area of BiH, largely inhabited by Bosniaks and Croats.

Brčko District is a third unit of Bosnia and Herzegovina with its own local government.

Banjaluka is a regional centre, Bosnia's second largest city and capital of Republika Srpska.

Sarajevo is the capital city of Bosnia and Herzegovina, besieged from 5 April 1992 to 29 February 1996 (1,425 days), acknowledged as the longest military siege of a capital city in the history of modern warfare.

INTRODUCTION

Biljana Plavšić, once a high-ranking political leader in Bosnia and Herzegovina (BiH), and president of Republika Srpska from 1996 to 1998, was indicted by the International Criminal Tribunal for the former Yugoslavia (ICTY) in 2001 for genocide, crimes against humanity and war crimes during the Bosnian War (1992 to 1995). In 2002, she pleaded guilty to one count of crimes against humanity: the persecution of Bosniaks and Croats on political, racial and religious grounds. When indicted and arrested, Plavšić was 71. She became the ICTY's oldest defendant and the first woman to be convicted by an international court since the end of World War II and the first female president to be sentenced by any tribunal in history.[1] Plavšić and Momčilo Krajišnik were the highest-ranking Bosnian Serb politicians convicted, sentenced, imprisoned and eventually released early. Plavšić was the first, and only, woman incarcerated in a detention unit in Scheveningen, The Hague. After more than twenty years in operation, the ICTY, the first international criminal tribunal since Nuremberg and Tokyo, closed down in December 2017.

Plavšić's life has not attracted the same attention as the lives of her male colleagues also indicted for war crimes during the Bosnian War. Why Plavšić pleaded guilty; how she spent her years in prison; and how she reflects on these events after her release encapsulates the direction and focus of my work in this book. At the time of publication, Plavšić was 95, and even after many years have passed since her detention and early release, she has remained unrepentant and untouched by the legal processes against her.[2] Remorse has never been part of Plavšić's story, just as it has not been for many in her cohort. In fact, remorse and acknowledgment of the crimes committed have not been a precondition for what was deemed by the Tribunal as 'successful rehabilitation' and early release. To this day, Plavšić stubbornly believes that she has done 'nothing wrong' and, as she told me many times, 'would do the same again'.

Before the Bosnian War, Plavšić was a university professor, respected scientist, biologist, the president of the Committee for Science in BiH and the dean of the University of Sarajevo's faculty of natural sciences. As dean, she earned the nickname 'Iron Lady' for her tough and cold demeanour. Plavšić was flattered by the comparison with Margaret Thatcher, the former British prime minister who was called the 'Iron Lady' due to her uncompromising politics and leadership style back in the 1980s. Plavšić chuckled mischievously as she recalled, 'I liked that nickname. It suited me well'.

Plavšić was a Fulbright scholar and, as such, spent two years at Cornell University in New York doing botany research. A highly accomplished scientist, Plavšić published over one hundred scientific papers, which have been widely cited in scholarly literature and textbooks. Perhaps this fact—her scholarly profession and higher education—is what makes most academics both uncomfortable and fascinated with her, because she is 'one of us'. Plavšić is a reminder that higher education does not necessarily mean that one is immune to committing crimes. Not only Plavšić, but the rest of the top Serb leadership during the Bosnian War consisted of highly educated people: Dr Radovan

INTRODUCTION

Karadžić, psychiatrist and the first president of Republika Srpska; Dr Nikola Koljević, the Serb member of the presidency of Bosnia and Herzegovina and the vice-president of Republika Srpska, also a well-known Yugoslav Shakespeare scholar; and Momčilo Krajišnik, the Serb member of Bosnia's collective presidency, an economist and finance executive before the war. As Alette Smeulers argues, this is perhaps the most frightening aspect of studying perpetrators of mass atrocities: not the fact 'that this could be done to us, but the idea that we could do it'.[3] As we know, many Nazi leaders were highly educated too.[4]

Described by the Western media as the 'Serbian Iron Lady' and by the Serb soldiers as the 'Serb Empress', Plavšić became renowned for the intensity of her expression of Serb nationalism during the war in BiH. She will continue to be remembered for her infamous and inflammatory rhetoric proclaiming Bosniak inferiority, and for defending the purge of Bosnian non-Serbs as 'a natural phenomenon' rather than as a war crime, justifying the policies of ethnic cleansing with theories of ethnic and racial superiority.[5] Some commentators have compared such statements by Plavšić, which equated a specific ethnic group with a disease or illness, to how the Nazis described the Jews. Julian Borger, for example, describes Plavšić as a professor of biology 'who believed in the genetic superiority of the Serbs. She was an enthusiast for ethnic cleansing ....'[6] Smeulers, in her typology of international perpetrators, defines Plavšić as a 'careerist' wanting power, fame and glory, believing in ideology[7] and ethnic purity.[8] My colleague Vladimir Petrović goes even further. His impression is that in a vitriolic spectrum of Serbian wartime rhetorics, Plavšić's statements are simply nearing proto-clerical fascism.

Plavšić was initially charged with two counts of genocide; five counts of crimes against humanity (extermination; persecutions on political, racial and religious grounds; deportation; inhumane acts); and one count of violations of the laws or customs of war (murder). Plavšić was the only high-ranking official and the first Serb leader to plead guilty to one charge—persecution—raised against her before the ICTY. After entering into a plea bargain and serving two thirds of her eleven-year sentence in a Swedish prison, she was released early and flown to Belgrade in 2009, where she has been living ever since. She was welcomed to Serbia with the highest accolades.

Representations of Plavšić's violent female identity and agency have been produced and reproduced by scholars and the media, shaped and governed by dominant discourses. During this time, Plavšić has become 'a story told by others' rather than being able 'to spin' her personal version of the events.[9] Although she had opportunities to speak to local media on several occasions in the past, this time she was acutely aware that her story would be written for and read by an English-speaking audience for the first time. Over the course of seven years, I have spent hundreds of hours doing semi-structured phone and face-to-face interviews with Plavšić. She was in charge of recounting her narrative.

I first contacted Plavšić in August 2017 with the aim of conducting an hour-long phone interview about her post-conviction life. I gained access to Plavšić through my aunt, her very close friend, for whom Plavšić has the utmost respect. After our first conversation, which lasted more than two hours, I received Plavšić's permission to call her should I like to speak to her again. Plavšić was open to telling me her story, on the record and without holding back. After ten hours of phone interviews, she invited me to come to Belgrade and spend time with her. I packed my luggage and flew to spend nine days with Plavšić.

During that time, we discussed all aspects of her indictment, and her life before, during and after her conviction at the ICTY. I attempted to investigate gaps in her accounts and corroborate her recounted memories with deeply researched historical accounts, extensive research in archives, documentation, photographs, film

INTRODUCTION

footage and recorded testimonies. In addition, artefacts, letters and diaries helped me reconstruct scenes she recounted. I studied old photos for clues. I tried to match historical data with what Plavšić told me. The documents helped validate anecdotes and memories. Still, establishing truth is not easy. Memories can amalgamate. My filling in Plavšić's silences and memory gaps risks imprecision. I am aware that Plavšić did not tell me everything she knows and that documents and archives lack data.

She, however, gave me permission to use and publish her personal diaries and letters that she wrote in the Swedish prison as well as other original archives and documents from her time in detention in The Hague and later in Swedish prison. These included trial transcripts, presidential speeches, her private photos, various artefacts from the time when she was president and her typed-up notes about forming the commission on the Srebrenica genocide with arguments why what happened in Srebrenica 'cannot be defined as genocide'.[10] The notes about Srebrenica were made several years after her early release, in the comfort of her two-bedroom apartment in Belgrade, Serbia.

Among her personal files were numerous clippings from local newspapers discussing why Srebrenica 'is not genocide'; original copies of letters sent from the International Committee of the Red Cross (ICRC) asking her for permission for humanitarian convoys to pass safely through the Serb-controlled territory; letters to the ICRC asking for electricity to be restored in some parts of the territories under Bosniak control; transcripts from the Office of the Prosecutor (OTP) in The Hague; letters to and from the United Nations Protection Force (UNPROFOR) to her as a vice-president of the self-proclaimed Bosnian Serb Republic asking her for a safe passage.[11] And so on. These documents are all now in my possession. Plavšić insisted that I take all of her carefully preserved and stored original documents.

In this book, I draw extensively on Plavšić's private archives, which largely consist of unpublished materials such as her speeches and letters, online video recordings, her diaries, wartime reports, and her memories, which are still very vivid and lucid despite her age. I also used court documents, diverse local and international media articles and academic literature to confirm events and timelines. I talked to her former personal driver, and also her media contact person who worked in her cabinet when she served as president. I exchanged several emails with Plavšić's priest, who regularly visited her in prison and who answered some of my questions about Plavšić in written form. Being a religious person, regular priestly visits helped her to cope with her prison experience. Plavšić wrote two memoirs while she was imprisoned in Sweden. These were also helpful to understand her views on her role in the Bosnian War since they cover her life in politics from 1990 to 1998 when she lost the election and withdrew from political life.[12]

The two-volume Plavšić memoirs were written in the Serbian language in Cyrillic characters, and as far I as I am aware, never translated into any other language. Both volumes of her memoirs have been out of print for the past two decades. Second-hand copies can be bought occasionally online in Serbia or at the street book stands in Republika Srpska. In order to decrease potential biases, and provide multiple perspectives, I cross-checked her stories with these secondary sources as much as I could and always found her to be consistent in what she was saying. The benefits of triangulation include reinforcing confidence in the research data and providing a clearer understanding of the problem.[13] Using triangulation as a method helped me to conclude that her views from the 1990s were the same in 2024 when I conducted my last interviews with her. She did not divert from her thinking and beliefs over all those years and decades.

The research has been conducted in both the English and Serbian languages. A significant portion of articles, media

INTRODUCTION

coverage, reports and official documents are exclusively available in Serbian. The inclusion of both languages ensures a comprehensive analysis of Plavšić's political life, subsequent imprisonment and post-sentence, peaceful life in Belgrade. All translations from Serbian to English are my own.

In the course of writing this book, I remained in regular contact with Plavšić. I often called her to ask for further clarification on the topics we discussed. Most face-to-face interviews with her former colleagues were conducted in the Balkans. I elected to protect the identities of my interlocutors by changing their names and the locations of our meetings. I draw on the perpetrators' literature, in particular the work of Gitta Sereny and her conversations with Franz Stangl, the commander of Treblinka,[14] and Albert Speer, Hitler's architect.[15]

The first phone encounter with Plavšić raised issues regarding a lack of remorse, her imprisonment and guilt, which led me to conduct a series of phone and then face-to-face meetings that amounted to fifty-two hours over a period of four months in 2017—all conducted in Serbian—and which provided only the beginning of the answers I sought. More was needed to complete the picture, and I came to realise that the picture may never be completed since there will always be places not visited, words not spoken, stories not shared.

When I started this project, I did not know where it would lead me or how many people close to her would be willing to talk to me. What my conversations with Plavšić demonstrated was that most human beings, even convicted perpetrators, wish to be remembered for the good they achieved, and would never stop trying to justify their acts and omissions.

Plavšić wanted someone (me) to record her story. One of the times that we met, she smiled at me warmly and said, 'I am too old, have no energy and my right hand is trembling. I cannot write. Writing does not bring me peace; it brings difficult memories back'. Seeing her as emotionally vulnerable for the first time, I could not see Plavšić as anything else than a human being. This, and many other subsequent encounters and human moments, would crack open my own prejudices and assumptions that I had about war criminals. I could never imagine them as fully human before.

The principal aim of this book is to understand Plavšić. Understanding her does not mean excusing or justifying her deeds, but redefining our understanding of atrocities. By dehumanising war criminals, we engage in the same categorising processes that helped them to commit the crime: we see them as they saw their victims, as 'less than human', 'as evil', 'as monsters'.[16] In other words, we are engaging in the same sort of reductive thinking that a perpetrator uses to view victims. It would be impossible to achieve this if I had only viewed her, and her actions and statements, in isolation from the external elements that shaped and influenced her life. Indeed, as it has been argued, most perpetrators of mass atrocity crimes did not become involved in violent actions because they wanted to commit mass violence, but rather found themselves enveloped at the frontlines of 'tribal passion' due to their work or group belonging.[17] One could argue that this theory applies to Plavšić. She never committed any crimes before the war broke out in BiH, on the contrary, but once the opportunity arose, her strong 'group belonging' pushed her to extremes. Plavšić told me on many occasions during our conversations that if the circumstances should arise again, she would most likely respond the same way.

Although demonisation of war criminals is understandable on a human level, perhaps even psychologically necessary, it reduces our ability to understand the phenomenon of mass violence and the reasoning of its architects, who are humans just like us.[18] Unpleasant as this is, a scholar of mass violence needs to acknowledge this, with all the risks that it entails. And

INTRODUCTION

the risks could be manifold. It is ethically, theoretically and methodologically difficult to interview perpetrators, and even more so to write about findings, since these can be vulnerable to various contextual and political interpretations. Researchers often confront significant and unique sets of challenges when conducting qualitative fieldwork among people who have been identified as perpetrators of mass atrocities.[19] Jessica Stern, in her book *My War Criminal: Personal Encounters with an Architect of Genocide* recalls a series of meetings with war criminal Radovan Karadžić.[20] She was exposed to harsh criticism for her work. Stern was faced with accusations that she fell under Karadžić's 'hypnotic spell',[21] and that she was 'seduced' by her interlocutor.[22] She was even accused of adopting his views and denying genocide in Srebrenica.[23] As Stern stated, 'The idea that anybody would see me as a genocide denier, which is what many Bosnian Muslims accused me of was just a shock. It was just not what I expected'.[24]

I am acutely aware that my work may be the target of politicisation and misinterpreted. Even before the manuscript was published, I received backlash about the title of the book from some of my acquaintances. To them, and I assume to many other Serbs, Plavšić should not be called a 'war criminal'. Even though she was found guilty of war crimes, some believe that her prosecution and sentencing was unjust. A question will be raised as to why I, an ethnic Serb, would be the one to tell this story. It will probably come from all ethnic communities including those whose members were victimized by Plavšić and her accomplices. I can understand that. However, I am not only a Serb. I am also a scholar trained in international law and transitional justice.

Despite the constant pressures I received throughout the course of writing this book, for me, it was important to find out how Plavšić, a seemingly decent, well-mannered and highly educated woman, could become a war criminal. Perpetrators are often portrayed only through their criminal actions and negative impacts on others, but there are also other realities that I unveiled in my talks with Plavšić that reflect and reveal how unsatisfactory reducing identities to a single label may be.[25] As a scholar, I was aware of the historical value of interviewing Plavšić by spending long hours with her in close contact over the years. On the other hand, and on a personal level, this book was the most difficult project I have ever done. Perhaps this was due to my being an insider during the dissolution of my home country Yugoslavia, and my complicated relationship with my family members, of whom some are fond of Plavšić. I was at a crossroads many times over the past several years and constantly asked myself: Could I simply archive all the interviews and research I have done and continue pursuing my academic career? Or could I explain why listening to people like Plavšić matters? And so I listened to her stories and jotted down notes.

I struggled to be a neutral and attentive listener to a woman who was prosecuted as one of the masterminds of terrible crimes committed in my homeland. Due to years of experience of interviewing victims of mass atrocities, I have learnt the skill of listening intently to my interlocutors without much interruption. I have also learnt to build trust and a rapport with an interviewee, which is an important skill necessary to be mastered for all qualitative field researchers.

With a perpetrator, trust also needs to be built and a relationship developed if the individual is going to be willing to talk freely about his or her experiences to the researcher. I do not judge an interviewee's worldview in the moment. Many perpetrators fail to see themselves as bad people and search for excuses as to why they have committed the crimes. They often do not perceive their deeds as crimes but as acts they had to perform during the course of their duty to protect themselves and their ethnic group. Many simply deny they have done anything wrong, as Plavšić does to this day. Plavšić believes she sacrificed herself

INTRODUCTION

for 'her people' and did not show any ability to critically reflect on her actions but persistently justified and rationalised her behaviour, which she always perceived as highly ethical, moral and legitimate. But some perpetrators wonder—as researchers of war criminals do—why they did what they did, and some will try to manipulate and get listeners on their side.[26] In my interviews with Plavšić, I experienced this too. She wanted me to believe her. It was evident to me that Plavšić felt a strong urge to reveal herself profoundly at the end of her life. During our conversations, I was able to silence my judgement of Plavšić as I listened to her stories, and it became clear to me that curiosity and decency are expected, and necessary, for people like Plavšić to open up.

My dialogue with Plavšić aimed to set her actions within a broader political and ideological context that encouraged and supported her crimes. The richness and complexity of this social context in which crimes were committed is important. And this was the context that Plavšić wanted to explain, wanted to tell, and wanted others to hear. She was convinced that the ICTY could not assess her actions justly by looking at them solely in isolation from all other factors. She told me that she tried to convey her arguments many times, but the judges did not allow her to do so. However, now she could convey them to me with the hope that I will convey them to the wider public. Plavšić could also try to rationalise and justify her own behaviour, which people normally have a strong urge to do, which becomes even stronger when their behaviour violates predominant social, legal or moral rules, and norms and values within a society.[27]

I finished the first rough draft of this book in four years, but it took three more years to finalise it and send it to the publishers. I could never work on it full time, only in between teaching and working on other projects. I kept editing, rewriting, adding new text over time and searching for the right publisher.

11

The COVID-19 pandemic also impacted my writing at the time, and months would pass when I didn't work on the manuscript at all. Ethical and methodological quandaries also impacted my progress. Political scientist Ethan Hollander describes his experience when interviewing a Nazi war criminal: 'It was a little bit like talking to somebody's grandfather and listening to stories about the war, only in this case with that caveat that it's not your grandfather, the decorated war hero, but ... the convicted war criminal'.[28] Plavšić could have been my grandmother or a nice old lady from the neighbourhood, and I had to sometimes pinch myself and remind myself that she is neither—she is a convicted war criminal. However, over the years of talking to her in person, I have seen two sides of Plavšić: one uncompromising, and the other which I was more afraid of confronting—a human being capable of crying, feeling and knowing pain. I struggled with mixed emotions of contempt one moment and empathy the next. I felt ashamed to humanise her to any extent. I tried to feel bitter all the time, but I couldn't.

I have read media and academic articles that portray Plavšić as an evil woman, while the image I have been carrying around is of an old and fragile woman sitting in her plush red velvet armchair, occasionally trembling and breaking down. I keep juxtaposing these images with accounts of the terrible witch hunts against non-Serbs. To experience some kind of understanding for someone who was convicted of persecution and still holds extremist views, as I did with Plavšić, puts one in a compelling and confusing relationship with the perpetrator. Especially when, as was the case with me, my personal and professional experience focused on victims, which placed me in a powerful, empathic relationship with them.

My professional interest has always been in how victims of civil wars made sense of their past and how they lived with traumatic memories.[29] In their narrative, perpetrators often played a prominent role and were painted as less than human because they had taken away all that was worth living for. To survivors, and to me, perpetrators were terrible people who needed to be punished for their deeds. There was no space to even attempt to empathise or understand them until a few years ago. And then my first interview with a war criminal happened to be with a woman who was an ex-president, a professor and intellectual known for being uncompromising and single-minded. I was petrified and nervous most of the time I was talking to her but also curious to find out what she had to say about the years that also marked my life forever. It was very important for me to hear her side, and in order to do so, I knew I would not be able to judge much of what she had to say. And that had its own cost, as I felt guilty for not standing up to her, confronting her more often perhaps, despite knowing that was not possible if I wanted to undertake a series of interviews with her.

At times when I confronted her with some legal facts and evidence, she would snap into a scolding-professor mode, frowning at me. One time, without skipping a beat, she snapped, 'I've already told you what I think of it'. I quickly realised that no matter what I said, she will never change her convictions. I found it hard to stomach much of what she ardently still believed was right, but I buried my emotions so I could wind my way through it all. It was hard to strike the balance and know how far I could go with interrogating Plavšić. I regret not questioning her more, but I was nervous she would have stopped talking if I probed and poked too much. I decided to let her cling to her version of the past, a narrative she has built on hope and fantasy that has allowed her to be welcomed back by 'her people' [Serbs]. Plavšić has sewn together her protective blanket by choosing and reshaping parts of the past safest to remember.

She is a living testament to the limitations of transformation in transitional justice and the failure of rehabilitation as a sentencing aim at the ICTY. Plavšić has neither been rehabilitated nor changed her beliefs after almost nine years spent in prison. I knew I would not be the one to shift her views. She is a complicated and still a very bright woman, and I was cognisant of the fact that if I lost her trust for one second, our conversations would finish immediately. Plavšić was clear about it. I felt like I was walking on eggshells the entire time I spent with her. For the most part, it was an emotionally draining experience. Still, that does not mean that I took on the project without knowing exactly who she was. I never stopped questioning myself and the ethics of my work while working with her. Towards the end of our project, she became increasingly eager to know when the book would be published and why it has taken me so long. She was disappointed and worried that she would die before she could see it. 'You could have written an encyclopedia by now!' the scolding professor exclaimed in one of our last conversations.

Many Serbs feel angry and uncomfortable about Plavšić's stand and admission of guilt in the ICTY. She publicly admitted that the Serbs also committed crimes, so some Serbs still see her as a traitor. 'She should have never done that. Never. Never admit that Serbs committed crimes', her 89-year-old close friend from Banjaluka told me angrily. He, however, never said this to her face. He was afraid of losing his friendship with Plavšić, whom he admired for all her other qualities, such as being 'a good and loyal friend' to him. Although she subsequently withdrew her confession and repentance, many Serbs who still deny any wrongdoing did not forgive her for staging fake remorse.

Another aim of this book is to put the crimes for which Plavšić was prosecuted and sentenced into context, in order to try to explain how she understands her life and role in the crimes of which she was accused. As Lisa Davis argues, 'It is not enough to hold perpetrators accountable for the crimes that take place during atrocities. Justice also requires an understanding

INTRODUCTION

of how perpetrators justify such acts—if justice is to root out discrimination and break cycles of violence'.[30] In that sense, this book will seek to understand what makes 'ordinary' people with no previous criminal record suddenly instigate or commit brutal acts of violence.[31] How could Plavšić, an acclaimed intellectual, be the instigator of radical nationalist politics that saw around 100,000 people die at its hands? How does one woman juggle all these identities? How can someone become the bearer of all of them, all at once? Douglas Kelly, a psychiatrist, observed that the Nazis were not uniquely monstrous and that they could be 'found anywhere'. He wrote:

> No, the Nazi leaders were not spectacular types, nor do personalities such as them appear only once in a century. They simply had three quite unremarkable characteristics in common and the opportunity to seize power. These three characteristics were: overweening ambition, low ethical standards, and a strongly developed nationalism which justified anything done in the name of Germandom.[32]

As will be shown throughout this book, Plavšić and the rest of the Serb leadership were ambitious, holding ultranationalist, extreme views. When historian Christopher Browning published his seminal monograph *Ordinary Men*, he put the perpetrators centre stage and laid the cornerstone for a micro-turn in the study of mass atrocities.[33] Rather than focusing on meso and macro levels, he introduced the individual perpetrator.[34] As Browning argues, in relation to the Holocaust, 'not trying to understand the perpetrators in human terms would make impossible not only this study but any history of Holocaust perpetrators that sought to go beyond one-dimensional caricature'.[35] While the research of perpetrators of mass atrocities has flourished over the last decade, close-contact qualitative fieldwork among perpetrators has remained 'comparatively rare'.[36] As Frédéric Mégret noted, contemporary defendants' perspectives have been considerably

15

neglected in research and literature, and only recently has interest exponentially increased.[37] On the other hand, qualitative fieldwork studies among survivors and bystanders in various post-conflict and post-genocide societies have flourished.[38]

Even more rare are qualitative studies of female perpetrators of mass atrocities. So far, there is scarce research focused on female war criminals.[39] This may be due to the fact that women, since they are less present in combat roles and as rank-and-file members of military groups, presumably commit less crimes than men. There are even fewer women at the top level of the chain of command. All the more interesting then that Plavšić rose to the top of the political and military hierarchy, and from that position profoundly influenced her social environment.

Due to stereotyping, we also rarely think of women as capable of committing ordinary crimes let alone 'extraordinary' crimes, such as crimes against humanity. Female agents are typically overlooked because of gendered assumptions that reinforce the myth of women's 'inherent pacifism'.[40] As Sara E. Brown argues, women have been capable throughout history of acts of heroism but also belligerence.[41] Yet, an overwhelming masculinised interpretation of war and mass atrocities denies women a role in the violence except that of bystander or victim.[42]

Genocide, in particular, for which Plavšić was also initially indicted, 'is more often than not characterised as a male crime, the outcome of contemporary notions of masculinity'.[43] And once women are accused of war crimes and stand trial, they are often regarded as deviant or 'freak mistakes', whose transgression of gender norms that represent women as peaceful, 'beautiful souls' is perceived as particularly shocking.[44] Therefore, this book may lay foundations to pursue further studies of individual female war criminals, especially high-ranking leaders, which would seek to uncover whether, and how, they differ from their male counterparts. This study of Plavšić is the first single monograph of a woman war criminal that is based on close fieldwork with the subject and qualitative research methods.[45]

The victims of Plavšić's politics are an important part of this book, but they are not its subject. I acknowledge that this book may retraumatise many of her victims and that some may find it offensive to give her space to express her views. Her false acceptance of responsibility for war crimes and staged remorse deeply offended her victims. Still, Plavšić's 'storytelling' provides an insight into why leaders choose a perilous path of war crimes and armed conflict rather than peaceful means of negotiation.[46] Psychiatrist Joel E. Dimsdale argues that 'the fine-grained analysis of *leaders* is unique' since we can gain a deeper understanding of not only why and how mass violence occurs, but also what motivates leaders to commit atrocities—and all of this not to exonerate them, but to learn how to prevent future atrocities: by being vigilant and learning how to recognise the signs of leaders sliding into darkness.'[47]

In this book, I reveal how Plavšić's childhood circumstances made her a fierce nationalist from a young age and gradually cemented her nationalist ideology over time. By the beginning of the Bosnian War in the 1990s, she truly believed in ethnic purity and that Serbs needed to protect themselves from the 'other', which transformed her from an ordinary citizen into a war criminal. I listened to her story and documented it to show how she makes sense of her past experience of war and mass violence, which is important when studying individual circumstances and the context in which mass atrocities occur.[48]

Talking and listening to perpetrators gives us perspective as to how they recall their actions, because perpetrators' behaviour is largely determined by the context in which they operate. During a period of mass violence, there is a specific social, political, and ideological context in which perpetrators such as Plavšić incite and/or commit their crimes. The context in which they find themselves can thus explain their crimes. However, once they are taken out of that context, they have an opportunity to look back and reflect on their deeds, often from a considerable distance both temporally and spatially. Such reflections can perhaps, in turn, give us a better understanding of who they are and how they perceive their deeds and make sense of them in their aftermath, as well as whether or not they are remorseful. Researchers in perpetrator studies do this work, not to downplay the war criminals' experiences or forgive their crimes, but to try to understand them.[49] As James Waller notes, 'explaining extraordinary human evil is not exculpatory'.[50] By recounting her experiences and providing a narrative, Plavšić gives meaning to her own behaviour and brings us closer to understanding her, and perhaps the psychological make-up of other war criminals.[51] While every personal history can be viewed from multiple perspectives, this is her account. Though unsettling, it warrants consideration.

1

MEETING BILJANA PLAVŠIĆ

'Madam President, are we going underground?' the man asked the tall blonde woman standing next to him as they took a lift to exit the building.

'It would never cross my mind. I would never do that,' snapped Biljana Plavšić, President of Republika Srpska, without looking at the worried eyes of her somewhat timid but long-serving and faithful bodyguard. Her sharp, clear response and her whole demeanour indicated the end of any further discussion on the topic. He knew his president well enough to never think of contradicting her. 'When she gets furious, you better not be around,' he told me with a wide smile.

This encounter happened in November 1999 when Plavšić and her closest allies learnt about the long-in-the-making indictment coming from the International Criminal Tribunal for the former Yugoslavia (ICTY). Moments such as this, among other intriguing and never-publicly-revealed experiences of his service as Plavšić's former personal driver and bodyguard (MT) were discussed with me over a coffee at the well-known 'Hotel

Bosna' in Banjaluka, the capital of Republika Srpska. It was an unexpectedly warm autumn day in October 2017.

I flew to Banjaluka from Belgrade to meet with MT and NT, Plavšić's former media representative. They both worked in the Plavšić presidential cabinet between 1996 and 1998. I quickly learnt that they had the utmost, almost sacred, respect for Plavšić. With her dark brown eyes fixed somewhere in the distance, NT, briming with joy, told me,

> She is the most generous person I ever met. She taught me how it is possible to live without taking from others. She is a reliable, hardworking, incredible woman. She is from a rich family of intellectuals. She was not thirsty for anything. She went to The Hague with two to three thousand marks (BAM).[1] She could not even pay her own lawyer. It is a shame that she does not have a national [Republika Srpska] pension ... that no one pays for her summer holiday, spa treatments, and that she does not enjoy the honours.

They both still refer to Plavšić as 'Madam President', and they call and visit her when they can. While they knew Plavšić very well, I didn't meet her until 9 October 2017. However, I could have met her before, if I had really wanted to.

Biljana Plavšić and I both come from Bosnia and Herzegovina (BiH), which is a country located in the Balkan region of south-eastern Europe. It is a multi-ethnic country with three constituent peoples: Bosniaks (Bosnian Muslims), Serbs (Orthodox Christians) and Croats (Catholic Christians). Throughout its history, BiH was usually a kingdom, but mostly occupied by foreign powers such as the Ottoman and Austro-Hungarian Empires. Sarajevo, Plavšić's birthplace, was the capital and urban centre of the Ottoman elites.[2] In 1918, BiH joined the country of the Yugoslavs (South Slavs), the Kingdom of Serbs, Croats and Slovenes, later renamed Yugoslavia in 1929. The Kingdom was dominated by Serbs, and the Serbian royal house ruled the new state. The Serbs controlled senior positions in government and the officer corps. During World War II, BiH became part of a fascist puppet state, the Independent State of Croatia (NDH).

After World War II, the monarchy relinquished power to the Communist Party, who controlled the country for nearly five decades. In 1945, the Communists renamed the country the Federal People's Republic of Yugoslavia, and in 1963 renamed it again as the Socialist Federative Republic of Yugoslavia (SFRY). By this point in time, Plavšić had lived in three different countries and experienced various political regimes without moving from the place where she was born. BiH became one of six republics of the SFRY, which lasted until 1992 when the Bosnian War broke out. BiH was ethnically mixed, often called a 'mini-Yugoslavia' because of the presence of a number of different nationalities living together in the small republic.[3] At the time the war began, 43 per cent of BiH's citizens were Muslims, 35 per cent were Orthodox Serbs, and 18 per cent were Catholic Croats. The remainder of the population was composed of significantly smaller minorities, such as Jews, Roma, Egyptians, Ashkali and Hungarians, which are less recognised and often subjected to socio-political exclusion and marginalisation.[4]

The three-and-a-half-year Bosnian War was the most disastrous armed conflict Europe has seen since World War II. Some 100,000 people were killed and 2.2 million people displaced. Families had been split into shards and scattered throughout the world. Sarajevo, the capital of BiH, was under siege from Bosnian Serb militias in what became the longest siege in modern history.[5] In 1995, the Dayton Peace Agreement brought peace to BiH and a new administrative and political structure to the country. The agreement, while confirming the independent state of BiH, internally divided the country into two entities: the Serb-dominated Republika Srpska and the Muslim-

Croat-dominated Federation of BiH, with the city of Brčko as a separate district.

At present, BiH has a population of around 3.15 million people, 1.22 million of whom live in the entity of Republika Srpska. By pure coincidence, and through a chain of war-related events, my aunt and uncle became very close friends with Plavšić during the Bosnian War, and they carefully maintained and cherished that friendship for more than twenty years until they both passed away a few years ago while I was still writing this book.

Plavšić fled her hometown of Sarajevo with her 90-year-old senile mother, and after shifting between a few temporary shelters, the two women settled in Banjaluka in 1995. Here they met my uncle, a well-known doctor, in the local hospital. He treated Plavšić's mother. I was not in the city at that time, having left the country due to the war and resettled for the time being in the south of Serbia. In the meantime, Plavšić became a friend and regular guest of my family. My aunt and uncle spent many afternoons and evenings with Plavšić and her ex-husband, sharing food and enjoying each other's company. At the time, Plavšić was the sole carer of her 92-year-old mother, and a member of the wartime presidency of Republika Srpska.

I only knew Plavšić as a friend of my aunt and as a well-known Serb nationalist politician, and later on as president. I never met her in person during this time. She was a high-ranking Serb politician admired by extreme right-wing Serbs, but despised by Croat and Bosniak ethnic groups for her extreme nationalistic views. She was a regular feature of local media, TV and radio, giving speeches about Serbs as racially superior people and calling on Serb men to take up arms in the war effort. As the years went on, I was both physically and ideologically as far away from Plavšić as I could possibly be.

When Plavšić entered politics, I was seventeen years old. She was sixty, a few generations ahead of me—the generation of my grandparents. My friends were of mixed ethnic origins, and I had never thought about their ethnic background. In fact, I didn't really know mine. My family never celebrated any religious holidays and did not talk about them at home. Ethnic belonging was never the subject of our discussions, but once the war started, my friends and neighbours of the 'wrong' ethnicity (Bosniaks and Croats) had to leave my hometown Banjaluka, typically overnight. I witnessed many of them packing up their possessions from their apartments, often only what could fit in two or three plastic bags. The rest of what they owned stayed behind. In these hurried goodbyes, my childhood friends from my apartment block gave me their memorabilia and souvenirs to keep safe until they could return. But they never did. I still have these 'gifts'. Little did we know back then that we would never live next to each other again. And some of those neighbours I never saw again. Soon after they left their apartments, Serbs who were displaced from other areas moved in. At the time, I did not have the language to describe what was unfolding before my eyes, but later I learnt that what I had witnessed was the beginning of ethnic cleansing and persecution on the basis of nationality: one of the crimes Plavšić was accused of and for which she admitted responsibility.

Back then in 1992, although I knew who Biljana Plavšić was and what she had become, I had no interest whatsoever in her life. I was too preoccupied with my own survival and that of my family and friends. To be honest, I had no interest in politics at that time in my life and had no idea that someone who would become so close to my family was heavily preparing the country to plunge into civil war. Nothing could prepare me for the murder and madness that was about to be unleashed. I could never have foreseen it.

My father, as well as parents of my close friends, could predict that the war and mayhem was about to start with full force. I was even told that I could not go, as I had planned, to study in

Sarajevo because 'Sarajevo will burn next year'. That was at the end of 1991. I dismissed this statement and thought that adults must have gone mad from consuming too much television and political discussions that were heating up during those times. But they were right: Sarajevo did burn next year.

It was not until 2017, when I was researching wartime perpetrators more intensely, that I started taking more interest in Plavšić. I wondered how her life had panned out after serving part of her eleven-year prison sentence in Sweden for war crimes and returning to Belgrade in 2009.

Before 2017, to me, Plavšić represented one of the few key politicians closely engaged in the Bosnian War effort, and whose public statements about nationalism and ethnicism had always sparked strong criticism. I never had the slightest desire to meet her personally; she belonged to a world that from my perspective created turmoil and chaos, and I belonged to a world that was the product of that chaos.

However, in 2017, I considered calling my aunt to ask her whether she thought her best friend Biljana would be willing to talk to me about her indictment and detention. I knew that I was totally unprepared for an interview if Plavšić agreed to talk with me. I convinced myself that I was just 'mapping the field' and saw this as exercising my curiosity.

This sudden interest, and consequent request to use my aunt as a middle woman, was sparked by my decision to edit a special journal issue on the ICTY and war criminals with a colleague.[6] We had several contributors who had committed to write, so, while reluctant at the beginning, I started contemplating the idea of finally embarking on this long-awaited project.

I had an urgent need to understand Plavšić, to unearth moral sensibilities buried under her 'Iron Lady' facade, as well as to hear her reflections on the destruction of lives and the country to which we both belonged. I felt a need to understand the

MEETING BILJANA PLAVŠIĆ

motives of one of the people (and the only woman) who had been intimately associated with the dissolution of my homeland of Yugoslavia before she died. Plavšić was directly involved in the greatest tragedy that the Balkans experienced in the 1990s. She had enjoyed an upper-class life until that time. The period that followed, however, was the most intense of her life.

I had no idea how my aunt, who was eighty-four years old but still a strong, light-hearted woman, would react when I called her from my home in Brisbane to ask her what she thought of my desire to talk with Plavšić. To my utter surprise, she was thrilled. 'Sure, I will ask her. I will call her now. We call each other every week'.

I did not expect such an enthusiastic reply. I told her that I would call her back in two days to see what Plavšić had to say. Neither my aunt nor Plavšić had a computer or internet in their apartments, so I had to phone back to hear the news. Two days later, excited and nervous, I dialled my aunt again and she reported with urgency, 'You can call her now. She is expecting you'. My aunt started to dictate Plavšić's landline number, which, after the first wave of shock and confusion, I clumsily scribbled on top of the pile of papers I had in front of me. I stared at the number while standing over my office desk with the phone squeezed between my head and shoulder.

'I always wondered why you never asked for her contact before', my aunt added in her soft, but slightly puzzled voice.

I stayed silent, but my mind was racing; I opened my mouth to say that I was not ready but the words did not come out. I was staring at Plavšić's phone number in disbelief. Finally, and quietly, I told my aunt I could not call Plavšić that day but I would in a few days. I was totally unprepared for this news. I thought Plavšić would say 'no', as she had said to many researchers before; however, I guessed (and I was right) her friendship with my aunt meant a lot to her, and she did not want to disappoint her.

And so, I spent the next few days building up the courage and clarifying the reasons for my decision to talk to her now. She was nicknamed the 'Serbian Iron Lady' for good reason, as she was well-known for her strong will and directness with her interlocutors, to whom she would bluntly say what she thought.

> When I was serving as the president of Republika Srpska, Kornblum was ambassador of the US in Germany who once came to my office.[7] He was giving a monologue, telling me what I needed to do, trying to boss me around. There were twenty people with him. After listening to him for two minutes, I interrupted him, 'I won't allow you to talk to me like that. You cannot talk to me like that.' I got up, walked towards the door, opened it and turned to him. 'Please, leave my office, you and your delegation.' There was silence in the room. I gave them a lecture. No one ever dared to speak to me like that, and you know what he said? They all got up, him too, and he said, 'Madam President, sorry if something upset you.' I closed the door and said, 'I accept your apology, now we can continue.' That did not happen with anyone else afterwards and that's why other people did not talk to me like that. After I left the presidential office, the ones who took over just did whatever these third-grade bureaucrats told them to do. And of course, money worked its way through too. They could all be bribed.

Plavšić was also known for her resolve to stand against any threat to Serb interests, and for not flinching when faced with death threats from her former allies. She openly spoke about crime and corruption in the highest echelons of Republika Srpska, despite continuous threats to her and her family. Plavšić was the only member of the presidency who paid regular visits to Serb soldiers in the trenches during the war, bringing them cigarettes, blankets and spare clothes. Because of her courage and care for the soldiers' well-being, she earned herself another nickname, which the Serb soldiers wrote over their tanks, *Carica* [the Empress].

MEETING BILJANA PLAVŠIĆ

They [soldiers] loved me, called me Carica, wrote my name over their tanks or simply called me Bilja [nickname from Biljana]. In those wet tranches, often under strong enemy fire, there was someone who could be their mother or sister. If I did not have a convincing answer to some of their questions, I told them that it's all in God's hands, they should pray to him, He will help ...[8]

Some, however, such as Sonja Biserko, a prominent human rights activist from Belgrade, believed that Plavšić had instead 'spent the war touring the battlefields, stirring up the troops,' spreading hatred and encouraging young men to fight.[9] I knew a few private things about Plavšić's life, as I had been asking my aunt and uncle about their close friend from time to time over the years. These enquiries were more out of respect and love for my aunt, as I knew that Plavšić's sentencing and consequent imprisonment was hard on her. I never wanted to know much, and my polite enquiries were superficial. Any conversation about Plavšić would die off quickly between us, and we would switch to another topic.

However, my interest was piqued while reading about international war criminals who returned home, knowing in the back of my mind that I could perhaps get access to Plavšić if I wanted to. After her early release, she settled in Belgrade. I began to imagine and give serious thought to the types of questions I would ask her if I could meet her face to face. And so, I became more curious and eager to talk to her. However, another two years passed from this initial intellectual interest before the phone call to my aunt posed the big question.

Plavšić could have easily died in the meantime due to her age and health, but I did not feel any urgency. Although I still conducted a wealth of research on victims of war crimes, I did not have the slightest interest in the lives of war criminals, apart from what I needed to know as a legal scholar. To go deeper and explore details of perpetrators' personal thoughts and feelings about the crimes of which they were accused did not interest me at all.

I started contemplating the idea gradually from time to time over coffees and lunches with colleagues, mostly international criminal lawyers. They all knew how significant Plavšić was; they were amused and fascinated by the fact that I could possibly sit and talk to her one day. Understandably, Plavšić sparked academic interest primarily in international criminal law circles, but also amongst other fields of scholarship interested in stories about war criminals. Fascination with Plavšić as a war criminal is even more momentous because she is a woman. I asked my colleagues what two questions they would ask Biljana Plavšić if they met her. From these casual encounters, I started to build concrete ideas in my mind. I also emailed my colleagues in different parts of the globe, asking them the same question. Having the same intellectual curiosity, but also the generosity to help me prepare for what was coming, their thoughtful questions to ask Plavšić continued to flow into my inbox. And I gladly collected those questions, knowing I would use them and many more when I finally spoke to Plavšić.

I read every published paper I could find about Plavšić, and watched endless clips, interviews and shows featuring her. I found a Master's thesis, a few academic papers and book chapters; however, curiously, no monograph about her life and work had been published.

On 1 August 2017, I finally called Plavšić. I was nervous and did not know what to expect. My heart was pounding so hard my lips tingled. I planned to talk to her for only an hour, but our first conversation lasted for over two hours. I told her that I wanted to write a paper about her post-conviction life. She was polite but distant. We did not know each other. But I had strong referees—my aunt and uncle—and she told me straight away that this was the reason she agreed to talk to me: 'You know that I would not talk to you if it was not for your aunt and uncle'. After that initial call, she invited me to call her again if I wanted more information.

A week later, I asked my aunt if it would be appropriate to call Plavšić again. 'Of course, do call her. She likes and needs to talk about those experiences. It does her good. Don't be shy. She is a wonderful woman and she won't mind at all', my aunt told me in one breath.

Encouraged by my aunt, I called Plavšić a few more times. After our fourth phone call, she asked me whether I had plans to come to Belgrade soon. I told her that I had just returned from the Balkans and that I planned to return 'next year'. 'I may not be alive by then. It would be easier if you come. I can show you some documents and it would be easier for me to talk', she said in a decisive voice.

I told her that I would try to return sooner than I had planned. Despite the moral dilemmas and traps I could fall into, I thought that it would be irresponsible to not interview Plavšić just for my peace of mind. As a scholar, I felt that her account could be of significant historical value, so I decided to pursue the project. Eventually, I made the decision to go to Belgrade and meet with her in person. I was partially urged by her age but also by her personal invitation. I thought it might be a unique chance to spend many hours, indeed days, talking to her about her life before, during and after the war. I called her and said that I was going to visit in October of the same year (2017) and spend a few days with her so we could go through all the matters she wanted to share with me. I don't think she was very surprised by my decision to rework my original plans and organise my visit to her earlier than I envisaged. Plavšić is a highly self-confident woman, acutely aware of her historical significance, and she likely assumed that, as a young researcher, it would be a once-in-a-lifetime opportunity for me. She was right.

I spent nine days in Belgrade with Plavšić, learning about her life before and after the Bosnian War. I hid the fact from all my friends that I went to Belgrade to talk to Plavšić. I knew I would have to explain my actions, and I did not want to have conversations as to why I was doing it. Plavšić is a controversial figure, and I wanted to avoid being asked about my work with her. At the time, even I was not sure why I had made such a decision.

My first face-to-face meetings with Biljana Plavšić

Nothing could have effectively prepared me for sitting with Plavšić in her loungeroom for nine hours each day, over the course of nine days. Never before in my career had I experienced the breadth and depth of facing such intense emotional, moral and ethical dilemmas. I wrestled with questions: Why was I doing this? Why was I spending my time and energy on this woman, rather than a female survivor of the war? I felt angry, curious, emotional and morally doubtful, but I also knew that there must be more to Plavšić's 'story' than she was charged with. I felt like an interloper but kept reminding myself that this story was not about me, but about perpetrators of mass atrocities, and, through a curious set of circumstances, I had gained access to one.

I rented a small, one-bedroom unit just around the corner from Plavšić's apartment in Belgrade. I needed seven minutes to walk to her apartment, which was in one of those old communist-style grey buildings situated in a narrow street full of coffee bars and artisan bakeries. I would wake up early, stroll down the busy street, have a quick coffee and breakfast and be in front of her door at 9.30 each morning. An extra bowl of cereal with fruit and a banana shake—a breakfast that she ate each morning—would wait for me.

MEETING BILJANA PLAVŠIĆ

'I eat cereals and shakes each day. Do you like them too? I made some for you', she informed me on my first morning.

Although I was not really hungry, I ate out of respect and to keep her company. Her name was not written on her doorbell, and on my first visit I did not know which one of the various surnames (but not hers) I should press. Standing puzzled in front of the building entrance, I had to call her from my cell phone to ask. Plavšić had a fake last name on her doorbell that she spelled out for me while I was waiting on the line. She explained to me once I'd climbed the stairs: 'The police said it is better this way, so people do not know where I live in this building'.

Plavšić lives on the fourth floor, and although the building had an elevator, I climbed the stairs most of the time. I needed to breathe, and it gave me more time to digest what exactly I was going to do and say once I entered her unit—into her world. From the first to the last day of my fieldwork, I was in a state of constant disbelief that she indeed *let* me enter her world, and did so with open arms.

The first encounter was particularly stressful. I was apprehensive and felt totally unprepared. After ten hours of speaking with her over the phone from Australia, there I was standing in front of her door, which had a fake surname. My anxiety built until I felt it could burst out through the ceiling above me. I could almost hear the rapid beating of my heart. I took a few deep breaths and knocked. As the door opened wide, I was bracing myself; my heart thumping, my palms sweating. She stood tall before me. Our eyes met, and she was clearly pleased to see me.

Feeling overwhelmed, my heart beating hard, I stared at her and apprehensively muttered, '*Dobro jutro* [Good morning]'.

In return, she stretched open her arms as if we had known each other for a long time, took a step back and studied me from top to bottom. A light blue cardigan hung loosely from her shoulders. She was beaming. Plavšić said in a soft, almost whispering voice, 'Olivera ... is that you? Olivera ... let me see you. Do you look like your aunt?'

They were questions that required no answers, just simple pleasantries. I stared at this tall, well-built woman with a deeply lined face, sky blue eyes and receding grey hair, the ends softly touching her shoulders. I knew the face—I had seen it in the newspapers, on TV shows and at public hearings screened by the ICTY—but this was the closest I had ever been to her. Here, the only woman who was prosecuted for ethnic cleansing and the tragedy of war stood joyfully smiling at me. I felt as if for the first time, the war took on shape and form. Suddenly, Plavšić flashed her broad smile and drew me into her arms, her warm flesh all around me. I felt like I was suffocating. I was frozen and could not feel my legs below my knees. I was unable to move, nailed to the ground. I had not imagined her to be warm and personal. I had not envisaged breaking the 'objective' and 'neutral' researcher code—even before I had started my research—at the very entrance of her home, on my very first visit. What was I supposed to do? Hug her back or push her away from me? Whatever I chose to do felt wrong. The choice wasn't really a choice.

In our shared culture, embracing someone you think fondly of is not unusual, yet I was still shocked. Of all the possible scenarios I could have imagined for this first meeting, being embraced by Plavšić never crossed my mind. I finally got myself together, returned her smile, and hugged her back meekly with one arm. Her breath warmed my cheek. I could do no differently, nor would it have been wise to do so. The trust would have then been broken before it was established. Still, no one prepared me for this scenario: what to do and how to behave if a war criminal meets you with a broad smile and open arms.

'Welcome, welcome. I am very glad to meet you. Shall we have a coffee?' Without waiting for my response, in her grey flannel

MEETING BILJANA PLAVŠIĆ

trousers and green silk blouse, she shuffled down the corridor to the tiny kitchen to prepare the coffee. I entered the spacious living room and sat on the three-seater couch pushed against the wall. The aroma of coffee and warm bread wafted into the room while I was waiting to be served. Plavšić loaded the silver tray with small coffee cups before me. This was a typical Balkan style of welcoming the guest, nothing out of the ordinary here, apart from who she was and who I was.

From that moment onward I was in a state of constant emotional and ethical turmoil. She did not *look like* a war criminal to me, but a well-mannered, elderly woman. This struggle had started from the first phone call I'd made to her from Australia two months earlier, but it would reach its peak during these intense face-to-face encounters.

I was challenged on many levels as she spoke: I thought about what it meant to be sitting in a living room with the only female ex-president ever prosecuted for war crimes. She did not sit behind her desk and give orders during the war, but went out in the trenches with Serb soldiers; she was in the hospitals visiting the wounded and meeting the displaced and refugees in collective centres. Plavšić was at the centre of the chaos, the blood and the killing, witnessing the forceful removal of entire populations from their homes. She had been convicted of persecution, but she pleaded ignorance to ethnic cleansing that was playing out before her eyes.

Over the next few days, and in particular over the last two days of my visit, we became very relaxed with each other. By the end of my visit, Plavšić—whom I interchangeably called 'Mrs Plavšić' (very formal) or simply 'Biljana' (very informal, which showed my confusion)—switched from using the formal You ('Vi') to the more informal You ('Ti'). I was instructed by my aunt that I should probably call her 'Madam President' or at least 'Professor', but I could not do so. I behaved as I would with any

33

elderly person. I went shopping to buy her groceries, and she insisted on paying for them herself.

Since Plavšić is a heavy smoker, I thought of buying her a box of cigarettes, but her story about Carla Del Ponte, the ICTY prosecutor, wanting to 'bribe' Plavšić with a pack of Marlboro when she arrived in The Hague held me back.[10] I was worried she may misinterpret such an act of hospitality.

Offering food or cigarettes for my interlocutors was nothing strange for me though. I sometimes brought small gifts as a demonstration of my gratitude for a person's generosity with their time. I knew that what I gave Plavšić must be read in the context of my usual fieldwork behaviour and not seen as something to encourage cooperation.

Plavšić had a modest pension and did not enjoy any luxury, at least not that I could see. Apart from a rich collection of books and neatly lined-up pictures—black-and-white and more recent photos in colour of her family—occupying a large wooden bookshelf, her two-bedroom apartment was simply furnished. It was, however, filled with different sizes of religious icons of Orthodox Serbian saints and miniatures of the royal Serbian dynasties.

During Plavšić's time in prison, her brother and his family took care of her home since she is unmarried and has no children. Her ex-husband, with whom she retained a friendly relationship even twenty years after their divorce, passed away while she was in the detention unit in The Hague. My aunt and uncle stayed in her apartment a few times when they visited Belgrade. I heard a lot about it from them at the time, but I never envisaged I would walk through it so freely, and spend many hours in its various rooms and spaces while conducting interviews.

All our conversations, apart from one, were recorded in the big, bright loungeroom and occasionally on her small veranda. She jokingly called the veranda a 'bar', and the lounge room the

MEETING BILJANA PLAVŠIĆ

'salon'. One of the other rooms we used to go through some carefully stored archives over two days was named the 'working room'. Since we spent so many hours in these spaces, she gave them these spontaneous names, and we changed locations frequently so we did not sit in the same place for many hours. It could be that since she spent most of her time in this spacious apartment that she imagined it as her old presidential cabinet, where she was always well-dressed, meeting guests and journalists in her loungeroom for interviews and talks and then having drinks with them on her veranda (aka 'bar').

Plavšić was not willing to go out to a restaurant or coffee bar, although I offered to take her for lunch or coffee. She preferred to stay home, sitting in her favourite plush red velvet armchair, where she spent hours talking to me. Next to the armchair was a small, round wooden coffee table that was large enough to accommodate a coffee cup, ashtray, cigarettes and a lighter—the essentials to get her through the day, as I fast discovered.

'I make one big coffee cup in the morning and then drink it throughout the day', she commented in passing on our first day. She was a heavy smoker, but that did not bother me, as I grew up in the Balkans where most people smoked, including my mother. It is still common for people to smoke inside their houses, even during winter when everything is shut due to the cold. On the right side of her armchair was a pile of newspapers. Plavšić sucked at the cigarette, gazing at the papers next to her. 'Every day I buy a local newspaper [*Politika*], a weekly newspaper, and one trash magazine to cheer myself up', she told me with a giggle when she caught me staring at the pile. I assumed she must spend a lot of time sitting cross-legged in her armchair, her thin, grey-white, silky hair falling over her face while she bent over the newspapers.

Regardless of the fact that we spent almost all our time in her flat, Plavšić never started the day without makeup. Her lips were always sharply defined by carmine-red lipstick, eyebrows plucked and hair neatly combed. A long, thick golden chain with its dangling cross hung around her neck. My impression was that if you treat Plavšić decently, she won't come across as repulsive, but as a likeable woman with a good sense of humour. Now when I think of her, there is an image of her sitting in that armchair in her comfortable training pants and bright silk blouses (she had quite an assortment), surrounded by papers and her coffee mug, with smoke curling around her face. This image is cut deeply into my memory.

Plavšić was well-known for her impeccable outfits and natural beauty. During her studies in Zagreb, she was admired by students and professors, and not just for her intellect. Plavšić was one of the favourite biology professors during her teaching career in Sarajevo; students from other science faculties would flock to listen to her lectures. 'My lecture theatres were always full. Students were often sitting on the floor—it was that packed. I never missed or cancelled one lecture in my forty-year career'. Her voice cracked with emotion. In the mid-1970s she won the award for best teacher.[11]

The living room in which we spent most of our time together was wide and spotlessly clean, sparsely decorated with wooden furniture. Plain chairs surrounded a wooden dining table covered with a snow-white linen cloth. We made use of this sizable oval table, which occupied a space at the entrance into the living room, turning it into what we called 'the office'. On the second day of my visit, Plavšić brought out from the other rooms, and from the chestnut wardrobe in the living room, several worn leather briefcases and carton boxes filled with confidential documents from her hearings and time in prison: newspaper clippings, books, magazines, photographs, albums and diaries. Before putting these on the table, she carefully removed the white tablecloth. The number of documents she piled in front of me was unexpected. These documents were scattered across that table during my stay until the last day when we carefully packed the documents back in the bags and boxes, cleaned it up and returned the white tablecloth as if nothing had ever happened.

But the history had happened. We spent many afternoons at this table going through each item with great care while Plavšić would explain the context. I would sit across from her and tentatively listen, rarely asking questions. I was gathering data, lots of it. I raised questions only if I had to, and occasionally took photos of her and the documents. I was looking at her most of the time, sporadically turning my gaze to the white wall behind her on which religious icons and paintings were hanging. I had to rest my eyes elsewhere when I started to feel dizzy. But these moments of reprieve were short ones, as Plavšić was always searching for my eyes when talking to me.

I fixed my eyes on a striking handmade wooden cross at the end of the table. Plavšić noticed me looking at it and said it was made by General Zdravko Tolimir, a Serb military commander who was handed a life sentence for his involvement in the genocide in Srebrenica in 1995. In 2012, he was convicted of genocide, crimes against humanities and war crimes.[12] A Communist-turned-Christian, Tolimir died in prison in The Hague in 2015, a year after his conviction for genocide was upheld by the ICTY. He became a mystic during his detention and was known for wearing a large wooden cross over his shirts in the courtroom. Tolimir often crossed himself with three fingers three times and occasionally under his breath seemingly cursed the court.[13] Tolimir was one of the most senior Bosnian Serbs to have a verdict handed down by the ICTY and one of a handful of defendants found guilty of genocide. Tolimir and Plavšić knew each other well since he served as a deputy commander for Intelligence and Security in the Bosnian Serb army. From November 1996 to January 1997, he was an adviser to Plavšić before retiring from the army of Republika Srpska. Tolimir and Plavšić spent time together in the Scheveningen detention unit where he made that cross for her. I learnt that a convicted genocidaire became a skilled woodworker, and his favourite craft was making wooden crosses for his fellow inmates. Tolimir was among Plavšić's closest friends during their detention in The Hague, and his passing had a profound impact on her. Her face brightens a little, 'He was a lovely, quiet man. We liked to spend time together and he did some woodwork while there. The wooden cross was his work and he made it specially for me'.

Plavšić loved to talk, and I grew more and more eager to listen to her. We would hardly notice that she often spoke for five hours with no breaks. Each of our days would consist of two 'shifts', as we called them. The first 'shift' would start around 10.00 in the morning and last until 3.00 in the afternoon, and then we would have a lunch break from 3.00 to 5.00 in the afternoon. I used those breaks to breathe and return to my senses. I did not talk to anyone during them, but took long walks trying to gather my thoughts. I would go over some of our conversations and make a few notes here and there. The second 'shift' would start at 5.00 and last until 9.00 in the evening. This is what we did each day for nine days during my first visit. I sat across from Plavšić and talked to her for at least eight hours a day, for nine days in a row. During this time, there were never any discussions about myself, only about her life.

On the second day, she made it clear that she wanted me to take all her original documents and archives. I was astonished. 'But I cannot do that. You must keep them. I will copy what I need', I said in bewilderment. She paused. 'No, you take them all. Why do I need them? To take them with me into the grave? My family told me many times to burn them down to ashes. They mean nothing to me anymore and they can mean a lot to you'. My stomach reeled. Plavšić was looking piercingly at me with her bright blue eyes, her voice gentle and decisive at the same time. Her face was a shade of white.

I very quickly understood why people called her the 'Iron Lady'. Once she decided and said something, it was the end of the discussion. I did not believe she would really give her personal archives to me. I thought she might change her mind as the days went by, but she never did. Still, I did not feel flattered or comfortable. I felt enormous responsibility to preserve those archives and was unsure of what to do with them. I also thought that maybe this move by Plavšić was to make me feel obligated to write a 'good story' about her because she had entrusted me with her private and confidential correspondence and documents. Just before I left, we split the piles of documents and packed them into two big garbage bags that could easily fit into my suitcase. She laughed with mirth at the irony and said, 'Yes, these are the perfect content for the garbage bags. That is how I always wanted to get rid of them'.

On the last day of my first visit, and upon her insistence, I stayed overnight with her. I slept in the small 'working room' in a single bed she made up for me, surrounded by ghosts from the past and present. Next to me, Plavšić slept peacefully in her bedroom.

Despite my internal struggle, the more I came to know her, the more I struggled with my feelings against her. I could see her now as a human being, not just as a war criminal. Notwithstanding her age and health, she took my visit seriously and went overboard to help me understand her life. She trusted me.

'What are we doing today?' was her usual morning greeting.

I could see that she was as organised and hardworking as her former employees and students had told me. I grew to like her work ethic the more time I spent with her, and we spent a lot of intense time together. I respected her wholehearted commitment to work with me, despite a suspicion that that commitment may be purely a result of her strong desire to tell her side of the story.

I found her to be polite, sympathetic and informative throughout all our communications.

During the first two months of my biweekly phone calls to Plavšić, and then across the nine days of our work together, she often consulted her archives and materials, books and photo albums. I was interested in all of it. She told me about her upbringing: how her father, whom she admired, and her close family members were taken away by the Ustaše, who were responsible for 'eliminating' Serbs during World War II.[14] Plavšić even shared, and at the end gave me, her personal diaries that she had handwritten while imprisoned in Sweden. I have used her diaries in this book to support her arguments, translating her handwritten notes from Serbian into English.

I have also seen and taken the handwritten correspondence from her Swedish prison manager and guards. Plavšić showed me letters she received in jail from hundreds of 'admirers' from different parts of the globe—people who simply wanted her signature next to her colour portrait photo that they would enclose in reply-paid envelopes.

She continues to receive such letters.[15] Although many people do not know exactly where Plavšić lives, they have found which building her unit is in. They also learnt that she buys newspapers every day from a local newsstand just a few steps away from the entrance to her building. Her admirers leave sealed envelopes with her photo, asking for her signature, with the newsagent who sells the papers. This is how Plavšić continues to receive letters. However, she kept only a few; the rest she threw away. Plavšić told me she received hundreds of them. I could not fathom how popular she was, and still is, until I saw and read those letters. She shrugged her shoulders and muttered, 'I never replied to any of these. I simply ignored them'. But she kept some of them for all these years, together with other carefully stored documents. They must have meant something more to Plavšić, otherwise she would not have held onto them. I realised later that the letters were telling her something that she wanted to hear: that she had done nothing wrong and that she was admired by so many.

By the time I completed my face-to-face conversations with Plavšić in Belgrade, a special collaborative relationship had developed between us that was to continue for years during the writing of this book. Out of courtesy, but also because we knew that our relationship was not ended by my return home, I called her to tell her that I had arrived safely in Australia.

After all those intense hours of conversation, I could not just take all her private documents with me and disappear. I do not consider that ethical. But was this ongoing working/personal relationship ethical? I still struggle to answer this question. When should/could I withdraw from such a relationship? Once I finished writing, our relationship gradually came to an end. At the time of publishing this book, almost eight years after our first personal encounter in Belgrade, Plavšić and I had spent countless hours talking over the phone. I also visited her in Belgrade three more times. Two years of the COVID-19 pandemic seriously interrupted my work on this book. In 2020, Plavšić contracted the virus and was hospitalised for two weeks. She was 90 at the time. She was in a critical condition but survived and recovered fully in the following months.

I have hundreds of hours of recorded and non-recorded conversations with her and had to select which ones to bring to readers due to the sheer volume of information. I respected her wish to keep some information that she shared with me private, but this was mainly about her encounters with prisoners in The Hague. Plavšić is eager for the world to know what she thinks and feels about her role during the Bosnian War in BiH, her arrest and her imprisonment. 'Will you finish the book while I am alive? I would like to see it before I die', she implored.

* * *

During my nine days with Plavšić in Belgrade in 2017, I treated our conversations as information gathering, and while aware and even in awe of some outrageous statements she made along the way, it was important to not interrupt the flow too often with critical comments, but rather trust the reader of this book to see each claim, each admission and each denial as one more detail in a complex mosaic, which in the end may provide a comprehensive whole.

I wanted to open my mind, if not my heart, and learn about her and myself. I was terrified of myself. I almost preferred to remain in a state of resentment. It felt more comfortable and safe. I was incapable of dehumanising her, and for that I felt guilty. This woman was dehumanised by many who could not look at her without a dose of resentment and disdain, and I felt like a 'traitor' for not being able to feel the same.

I realised how hard it would be for victims wanting revenge. But where would such emotions lead us? Replacing enmity with at least regard for other human beings is important in post-conflict societies such as BiH, where the majority of war criminals returned after serving two thirds of their sentences. I felt revulsion and fascination at the same time. My academic training certainly did not prepare me for how to conduct such interviews and face the woman accused of some of the most horrific crimes.

However, I did realise why I felt so uncomfortable—because she treated me courteously, and I responded as expected–normally and politely. I was almost certain that I would have felt much better about the whole situation if she was terrible to me, but she wasn't. She has never offended me or treated me with disrespect.

Whenever I would slip into sentimentality, I would pinch myself and remind myself of what she 'had done'. I kept reminding myself that my mandate is to contribute to an understanding of why she did what she was accused of and to learn how a woman, a professor like me, became a notorious war criminal. Most disconcerting was when there were moments where our lives connected—talking about academia, university, publications and teaching. You do not expect war criminals to talk about literature, science, the arts and travelling—to have similar interests as you do.

Every time I entered her apartment in the morning, I walked straight into the living room and put my pen, notepad and audio recorder on the table while Plavšić was busy in the kitchen making coffee or sipping homemade cherry brandy, with which we would start our 'second shift' in the afternoon. At the end of our first visit together in Belgrade, while strolling on the street, Plavšić reflected on our long, and often unpleasant, conversations that took place over the last several days. She glanced at me once and said, 'I feel as if I have thrown some garbage out of me. As if I managed to release a big garbage bag that was sitting in my body. I feel better now, I think our talks helped me'. Her declaration made me realise that she'd experienced our conversations and her long monologues as therapy sessions, which wasn't what I had intended. This is one of many quandaries when conducting interviews with perpetrators: they see the interviewer as someone ready to listen attentively to the things that they may have never said before, which in turn can be cathartic for them.

Unintentionally, I found myself in this role of confidant with Plavšić, simply by doing what I have trained myself to do: listening to the interviewee who has given me her time and feels safe enough to tell me things that may not have been revealed before. So, in the end, our conversations were mutually beneficial. I saw this as a unique opportunity to interview someone of her standing. She, on the other hand, saw my interest in her views as a unique opportunity to promote a narrative aimed at convincing the world that she had done nothing wrong.

2

PERSONAL AND PROFESSIONAL LIFE

Biljana Plavšić was born on 7 July 1930 in Tuzla, in the then-Kingdom of Yugoslavia.[1] She was only four when her family moved from Tuzla to Sarajevo, the capital of Bosnia and Herzegovina (BiH). Plavšić was the second child of her father Svetislav, a professor of biology at the local high school, and mother Živana, a housewife. Živana was a tall, dark-haired woman, but pale in complexion. Plavšić told me that all the males in her family were blond and her last name was coined due to that fact. *Plav* [šić] means *blond* in Serbian. The Plavšić men all married women with dark features like her mother. Biljana Plavšić took on her father's traits: she is blonde with blue eyes.

    Her brother Zdravko, to whom she was close, was a year and a half her senior. Every time she mentioned him during our conversations, her face would crumple, and she would shed a tear. Zdravko, once a professor of sport at Sarajevo High School, died just a few months before Plavšić and I met for the first time at her home in Belgrade, and she was still mourning him. The bond between them was obviously strong, and the pain from that loss was still raw at the time. Zdravko had lived with his wife, a retired ophthalmologist, just around the block from Plavšić's apartment, and they had had daily encounters with each other until he, and then his wife, passed away. Zdravko was a rock of support throughout Plavšić's life, especially after her arrest and while she was serving her time in The Hague and later in Örebro, Sweden.

Zdravko and his wife had two sons who both migrated to Canada during the Bosnian War where they settled with their families. One son finished his Master's degree in law in Sarajevo and was about to defend his doctoral thesis when he had to flee. Plavšić told me that his dissertation was printed out and left behind in his briefcase in Sarajevo. 'He typed up his thesis with a typing machine and he had only one copy ... the one he left behind in their apartment'. Her other nephew has a degree in mechanical engineering. Plavšić is close to both of them, and they pay her visits whenever they come to Belgrade. Once they left the country, like many others, they never returned to live in it.

Throughout the war in BiH, Radovan Karadžić as president and Plavšić as vice-president of the self-proclaimed Republika Srpska called on Serbs to take up arms against their Muslim and Croat neighbours with the slogan 'Only Unity Saves the Serbs'.[2] I knew that Plavšić was very active in mobilising Serbs in and out of the country to take up arms and fight in the war. I asked her what she thought about the men who refused to take up arms. 'It was a war and they ran away from it. They should have all returned and fought for their country. I lobbied all the time for men to come back and fight. Our key problem was that we consistently missed people capable of bearing arms and fighting'.

When I pressed her about her two nephews, who were of military age at the time, she hesitated, looking a little peaky. I glanced up at her frowning face while she was taking time to respond. Silence. 'Hmm ... the older one was in Switzerland back then ... the other one in Belgrade helping me to disseminate

PERSONAL AND PROFESSIONAL LIFE

truth about crimes against Serbs ... he was delivering reports I was sending him about these crimes to the embassies that had a presence at the time in Belgrade ...' Her voice tapered off. Heat rose to her cheeks. I hesitated to push the point. Plavšić opened her mouth as though to speak, but no words came. She shifted her eyes, mumbling something under her breath. 'Would you like another cup of coffee?' she asked.

***

Plavšić comes from a well-educated, urban and affluent family; her father was the first Doctor of Science in Sarajevo, having completed his doctorate [degree in biology] in Vienna in 1934. Tall with blond hair and piercing blue eyes, Svetislav was a prominent biologist, a director of the natural science department at the Sarajevo Museum and custodian of its botanic collection until 1946.[3] He was a respected scientist who published in German and other languages.[4] He is renowned for his research on the *Pančićeva omorika* [Serbian spruce], a tree endemic to the Drina River valley.

Plavšić is proud of her father's work, contentment bathing her face every time she mentioned him:

> When I worked at the faculty, one famous biologist came from abroad and told me how my father researched 'the most beautiful tree in the world', and how I research something that is impossible to see with a naked eye—viruses [she laughs]—pointing out our polar different interests. No one at that time did such research. It was his original thesis. Our family apartment was full of scientific papers and various plants that he studied. Lots of it was left behind in our home and most are now archived in the museum in Sarajevo.

Plavšić's grandfather, Dionisije, was a well-known merchant who exported a local plum brandy to Austria and Germany. This wealthy merchant family was widely recognized among local people at the time. However, while Plavšić's father was respected for his work, his career suffered, because according to Plavšić, he was a monarchist and refused to join the Communist Party. Although he had a doctorate in biology at the time the Faculty of Science was established in Sarajevo, he was consistently overlooked due to his 'political dissent'.

Svetislav ultimately lost his job because he chose to follow his Orthodox tradition and religion over the Communist Party's ideology. The Serbian Orthodox Church is one of the ecclesiastically independent Eastern Orthodox Christian churches. The Orthodox religion, anti-fascism and anti-communism shaped, according to Plavšić, his general orientation and political views. After the war in 1945, Yugoslavia was renamed the Federal People's Republic of Yugoslavia when a communist government was established. The newly established government saw the danger in people like Svetislav holding anti-communist views. He did not believe in the communist ideology which advocated a classless system and common ownership of means of production. He opposed the idea of the working class running the country and the communist resentment of religion. Religion was to be substituted with 'scientific atheism', a key feature of communist ideology. Atheist or intentionally secular ceremonies and rituals replaced religious ones both in public and private life.[5]

Svetislav was a democrat who believed in personal freedom and equality, and ruling by the majority. He believed that people should choose their leaders by voting in free democratic elections. Communist Yugoslavia, with its one-party, state-controlled economy and totalitarian government, stood in stark contrast to the capitalist, democratic nations. For being stoic in his convictions and refusing to become a member of the Communist Party, Svetislav was forced to retire from his work in 1948. He was told that he would be teaching members of the Communist

PERSONAL AND PROFESSIONAL LIFE

Party at evening school. With a grim face and a harsh tone in her voice, Plavšić held my gaze for a moment, then recalled:

> At that time few people attended high school, and they appointed him [her father] to teach the evening courses to the Udbaši.[6] He had to do it to earn some income, but also because he was ordered to. To humiliate him even more, they replaced him with a man who was a gardener now promoted to the leadership role.

She winced, her voice full of sarcasm. Svetislav died not long after these events in 1949. As a young woman, nineteen years old at the time, seeing her father humiliated and degraded by the Communists sparked even more indignation towards the Party and its ideology. Following in his footsteps, Plavšić never joined the Communist Party of Yugoslavia.

Plavšić was only eleven years old when World War II started, and her teenage years were marked by harrowing events such as her family members being either killed or deported to Ustaša concentration camps or expelled to Serbia.[7] Plavšić spent the war with her family in Sarajevo, bearing witness to the crimes against her family and fellow citizens. She lived with her parents and brother in a two-bedroom unit in Magrabija Street in the Marijin Dvor neighbourhood. It was a small building with four floors, and their apartment was on the second.

> I spent my childhood and youth there. I left when I married, as my brother did. Mum stayed to live in that unit until 1992 when we all had to flee from Sarajevo. I lived in that city for fifty-five years. My family have strong roots in that part of Bosnia. Everything that happened there worried me deeply ... I have been connected to that city for generations. For a long time, I kept the keys of my apartment hoping that one day I would return and watch the domes of God's house, the Orthodox church, which would be in my neighbourhood as it was planned once. But nothing happened from it all. The church was never

49

built. Sarajevo was given to the Muslims. I threw away the keys. There is no return to Sarajevo for me.

Plavšić removed her glasses, bowed her head and prayed. She collected her three fingers and quickly crossed herself. The Kingdom of Yugoslavia was invaded by the Axis powers in 1941, and BiH was controlled by the pro-Nazi Independent State of Croatia (NDH).[8] Plavšić's eyes narrowed as she looked at me.

> Planes flew over the city. In Sarajevo, in our house, I watched through the window almost daily bombings of my city. One day, I remember bombs were raining near our house—six of them. Rattling. There were sounds of continuous explosions. I could hear the bomb shriek as it plummeted. I could hear shouts and screams. My grandfather did not want to go to the basement to hide and neither did I. I was a kid and would get excited with bombs, smoke and all that.

I was confused for a moment, unsure of which period she was referring to. Then I realised that she had switched to 1941, as she often did. Sometime, in the same breath, she would speak of events from 1941 and 1992. In 1941, her seventy-eight-year-old grandfather, Dionisije, and twenty-two family members were sent to the Slavonska Požega detention camp.[9] Seven households of the Plavšić family were taken there overnight. According to Plavšić, her grandfather was 'forced by the Ustaša to dig graves for his children, and then his children had to do the same for their young ones'. She listened to stories of survival that were told to her by her family. After starvation and torture, some of her family members were forcibly transferred to Serbia, never to return to Sarajevo. Plavšić glanced down for a second, then her eyes met mine. 'The Ustaša took all their property, they lost everything'.

Plavšić's mother was originally from Livno, Herzegovina, and most of her family members were killed by the Ustaša rather than expelled. Plavšić said she lost thirty-four members of her family at the hands of the Nazis' wartime Yugoslav allies. These events marked her formative teenage years and instilled fear and resentment toward Croats as an ethnic group. 'These events and stories my family recounted marked my life forever. Croats and Muslims always sided with occupying forces—in World War I and II, and in this last war in the 1990s too. Serbs were on one side and they were on the other'.

In our conversations, Plavšić often referred to 1991 as the continuation of 1941, when war between the Ustaša and the Chetniks started, and according to her, 'never finished'.[10] The memories of her teenage life in Sarajevo during the war were heavily imprinted in her mind:

> I entered politics because although I was only a child during the Second World War, I was old enough to understand that only Serbs [were] getting killed. Bosnia and Herzegovina were part of the Nazi puppet state, so-called the NDH. We knew that meant for Serbs our death sentence. The politics of the NDH at the time were that one third of Serbs should be killed, one third baptised, and one third expelled to Serbia. All of my Plavšić family members, except my immediate family in Sarajevo, were either killed or expelled during the Second World War. This was my sole reason for entering politics in 1991: to prevent that from happening again.

Her chin dropped, she closed her eyes for a moment, and took a deep breath. Plavšić then told me that she would sometimes be asked about her origins during her pre-war academic career when she travelled abroad on business. Once when she was a Fulbright scholar in the US, she was asked by her good friend and colleague Karl Maramorosch, a famous scientist, whether she had 'some nobles in her family'. She told him that her aunt from Livno was married to the brother of Gavrilo Princip. Her family had ties (though not through blood) with the infamous

Princip, who was a Bosnian Serb member of the Young Bosnia Movement, a Yugoslav organisation that was seeking an end to Austro-Hungarian rule in BiH.

Princip assassinated Archduke Franz Ferdinand, heir to the Austro-Hungarian throne, and his wife, Sophie, Duchess von Hohenberg, in Sarajevo on 28 June 1914. This event was described as the trigger that sparked World War I. He was only nineteen at the time. Princip was promptly arrested and imprisoned within the Terezín fortress, in what was then Czechoslovakia, where he died of tuberculosis in 1918. Plavšić went on to tell me that Gavrilo Princip had an older brother, Jovan, and a younger brother called Nikola (Niko). Niko married Plavšić's aunt—her mother's first cousin, Aunt Mirjana. They had two sons.[11]

> We had these photos of them ... I remember one big photo of Gavro [Gavrilo's nickname] that my grandfather kept in his house in Dubrovnik. Gavrilo was considered a saint in my grandfather's house. He was so respected. Niko, his brother, was a doctor. Gavro considered himself, as did Niko, Yugoslavian. My father considered himself a Serb and there were all these endless discussions in our household about religion and communism. Dad was not 'veliki Srbin' ['a big Serb', meaning an ultra-nationalist], but he was a Serb.[12] He was not a member of any Serb nationalist organisation. He was always honest and direct: when something was not right, he would say so. But as is the case with all regimes, the only people who did not have any troubles were poltroons [who sided with the government]. For example, my uncle was in Stojadinović's government, but my father despised Stojadinović, although he was very clever. My father simply hated regimes ...[13]

Niko was a doctor in Čapljina, and he was a regular guest in Plavšić's family home in Sarajevo. One day in 1941, he came to visit the Plavšić family. On his way to the city to have a short stroll before returning to Plavšić's home, a man riding on the same tram, pointed at him and shouted, 'This is Niko, brother of Gavrilo Princip!' A police officer stood up from his seat, approached Niko and arrested him. Princip did not return to Plavšić's home that day, where the family was waiting for him for lunch.

Visibly excited by these memories still so fresh in her mind, Plavšić paused and lit another cigarette. She looked down, wanting to move the conversation along, it seemed. Then her eyes narrowed in slits. 'Gavrilo died in terrible pain, but Niko was worse off. The Ustaša torturers cut him into pieces and gave his meat to the Serb prisoners in Čapljina to eat. Terrible.' Plavšić took a long drag on a cigarette before exhaling slowly. This story was told to the Plavšić family by Niko's fellow prisoners. Plavšić firmly believes that the story is true.[14] Niko was executed for no other reason than he was a Serb and for his family connection with Gavrilo.[15] The house where Princip lived in Sarajevo was destroyed by the Ustaše during World War II.[16] Between two cigarette puffs, she continued:

> My father tried to warn him [Niko] several times that he was not safe. He told him that he needed to leave Bosnia because he was not safe in Čapljina because he was a Serb and a brother of Gavrilo. He [Niko] sent his wife and two children to his brother-in-law in Sopot, Serbia, and thanks to that decision they survived the war. Unfortunately, he did not go with them but stayed.

The German embassy was based in Sarajevo, and according to Plavšić, 'Germans were arresting Communists on a daily basis'. As her father was not a member of any political organisation, she thinks that saved him from certain death by the Ustaša, and by the Germans too. Svetislav would sometimes go to the Old Orthodox Church in Baščaršija, which was built during the Ottoman Empire.[17] However, Plavšić said that he was doing it more out of 'defiance than belief'. During one of his visits to the church, he was approached and questioned by the Ustaša, and after some time they let him go free.

Her memories of events that happened almost seventy years ago are vivid and still painful to her. She struggled with emotions when she spoke about those times, which affected the rest of her life and, according to her, influenced some of her future decisions, such as to leave a successful academic career and 'jump into' politics, as she liked to say.

> Before the Second World War ended, from the house where we lived straight to the museum, there was a long line of trees. One day my dad was about to go to work. I saw him standing tall and peering through the window. He called my mum to come to show her something. 'Why are these people standing next to these trees?' Mum looked at him nervously and said in a low voice, 'No, these people do not stand there, they are hanging from the trees.' They froze there and watched. I remember silence. Nobody talked. On each tree, two to three people were hanged to death. One of the young women hanging there was a daughter of a doctor gynaecologist we knew. She was the only child in that family. I heard later that she was raped by Ustaša men and then hanged. One of them was in love with her, but she did not want to have anything to do with him. They raped and then hanged her as a punishment. She was blond and had a coat on her the same colour as her hair. One shoe was on her foot, another one was on the ground below her.

I could picture ten-year-old Plavšić peering through that window. I was there with her as she looked at those hung bodies. I grew up with similar stories. Her eyes moist with tears, Plavšić shrugged and paused. Her face reddened. I pulled myself together and straightened my back. Her features were distorted as she recalled the incident, staring out the window into nothingness. She rubbed a callus near the top of her middle finger, and then abruptly returned to her story:

How can I forget these things? I later found out who the people were who hanged her. Our mum tried to prevent my brother and me from seeing this; she tried to lock us in the house so we could not get out and look at the corpses. This was a warning to Serbs. My mum was crying a lot during those years. This is how I remember her: crying. 'Mum, why do you cry? Stop, please,' I remember telling her. Every now and then she would get terrible news about someone from her family or people she knew being killed by the Ustaša. In Livno,[18] they killed almost all Serbs. All of them. My mum told me about her cousin's husband, Dr Mitrović, who had three children. His daughter, eighteen at the time, was raped in front of her grandmother and parents. Her grandmother, mum's aunt, survived by emerging from under the corpses in the mass grave. She watched as her granddaughter was raped and went mad after that. Italian soldiers picked her up and took her to the military hospital in Split. Her husband, as well as Dr Mitrović and his two sons, were killed, and his daughter raped. The grandmother was transported to the psychiatric hospital in Belgrade and died there. You can forget some things, but some like these are engraved in your memory so that while you live, you won't be able to forget them ever.

When Plavšić talked about her parents and family, a veil of sadness seemed to wrap around her like a cloak. One could see the painful imprint of these traumatic memories on her. Due to such an upbringing and childhood, Plavšić was very aware of her Orthodox religion and traditions from an early age. When she was in high school, one professor asked her class to fill out forms that requested them to state which ethnic group they belonged to. She notes in her memoirs that while her Bosnian Muslim friend, Mina, did not know how to answer that question, Plavšić was proud to always state 'to which nation I belonged'.[19]

In 1986, when I was thirteen, I was asked the same question by my teacher and received a similar form to fill out. Contrary to Plavšić, like Mina, I did not know my ethnic origin. I was raised by communist parents and born in Tito's Yugoslavia in the early

1970s.[20] I did not practise my religion or know anything about it. I was totally oblivious to it at that time. I buried this event deep in my memory and have only started to reflect on it in the last decade or so.[21]

Plavšić followed the family tradition. After completing her elementary and secondary education in Sarajevo, she received a Bachelor of Science, majoring in botany, at the Faculty of Mathematics and Natural Science in Zagreb, where she subsequently also earned a Master's degree and a PhD. She spoke fondly about the time immediately after World War II and how she enjoyed her youth with her family and friends in Sarajevo. As a high-achieving student, she received a full scholarship from the BiH government to study in Zagreb. These were all great achievements for someone who was not a member of the Party. Each time I probed Plavšić as to how it was possible to obtain such opportunities despite openly despising the Party, she struggled to find any explanation apart from stating that she deserved it 'on merit'. 'Dad wanted me to study in Belgrade, but I wanted to go where everyone else was going. Sarajevo students who received stipends were sent either to Zagreb or Ljubljana', she said between two sips of what must had been by then a cold cup of coffee.

Plavšić finished her first degree within the deadline and with the best grades. She then stayed in Zagreb to do her PhD. Contrary to her father, she specialised in virology. Her father's first cousin also studied biology. Plavšić told me, 'People were often saying: the Plavšićs are obsessed with biology'.

Academic career

Once Plavšić returned from Zagreb, she secured a position as an assistant professor at the University of Sarajevo. Plavšić remembers these times fondly, but some of her colleagues were unhappy with her publicly holding onto her religious views and practices. At work, two female professors warned her that she 'had a bad habit' of telling her colleagues that if something was meant to happen it would happen only 'with God's will'.[22] Plavšić was disappointed that it was 'usually Serbs warning her' because 'they wanted to prove themselves to be good communists'. Yugoslavia, which was characterised by one-party rule, placed some restrictions on practising religion until the mid-1980s. It was hard, if not impossible, for people employed in state institutions to be promoted to higher ranks if they were openly religious.[23]

In the early 1970s, Plavšić completed her post-doctoral studies on the Fulbright Fellowship in New York at the Boyce Thompson Institute for Plant Research. 'I had a wonderful time in the USA, a fantastic experience. The colleagues there appreciated me, and once I finished, they sent me an invitation to rest for a week in Florida and then to visit their institutes across America'. She then specialised in electronic microscopy in London and plant virology while in Prague and Bari. Plavšić has published over one hundred studies, articles and papers, which have been widely cited in scholarly literature and textbooks. As a tenured professor in the University of Sarajevo's Faculty of Natural Sciences and Mathematics, she was elected as dean in 1987. She told me in a scholarly tone that this was 'impossible for someone who was not a Party member'. Her face beamed with pride, her lips locking into a mischievous smile.

At the time, these were great achievements, since women across Yugoslavia, and in particular in BiH, had a high rate of illiteracy, and the majority worked on the land in agriculture. When Plavšić was sent to Zagreb to study, 80 per cent of women in Yugoslavia were working in agriculture, with 40 per cent of them between the ages of 13 and 21.[24] In 1971, when Plavšić became a full professor, just over 35 per cent of women were still illiterate.[25] Yugoslavia was a patriarchal, traditional country where education was not encouraged for girls, who were expected to work the land and help with chores in the household while waiting to get married. Children of professors and merchants, like Plavšić and her brother, were among those who had an opportunity to school themselves.[26] Although few women in Yugoslavia were educated at this time, even fewer could achieve a position of power.

Plavšić is remembered by her students for her stunning wardrobe and her strictness, but also for her excellent teaching skills. One of her ex-students, now living in Australia, told me:

> She was a fantastic teacher. All the students respected her greatly. Her lecture theatres were always full. She was a strict, but fabulous teacher and scholar. She was always generous with her time if students wanted her to provide more explanation. A fair-play and approachable professor, one of very few women professors and the only real lady; different from all other professors. She always looked professional and was a beautiful woman and expert in her field. I could never imagine her in politics. She loved her subject and was passionate about plants and botany. She never discriminated against Muslims and Croats. I never heard of such discrimination. Professor Plavšić was also a professor whom students knew they could not bribe to pass exams.

Another former student, now in his sixties, approached Plavšić as we were strolling down the street in her neighbourhood. He stopped in front of her with a sparkle in his eyes, corners of his mouth curving up showing his teeth. He gushed, 'Professor Plavšić, I was your student once, a long time ago. I just want to tell you that you were such a great teacher. The best. I enjoyed your classes so much'. Plavšić beamed, obviously pleased. I think she is used to receiving such flattering compliments.

Despite repeated offers, Plavšić never wanted to become a member of the Communist Party, although membership was generally a pre-requisite for advancement in an academic career.

She stayed loyal to her family's convictions and was raised to follow and practise her religion. Plavšić had witnessed her father being humiliated and degraded by the Communist Party and could never forgive them for that, which she illustrates here:

> When I finished my studies in Zagreb, they wanted me to stay there to work. My father passed away at that time, and my poor mum was trying to survive with her little pension. I loved Sarajevo so much and did not want to live anywhere else. I said to them, 'No way, I must go back.' The Faculty of Philosophy had just established the Department of Science, which after five years became the Faculty of Science and Maths. I became the deputy dean for Finances. I then applied for an assistant professor position.[27] One of my colleagues, a professor, told me: 'Do you know how much we discussed your application? I think if we were to elect the president of the Republic, we would not deliberate that much. They discussed the fact that you are not a Party member and how your father was a famous anti-communist.' I got up and said, 'Are we electing the father of Biljana Plavšić as an assistant, or her herself?' It was ridiculous. I had all the requirements fulfilled and even more. I had finished my studies, and published two papers in international journals. No one had that at the time. And they discussed whether they would accept me or not based upon my political convictions, until he, the respected professor, stood up to defend me. I also applied for the Fulbright stipend and got it. I could have applied for the Humboldt research fellowship[28] too and I am sure I would have got it, but I did not want to go to Germany. The wounds from the Second World War were still fresh.

Plavšić lifted her eyes and looked at me. She drew a long, silent breath then continued to tell me that she later became Dean of the Faculty of Science at the University of Sarajevo and successfully managed to obtain funds for new laboratories for chemistry, biology and physics. In her memoirs, she wrote that she built up her career gradually,

> ... never skipping ranks, unlike some individuals involved in politics. I built my career in studious ways and based on merit; not because I followed the [Communist] Party lines. I wanted to prove to everyone out of defiance that I can achieve it all without being member of the Party and I succeeded in it. This was rare and difficult to achieve at the time. Still, I have to admit that my colleagues at the faculty were tolerant.[29]

Plavšić was aware that her colleagues knew she was religious, and that she regularly went to church and celebrated religious and national holidays.[30] Her behaviour obviously challenged the dominant communist ideology, which strongly discouraged the public embrace of religious celebrations.

While she was serving as dean, and on her invitation, a Japanese firm came to install the first electronic microscope in her faculty and the first in BiH. The microscope was already in high usage overseas. Plavšić was nominated as the president of the Electronic Microscopic Association of Yugoslavia, and all representatives of the major government ministries were invited to the celebratory opening of the laboratory. Hamdija Pozderac, a Yugoslav communist politician and the president of BiH from 1971 to 1974, came to the opening and, according to Plavšić, told her:

> Comrade Plavšić, congratulations. You know, if you were a member of the Party, I would dismiss you from the Party because through our self-management system this could never be done. It would have to go through an electoral process where each member of the Party would have to vote whether an electronic microscope should be bought, even people who work as cleaners at the faculty. It would not be possible to do what you did and in such a short period of time. If you were a member of the Party, I would personally sack you from the Party, but also build you a monument in front of this building for your achievement.

Plavšić's eyes lit up, and a slight air of mischief appeared on her face. She was amused with this anecdote, clearly proud of herself for having accomplished great things without being a member of the Party. Plavšić saw Pozderac's comment as her victory and a defeat of the mainstream ideology.

The late 1970s and '80s marked the pinnacle of Plavšić's career. During that period, she specialised in electron microscopy and became a highly accomplished scholar, publishing her studies in English, French and Spanish.[31] In his memoirs, Karl Maramorosch, Austrian-American professor emeritus and a world-renowned scholar in biology and ecology of plant viruses, wrote highly of Plavšić's original contribution to science in electron microscopy findings.[32] Plavšić was regularly invited to present her work at conferences around the globe and was friends with Maramorosch, with whom she collaborated on scientific projects. In 1976, she took an unpaid leave of absence and went to Al Fateh University in Tripoli, Libya for a two-year work placement as an academic. She helped her colleagues establish a laboratory for plant pathology.[33] She returned to her university department in Sarajevo after these two years and continued teaching and researching viral diseases and plant phytoplasma.

Plavšić's scholarly work can still be accessed online when searching the internet under her married name Plavšić–Banjac.[34] She is one of the most highly educated war criminals on record.[35] In 1963 she married Žarko Banjac, one of the leading criminal law attorneys in Sarajevo. She studied in Zagreb, and he undertook his law degree in Belgrade. Karl Maramorosch (in his memoir) describes the couple as seemingly happy and living a comfortable life. However, they divorced after fourteen years of marriage. According to Plavšić, they were both too dedicated to their careers, and because they had no children, they decided to separate. My aunt explained that despite their separation, they spent a lot of time together and would often come together to visit her and my uncle. She told me:

> During Biljana's presidency, they [Plavšić and Banjac] often came to our home and we had lunch or dinner together. Our house was always full of laughter with them. They were friends and cared a lot about each other. Žarko came from Belgrade, where he'd fled to during the [Bosnian] war, to Banjaluka to visit Biljana and help her arrange her library and other stuff in her unit. They were happy together. He was meant to help her with her trial but he suddenly died. He was a nice man.

Regardless of their separation, Plavšić and Banjac stayed close friends, and neither of them remarried. During our conversations, Plavšić would sometimes refer to him as 'my husband'. Banjac even tried to help Plavšić's attorney prepare her defence while she was in detention in The Hague awaiting trial. Banjac was not an expert in international criminal law, so he struggled to understand the accusations and evidence against Plavšić. However, Banjac's health unexpectedly deteriorated, and he died during her time in detention. Plavšić expressed deep sorrow that they had no children. She confessed to me that she loved children and wanted to have her own. She tried for years, but with no success, and she did not believe in in-vitro fertilisation.

> It was God's will. I did not want to become pregnant artificially if I could not become pregnant naturally. It was a sign that it was not meant to be. And I was not going to do it against His will, although I wanted a child desperately. It was heartbreaking for me to accept that I could not have children. I adore kids.

Political career

During the time Plavšić was serving as the first female member of the Bosnian presidency at the first multiparty elections in 1990, she was still working as a full-time professor. Plavšić held both these roles for some time, but she eventually realised it was too difficult to continue managing both. She told me, 'I could not do two jobs at the same time anymore. I had to make a decision. I decided to let go of the academic position and resigned from being a dean'.

In 1990, with the first democratic elections and multiple parties, Plavšić decided to join the Serb Democratic Party (SDS). The first president of the SDS was Dr Jovan Rašković. Plavšić wrote in her memoirs about how impressed she was with Rašković, whose ideas she'd admired for a long time. On her flight back from the USA in 1985, where she was on a one-month fellowship, she read an interview with Rašković in the popular tabloid *Duga*. He was concerned about the political situation in Yugoslavia.

Of all three nationalist parties, the SDS was the last to be formed, after the Croatian Democratic Party (HDZ) and the Party of Democratic Action (SDA) were established. It is interesting to note that the SDS leadership was composed of elite intellectuals at the time: Dr Jovan Rašković (psychiatrist and academic), Prof. Nikola Koljević (a Shakespeare and literary scholar), Dr Radovan Karadžić (psychiatrist and poet), Prof. Milutin Najdanović (doctor), Prof. Slavko Leovac (philosopher and literary scholar) and Momčilo Krajišnik (economist). Both Karadžić and Krajišnik were jailed for embezzlement and fraud before the war.[36]

On 12 July 1990, the SDS had its first public and constitutive meeting in the Skenderija Cultural and Sports Centre in Sarajevo, and Plavšić decided to attend to hear Rašković's speech. She was dean at the time, and she walked away from this meeting determined to become a member of the SDS. Koljević, who was already a SDS party member, invited Plavšić to attend a meeting of the Political Advisory Board to the SDS, which brought together an exclusive group of Serb academics from the

University of Sarajevo. Plavšić met Slobodan Milošević, who was the president of Serbia at the time.

On Karadžić's invitation, Milošević attended a meeting while he was visiting Alija Izetbegović in Sarajevo. With her eyes resuming their focus on her coffee cup, Plavšić commented that everyone at that meeting complimented him. She was the only one who stood up against Milošević. She openly attacked him at the meeting for refusing to return property taken from the Serbian Orthodox churches after World War II to their original owners.[37] Milošević answered, 'But if I did that then everyone would ask for their property to be returned'. She told me that she did not flinch, and said to him, 'So what? It is not yours but theirs, and it should be returned'. She said she was 'marked' from then on as 'an open opposition' to him.

In October that same year, Plavšić and Koljević were elected by the SDS to become representatives of the Serbian people in the presidency of BiH. From each ethnic group, two people were elected as representatives of their people in the presidency. People from all over BiH came out to vote. Plavšić cast a quick glance towards me, and her cheeks coloured. 'It was a surprise. I did not expect that at all'.

Plavšić said that a journalist recently asked her how, as a woman, she could go through the ranks with all these men around her. Plavšić giggled and added, 'I did not have to struggle for attention. They wanted me. They were asking for me'. There were five candidates altogether, but Plavšić got the highest number of popular votes. 'I received those votes from Croats, Muslims and Serbs. One night during that time, I received a late-night phone call from [a member of] the Catholic parish in Modriča, who told me, "Professor, all my parish voted for you."' Her smile mellowed as she continued:

> I think people voted for me because I simply wanted prosperity for the people. I was always a good, hardworking person who supervised

generations of students. Some people considered me apolitical. I did not belong to any party until the 1990s. I did not look for any differences between people. I only differentiated between the just and the unjust, and truthful and untruthful people. My students were of mixed ethnic origin. I was not guided by differences in ethnicities of people. Maybe I had such principles because I was religious.

At the time, Plavšić was about to be elected as a member of the Academy of Sciences and Arts of Bosnia and Herzegovina, the most respected science institution in the country, which only included elite intellectuals. With an ominous tone underscoring her words, she commented that she knew that if the Academy found out that she was to be nominated as a Serbian candidate for the presidency, they would have immediately withdrawn her candidacy. With a hardened expression, Plavšić said that while the Academy would have been the final and ultimate achievement in her academic career, it would only bring 'a personal gain and satisfaction'; however, she believed that her nomination as the Serbian representative was in 'the wider interest to the Serb people'.[38] This is how the perception of her sacrifice for the Serb people began: by giving up her successful academic career to take up an unpredictable political career. All this was done, not for her own sake, but 'for her Serb people and their nationalist interests'. At that time, little did she know that she had set herself on the path to become the first female president of Republika Srpska and the second woman in the history of the Serb people to be the head of state.[39] Plavšić could also never imagine that as a high-profile intellectual and president she would one day find herself behind bars, convicted for war crimes and crimes against humanity.

Some commentators, such as Slavenka Drakulić,[40] suggested that the real reason Plavšić entered politics was because she was in her early sixties and close to retirement age. According to

Drakulić, Plavšić was 'ambitious and intelligent, with no family commitments and full of energy; the prospect of retirement to her was not so attractive'.[41] Once Plavšić was elected as the Serbian representative, she decided to accept a candidacy in the presidency and consequently was not elected into the Academy. That was the beginning of the end of her academic career. Soon she would abandon it completely and become a full-time politician. She raised her head and stared blankly ahead, saying quietly, 'This is how I glided into politics'.

Life during the Bosnian War

BiH received international recognition on 6 April 1992, and the most common view is that the war started on that day. However, Plavšić considers 1 March 1992 as the beginning of the Bosnian War. On that day, a Serb wedding procession was attacked in front of the Orthodox church in Sarajevo when the father of the groom was killed and the Serb Orthodox priest wounded. At that time, Plavšić was living in Sarajevo. She is still convinced that this crime was committed by the members of the Patriotic League, the then-Bosnian Muslim organisation.[42]

> Alija Izetbegović publicly condemned this crime at our National Assembly meeting and guaranteed that attackers would be arrested. He, of course, speculated that Serbs could potentially have committed this crime as a provocation. The groom was from an old Serb family, Gardović, and this gruesome event happened in front of the church that was built during the Ottoman Empire. The church has a very special meaning for Serbs with its rich religious symbols and a space where Serbs have gathered through the centuries in times of troubles …. My aunt was also married in that same church … My grandfather, Dionisije, also went to that church as a child, and in my childhood, I regularly passed by or entered the church. I had a special respect and admiration for it, a feeling that grew as I was growing up. [Plavšić's

eyes narrowed to slits]. The war started right there on that day. The Serbs were the first victims of the war ... This was a warning and a call for Serbs to prepare and defend themselves from an enemy.

This is how Plavšić perceives the beginning of the war: the Serbs were attacked and provoked, and they needed to organise and defend themselves against their 'enemies'—Bosnian Muslims and Croats. Plavšić was not the only one who held such an opinion—the majority of Serbs shared her view.[43] Only two days later, on 3 March 1992, independence for BiH was formally declared by the Bosnian parliament. Serbs were against the republic's independence as they wanted to stay within the borders of what was then Yugoslavia. During the month of March, Plavšić travelled to Herzegovina to visit a few Serb-majority villages in the vicinity of Čapljina, a town close to the border of Croatia and largely populated by Croatia. As a member of the presidency, she recollects how she organised a meeting in a community hall in Čapljina because the presidency had been informed that young recruits of the Yugoslav People's Army had been cut off from electricity and water.[44] Plavšić wanted to plead with the people of Čapljina not to harm young soldiers, and at some point in her speech, she said in front of the gathered residents, 'Can you please imagine how you would feel if this was done to your children?' Plavšić's cheeks were red, her voice cracking. She glanced at me.

> Everyone was angry at me. The women were terrible. They were casting threatening looks at me and expressed their hatred with their words and gestures. When I told them to think how they would feel if someone was hurting their children, one big woman screamed at me from the top of her lungs, 'What do you know about children, you Serb cow!' I left the hall and my driver said we needed to leave immediately since these people may try to kill me. I jumped in the car and we left the town. As I was running away from Čapljina, I was thinking about my aunt and uncle, Niko Princip, brother of Gavrilo

> Princip ... I remembered how my father tried to convince him to leave Čapljina before it was too late but he believed no one would hurt him. He trusted his neighbours and local residents ... And they were the ones in the end who killed him ...

On 28 March 1992, a massacre was committed in a small, ethnically mixed Bosnian village called Sijekovac, situated within the municipality of Bosanski Brod. The majority of the Serb civilian population was brutally killed. The massacre happened in 'peace time', as war had not yet been officially declared. A day later, on 29 March Plavšić, as a representative of the Bosnian presidency delegation, went on an official visit to witness and investigate what happened a day before. She saw houses destroyed; the village was razed to the ground. People were lying dead around their houses. This massacre was carried out by paramilitary groups consisting of local Bosniaks and Croats.[45] Only one man, Zemir Kovačević, has ever been held responsible for this crime in Sijekovac.[46] These events were imprinted on Plavšić's mind, and she talked vividly about them when describing the beginning of the war. However, her remembrance is selective, as she only recalls crimes committed against Serbs. These selective memories convinced her that the Serbs needed to defend themselves. She held my eyes as she spoke.

> As in the Second World War, people were saving their lives by migrating and running to safer places. I was watching these poor people on their carts going somewhere they even did not know where with their children and few belongings. I had flashbacks from 1941 when my grandfather Dionisije and my uncles and other male relatives were taken by the Ustaša and how I was running as a child after the carts they were forced to climb in. That image of me running and crying as a child was mixed with pictures before me of these people fleeing for their lives. This is what the international court [ICTY] calls 'ethnic cleansing' but it was only natural to run for their lives. I could never understand that

term, really ... [Plavšić said, her voice skewered with spite]. The war really had not yet begun at the time of the Sijekovac massacre, at least not officially. There was a presidency and other institutions. Seemingly everything functioned but the killings had started ...

Plavšić tells me about her first encounter with Željko Ražnatović, better known as Arkan, who told her that he 'loved and appreciated her'. Arkan was a notorious paramilitary leader of the Serbian Volunteer Guard, aka 'Tigers', and a criminal who was indicted by the ICTY in 1997 for murder, rape and other inhumane acts.[47] He was assassinated in 2000; his murder ensured that he would never go on trial.[48] Verdicts at the ICTY have established that at least forty-eight people were killed in Bijeljina by Serb paramilitaries led by Arkan in the first two days of April 1992.[49] But thus far, only one of his fighters, Boban Arsić, has been convicted in absentia in Croatia.[50] Plavšić's photo, in which she and Arkan embraced in Bijeljina, which the Serb army occupied, was widely used as evidence of her close relationship to one of the most wanted and notorious criminals. Arkan and Plavšić met in Bijeljina after the city fell to Arkan and his people. Plavšić tells me she'd never heard of him before. She puffs on her cigarette and says, smoke filtering from her nostrils,

> One late night Colonel Jankovic called me and said that three men from the presidency, Fikret Abdić, Jozo Doko and Miodrag Simović, who were sent to Bijeljina, were in difficult situation. I asked where they were and he said with Arkan. I thought Arkan was the name of one of the villages around Bijeljina. I knew all those small villages around the town of Bijeljina because of my biology profession and plants that grow in that area. I was thinking, but could not remember any village called Arkan. I said to the colonel, 'I have never heard about village Arkan. Where is it?' He said, 'Ms, it's not the village. It is a man'. I asked, 'What kind of man?' He said, 'Dangerous!' He then asked me to call Arkan and ask him to free up the men from the presidency cabinet. It

was night and I called the number he gave me, which was apparently in an office space in one of the municipalities of Bijeljina. A woman received my call. I asked if I could talk to Arkan. She said, 'You mean with the commandant Arkan?' I was surprised that she called him a commandant. He took the phone and said, 'Ms Plavšić I respect you and love you a lot'. I said, 'Mr Arkan, I don't know you but if you love me and respect me, please release those three men. They told me they are with you'. He replied, 'Maybe, if it is not too late, *if they haven't already eaten the grass* [meaning they haven't been killed already]'. I said, 'What does that mean?' I was shocked. 'If they haven't eaten the grass, I will release them but you will regret asking this'. I said I wanted to see them in the morning in my cabinet. Doko, Simović and Abdić were released. Arkan told them that they could thank me for their release. Abdić later gave a report on the situation in Bijeljina.

Arkan was, according to Plavšić, a freedom fighter, a Serb hero rather than a terrorist. She stared at me for a moment.

> He came with his fighters to places where we did not have enough men of our own to protect our borders, to fight for our homeland. He and others were there to fill in the gaps in our own ranks. They had bravery and determination, and sacrificed themselves for the Serb greater good. I told you before that we were missing people who would fight for us. [A corner of Plavšić's mouth twitches]. So, yes, Arkan was impressive and I am thankful to him and his men. He kept discipline. His men could not steal or similar. He established peace and stability in the region.

She paused. What Plavšić did not say was that Arkan and his men were accused of war crimes, including mass murder, rape, cruel treatment, inhumane acts and other 'grave breaches' of the Geneva Conventions of 1949. At the time of his death in January 2000, Arkan was under indictment for numerous crimes committed while acting as leader and supervisor of the Serbian Volunteer Guard, also known as 'Arkan's Tigers'.[51] But, he—

Arkan—also saved Plavšić's nephew from besieged Sarajevo who, at the time, was an assistant at the Faculty of Law. She was worried that 'he may be a target for Muslims ... that they would arrest him and force him to enlist in their army' and then blackmail Plavšić in order to release him. In her memoirs, she describes the evacuation of her older nephew together with his wife and young daughter from besieged Sarajevo. After their first meeting, Arkan gave Plavšić his phone number and told her she could always call him if she needed anything. She remembered this offer and called Arkan a few weeks later to ask him to help her organise the evacuation of her nephew and his family from Sarajevo. Arkan responded immediately. He arranged their evacuation from the city to the Sarajevo airport in twenty-four hours. From there they flew to Belgrade.[52] None of Plavšić's family returned to live in Sarajevo after the war.

On 4 April 1992, a delegation from BiH's collective presidency consisting of Plavšić and Fikret Abdić as the Serb and Muslim representatives went to Bijeljina after its seizure by Arkan's paramilitary unit. On that same day, Plavšić met Ljubiša Savić, nicknamed 'Mauzer', who was another paramilitary warlord from Bijelljina whom Plavšić adored. In her memoir, she called him a 'celebrated hero of Semberija'.[53] During the war he was a leader of the 'Panthers', Serb volunteer fighters. 'Mauzer never disappointed me—in war or later on in peace. He was a fighter for the Serb cause'.[54] Plavšić lowered her eyes to the floor.

> All these paramilitary units, and in particular Chetnik associations, were important. I paid attention to Chetniks who had their units across our territory. I was in touch with them regularly during the war. These martyrs suffered a lot during the communist regime since they did not want to give up their religion and traditions.

Once again what Plavšić omitted to mention was that Mauzer and his paramilitary group, according to many witnesses, were responsible for much of the 'ethnic cleansing' in the Bijeljina area. Mauzer also introduced himself to Human Rights Watch as the commander of the notorious Batković detention camp north of Bijeljina. The Batković camp, jerry-built on a farm cooperative, was the latest Serb-run detention site to be opened to journalists and human rights groups.[55] Mauzer's involvement in war crimes in the Brčko area was documented too, where a brutal campaign of 'ethnic cleansing' and mass executions was carried out in May 1992. This was around the time when Plavšić and her delegation met Arkan in front of the municipal offices in Bijeljina. According to an eyewitness, Plavšić kissed Arkan on the cheek and called him 'my child'.[56] Plavšić proclaimed 'the liberation' of Bijeljina on that day.[57] Plavšić told me that she never called Arkan 'her child' but the kiss she planted on his cheek 'was one of the two crucial proofs' against her in The Hague.

> They took a photo of me kissing Arkan on that day in Bijeljina and used that as crucial proof that we must have known each other from before otherwise we would not have embraced and kissed. That is ridiculous. They don't know our traditions and rituals. We sometimes embrace people and kiss them on the cheek even if we don't know them but if we just think fondly of them.

It is true that embracing people is part of the tradition, but it is not true that she did not know him. She had spoken to him on the phone before they met, and Plavšić had also been told that he was 'a dangerous man'. She continued to tell me how she spent that day with Arkan in Bijeljina.

> We entered the Muslim houses and were greeted by their residents. They all welcomed us. Women even kissed Arkan's hand as if he was some kind of a priest. It was Bajram, and we sat with people to have coffee and baklava.[58] They were all grateful to Arkan because they felt he kept them safe. There was no massacre of Muslims in Bijeljina;

that was all a lie. But from that visit, journalists and others were only interested in that photo where we embraced and kissed each other ...

Plavšić still denies that massacres of Bosniaks took place in Bijeljina despite the ICTY's evidence of the crimes and more than forty murders that happened there at that time.[59] When I contradicted her views with the ICTY findings, her thin eyebrows lifted, and she cut in, hissing, 'That was all a lie. I personally talked to Muslims in Bijeljina, and they all praised Arkan and his fighters.' She waved me away, dismissing my proposition. She was a master of brushing off questions to which she did not want to respond.

A few months before these events, Republika Srpska marked 9 January 1992 as the day of its establishment. On this day, the National Assembly proclaimed the republic of the Serbian people as an independent entity within BiH. Its aim was to stay within the borders of former Yugoslavia. But the tensions between Serbs, Croats and Muslims (Bosniaks) had already started in the second half of 1991. Radovan Karadžić, the SDS leader, in his infamous speech in the Bosnian Assembly was addressing Bosnian Muslims. The speech was later on used against him by the ICTY.[60] Karadžić stated:

> I ask you once again, I am not threatening, I am pleading that you take seriously the political will of the Serbian people represented here today ... The road you are choosing for Bosnia and Herzegovina is the same highway to Hell and suffering that Slovenia and Croatia have already taken. Do not think that you will not take Bosnia and Herzegovina to Hell and the Muslim people maybe into extinction, because if there is a war, the Muslim people will not be able to defend themselves.[61]

He gave this speech on 15 October 1991 when the Bosnian multi-ethnic assembly was discussing the future status of BiH, which was then still part of Yugoslavia. Karadžić was determined to prevent Bosnian Serbs from being separated from other Serbs in the former Yugoslavia by the establishment of a sovereign and independent BiH. His speech, and Plavšić's lack of protest against it, was used as another crucial piece of evidence against Plavšić by the ICTY. Plavšić was present at the time, sitting in the first row and listening to Karadžić. She recalls, looking puzzled:

> They [the prosecutors at the ICTY] told me that I was responsible for Karadžić's speech. I asked how can I be accountable for what he said? I had no idea what he would say. They just said that since I was sitting in the first row and did not object to his speech but rather stayed silent meant I fully supported what he said and how he threatened Muslims with extinction. They literally told me I was supposed to get up on that podium and tell everyone, 'Not all Serbs think like you'. Can you believe that? How could I do so? And, in any case, I think he was just warning them what could happen if they decided to go to war against us. He was telling them the truth and pleading with them not to go to fight with us. There was nothing malicious there but a friendly warning and concern for their welfare. He did not threaten that he would drive Muslims to extinction but that they may do that to themselves if they went to war since he knew they would end up as losers. They were not capable of going to war. They had no tradition of bravura and heroism as the Serbian people have had for centuries. And since they had no history, they needed this war to create some national history of bravura for themselves. We all knew they could not fight us; they had no army, no weapons, no heroes or military spirit as the Serbs have had throughout centuries of fighting the biggest powers in the world for their freedom. And they [the Muslims] ended up being killed in the highest numbers as they did not want to listen ... They could have stayed with us, but no, Alija [Izetbegović] wanted his independent republic, and he said that he would 'sacrifice peace for a sovereign Bosnia'... He was preaching for war, not us [Serbs]![62] But no one cared what he said ... Only the Serbs were accused and prosecuted for the mayhem ... How were twenty thousand or more Serbs killed then? We did not kill ourselves.

Plavšić did not object to Karadžić's infamous threat of genocide—simply because she supported it. She treated his threat as a 'friendly warning', something to be appreciated rather than condemned. Her thinking and interpretation of almost all war-related events represents a case of historical revisionism. She continuously introduced contrary evidence or reinterpreted events to fit her narrative. The international community recognised BiH as a sovereign state on 6 April 1992, which launched the war in BiH. Serbs were against Bosnian independence, and according to Plavšić, did not want to be 'raja' to the Muslims.[63] On 7 April 1992, Plavšić signed her presidency resignation. She left the presidency building and her cabinet, and never returned to its premises. She did not accept the referendum results, or believe in a newly established independent state of BiH. 'Serbs did not want to be part of it. I followed my people and left that presidency for good'. Since the city was under siege, Plavšić stayed in Sarajevo in her apartment with her senile mother, without water and electricity. 'Serbs were forced out of the city, expelled. The only way to fight for the city was from the surrounding hills where they were forced into exile'. She told me they hardly had any food. Sarajevo experienced bomb and sniper attacks all the time.

However, Plavšić did not mention that the Serbs occupied the hills surrounding Sarajevo and were shooting at the city and its residents. Bosnian Muslims were defending their city from the urban areas they occupied. During the longest siege in modern European history from 1992 to the beginning of 1996, Plavšić told me that while the majority of telephone lines in the city were cut, hers was intact until her last day in Sarajevo on 22 May 1992.[64] 'They [Bosnian Muslims] made sure my lines were working so they could record my phone calls. Many of these recorded phone conversations from that period were used as evidence against me in The Hague'. Her decision to leave abruptly and 'in twenty minutes' was prompted by the arrest of her brother and sister-in-law.

> My brother and his wife were detained in Ramiz Delalić Ćelo's private prison in Sarajevo. Ćelo called me one night to tell me so. He said I needed to come and get them, and if I did, he would cut me into three pieces. I said I would come tomorrow morning. I was desperate to help them since I knew that he was a dangerous criminal. My friend Jerko Doko, a Croat and Minister of Defence, helped me to get them out and they were put into a car and driven to my apartment. I organised for them to leave Sarajevo the day after. My brother did not want to leave me and our mother but I forced him to go ... I was the last one to leave. I left my home city in twenty minutes with my disabled mother ... I packed in a rush some nappies for my mum and some clothes. My Muslim neighbour, who was a good man, came to my door and just said, 'You have to leave in twenty minutes. The ambulance will come to take you and your mother. You cannot stay here overnight'... And that was it. I left. I think this man appreciated that I took care of his old mother, helping her regularly with her groceries from the market place and having a chit chat with her ... maybe he helped because of that ... I don't know ... I was 'ethnically cleansed' from Sarajevo, but they [the ICTY] did not care. There are different types of cleansing but some of them are obviously not the subject of criminal investigations ... What do they call it when people run for their lives from bombs and bullets? They have no idea about wars in the Balkans. They are coming from nice countries. I tried to explain to them [the ICTY] about our destinies; that is not what they imagine in their nice West ...

Ćelo was a Bosnian gangster and warlord, and commander of the 9th Mountain Brigade in Sarajevo. He was one of several prominent underworld figures engaged by the Party of Democratic Action in preparation for the war in BiH. He gained notoriety as the main suspect who stood trial before a local court for the killing of Nikola Gardović on 1 March 1992. Plavšić refers to this killing as a marker of the beginning of the war in BiH (the Serb wedding killing). In May 1992, Plavšić left Sarajevo.

> All my belongings were left in my apartment that I never returned to. I took only three fur coats. I loved fur coats ... One was a tiger's fur. I remember showing up in it on the frontline among the poor soldiers ... But that was one of the few things I took with me from my unit ... I loved jewellery, had a lot of it, but could not take it all with me ... I never submitted a request to return to my property. I did not want to ask Alija Izetbegović to give me back my unit and humiliate myself. I have my apartment in Belgrade, and I don't need that one in Sarajevo although I owned it. I needed to submit a request for them to return it together with their new Bosnian ID legitimation which I never wanted to apply for. I heard that someone from my former faculty where I was a professor and dean now lives in it, and that is okay with me.

I found it perplexing that Plavšić showed no emotion when speaking about how one of her colleagues is now living in her apartment. She told me that she never received any compensation for it. I expected some emotional response to reflect such a loss. Losing a home, one's personal belongings and being displaced is considered a deeply traumatic experience. I came to realise that this emotionless reaction to losing her home fits within Plavšić's deliberate normalisation and relativisation of ethnic cleansing. By seeming indifferent to someone else occupying her home, she was perhaps telling me that the Serb cleansing of other people's homes was 'normal' too during the war. But also for Plavšić, losing her apartment in Sarajevo did not mean having to live in a collective centre or rent an apartment she could not afford. Many people displaced by the war lived for years—even decades—in collective centres or rented apartments, or were forced to move abroad to start from scratch. From her position, losing a home was acceptable since there was another home and privileges that came with it.

During this time, Plavšić received a humanitarian portfolio as a member of the newly established Republika Srpska presidency. She wrote to the Orthodox churches abroad asking them to organise help in the form of food and medications for Serb soldiers but also for other Serbs in need. She was often in the field, going to the trenches to visit soldiers.

> I once went to visit soldiers on the Jahorina mountain. It was winter, early morning. It was freezing cold. They were poorly clothed, around one hundred of them. They were armed, some wrapped in blankets ... I met their commandant called Švaba. He was red-headed, almost two metres tall, with blue eyes. He looked like some Viking hero in full strength and beauty. Someone came and wrapped a blanket around my arms as it was so cold and I was poorly clothed. We all drank a morning coffee. When I returned to my accommodation in the mountain, I called my cousin Slobodan Plavšić in Frankfurt and told him where I was and asked him to help me. He kept asking what my family and I needed and I told him to send me two hundred warm woollen pants, singlets, socks ... I organised donations for young soldiers many times. I also visited them in hospital, crippled and wounded ... I spoke to women, men and children who were victims and tried to help them as much as I could ... This is what I was doing during the war. I had no other power, nothing in my portfolio, apart from doing humanitarian work, which I did ... I did not know anything about Karadžić and his decisions ... He hated me, called me *baba* [grandmother].[65] He and Krajišnik never invited me to any of their meetings. They believed conversations and negotiations are men's business ... according to their traditional thinking, in peace times, and especially in times of war, there is no place for a woman.

In 1995, after one of her regular visits to hospitals occupied by disabled veterans, paraplegics and quadraplegics, Plavšić agreed to give an interview on the local radio station. She will be remembered for relating something that one of the veterans told her that day when she paid a visit to the hospital in Slankamen. This event fuelled the pre-existing tensions between Plavšić and the then-Serbian president Slobodan Milošević.

> I entered the hospital room full of young disabled Serb soldiers, many with no limbs. I came close to one of these soldiers with no legs who was sitting in a wheelchair. He was distressed, and he told me, 'We Serbs have had enough wars in our history. We should finish them all now and for good. There are twelve million Serbs and even if six million die, six will remain to live in freedom'. I remember I was so shocked by what he told me that his words stayed imprinted on my mind. After talking to him and others, I was invited for an interview on the radio, and I recounted what this young soldier told me after I was asked what do these young wounded soldiers think of war. The next morning, I saw the cover page of *Politika* [Serbian daily newspaper] with the heading printed in capital letters and the statement from this young veteran on its front page. The only difference was that my name was ascribed to the statement, as if that was something I said. Below the title, Mira Marković's statement was also printed as a reply: 'The person who dared to say something like this has to be expelled from social and political life for good'.[66] She also called me 'the psychopath'. I was shocked. I went straight to that radio station to listen to the recordings and see whether what I said was not clear and could be taken out of context. It was perfectly clear that I was just repeating what I was told. However, that rumour spread like a fire, and to this day I keep being asked why I said this ... I was so angry with Milošević ... he was terrible for our people, a real Communist. I told him to his face that it is a pity that Serbia does not have a strongman like Tudjman, and that Croatia was a lucky country.

She took another drag on her cigarette and glanced at me with a bemused smile. Plavšić then said that she met Slobodan Milošević in person only twice: the first time at a Serbian party meeting in Sarajevo before the war broke out, and the second time in Jahorina at the end of the war. She had no respect for him and his wife. Plavšić considered them Communists and bad politicians with whom she strongly disagreed. 'They both hated me. I did not like them either,' she said with a cough. Plavšić claims that she never met Milošević during the war, only when he came to Jahorina to meet with the Republika Srpska leadership before he travelled to Dayton to sign the peace agreement. This meeting, and Plavšić's action, entered into history. In front of all the journalists and diplomats, Plavšić turned her back on Milošević when he came to greet her. His hand that was meant to shake hers stayed hanging in the air. Plavšić considers the end of the cigarette as it glows orange and then suddenly crushes it into a crystal ashtray sitting on the coffee table next to her.

> In 1993, Slobodan Milošević came to a meeting in Jahorina to talk about another proposed peace agreement that eventually failed. It was very soon after that infamous *Politika* news about my so-called statement on the radio and his, and his wife's, declaration that I was a psychopath. I was furious with him. Karadžić did not tell me that he was coming. If I knew I would never have gone to Jahorina. When his turn came to greet with me, I turned my back on him. Just before the war ended, Karadžić could not go to Dayton since there was an indictment against him, so he was asked to give Milošević authorisation to represent the Republic Srpska. Krajišnik, Karadžić and I signed the paperwork and Milošević represented the leadership of the Republic Srpska. I have to say he did a good job. My only regret was Sarajevo. I loved Sarajevo. Now I am over it, but for my whole life I was returning to it. But Milošević gave it to Alija [Izetbegović] and that was right, I guess, since the Serb leaders fled from the city too early. They were *pobjegulje* [escapees], and this is what Milošević called them [Krajišnik and Karadžić]. I did not even know they had left Sarajevo before me. But Milošević knew nothing about Sarajevo, it meant nothing to him. Milošević said to Alija in his whisky-drinking session during negotiations of the Dayton Peace Agreement, 'Here you go Alija, Sarajevo is yours, you deserve it'. With his 'gift' to Alija, hundreds of thousands of Serbs who had built their

lives for generations in that city had to flee after the peace agreement was signed ... those Serbs who stayed in Sarajevo during the war, who did not want to leave their homes, now left it as they were afraid to stay and live in Alija's kingdom. The tribunal never talked about this ethnic cleansing in peacetime ... We met once soon after Dayton was signed. Alija came to me and said, 'Congratulations, you got a state [Republika Srpska]!'

During the war, Plavšić made regular oral and written invitations to Serbs and others to join the army of Republika Srpska in their fight against Muslims and, later on, Croats. 'It was normal that I used my position to call dispersed Serbs to return to their homeland and fight for their people's survival. They [the prosecutors at the ICTY] used these patriotic calls as evidence of incitement of hatred. I found it ridiculous'. During the four years of war, Plavšić gave a number of inflammatory and racist speeches against Bosnian Muslims in particular. Employing her biologist expertise, she spoke with conviction that 'Muslims are genetically spoiled material'. Some of her infamous quotes that the ICTY also used as evidence of her incitements of hatred were, for example,

> It was deformed genetic material that embraced Islam. And now, of course, with each successive generation it becomes concentrated. It gets worse and worse. It simply expresses itself and dictates their style of thinking, which is rooted in their genes. And through the centuries, the genes degrade further.

Her derogatory views about Bosniaks have not changed after all these years. Dario Kordić's judgment recognised that people's mindset during war is altered; 'the unfortunate legacy of wars shows that ... many perpetrators believe that violations of binding international norms can be lawfully committed because they are fighting for a "just" cause'.[67] But Plavšić's views have never altered: they have been the same before, during and after the war. Plavšić is still against any 'mixing' of Serbs and Muslims, and she never supported 'mixed' marriages that were normal practice before the war. In 1994, she stated, 'We are upset by a rising number of mixed marriages between Serbs and Muslims, for they allow genes to be exchanged between ethnic groups, and lead subsequently to the degeneration of Serb nationality'.[68] Plavšić publicly called for mass displacement of Muslims.

> I would like us to cleanse Eastern Bosnia ... To tell you the truth I am not very well disposed towards them [Muslims]. But if I want to be at peace, I must give them something ... because then they would not keep disturbing me. This is how I perceive that thirty per cent [Bosnian Muslim population].[69]

In 2023, she told me, 'It is impossible to live with them [Muslims]. Serbs and Muslims are like fire and water; they cannot and should not mix'. Her voice was clear and assertive, leaving no room for negotiation. Plavšić said she never made any decisions with Karadžić or Mladić, the highest-ranked political and military decision-makers.[70] She told me that Carl Bildt, who acted as a witness in her trial, confirmed that she was never present during the talks on war and peace. Plavšić claims she knew nothing about crimes committed against Muslims and Croats for a long time and still firmly believes that detention camps established by Serbs during the war did not exist. She also confirmed that once she was told about them, she didn't do anything, and this is why she accepted guilt for the 'persecution'. Plavšić thought, and still believes, that they weren't detention camps but 'camps for war prisoners'. Despite overwhelming evidence, Plavšić continues to deny their existence.

Once the war was over with the signing of the Dayton Peace Agreement, the tensions between Plavšić and Karadžić continued to escalate.[71] She publicly talked about his criminal activities during the war and promised she would uproot corruption from the echelons of Republika Srpska. Plavšić accused Karadžić of having amassed a fortune through an illegal smuggling ring. Plavšić openly accused Karadžić of trading cigarettes, fuel, arms and ammunition and other goods on the black market during the war, and of gambling and embezzling funds for his own good. She also disclosed that he wanted to kill her due to her public accusations against him.[72] This was the political move that enabled her to become the next president of Republika Srpska.

Becoming Madam President

Plavšić was one of the founders of Republika Srpska and its second president, elected to the position in September 1996. Plavšić told me she didn't see it coming. She was surprised when she found out that she was on the list of SDS candidates for the next president of Republika Srpska. She took a sip of water and put the glass down.

> I came to attend the General Assembly of Republika Srpska and learnt during the meeting that I was one of the suggested candidates for the position of president in the forthcoming elections. I was confused. I did not expect to be one of the candidates since they knew that I didn't compromise, but criticised all the illegal activities carried out by the SDS party members and especially Karadžić, the president of the party. No one asked me if I agreed to be one of the candidates. I was surprised that they wanted me for a candidate and not professor Koljević and I only later found out why. They [the SDS Party] were afraid Koljević would extradite Karadžić since they perceived him as too close to the international community. This is how I became a choice for the president. I was also suitable because according to the constitution, I was the only one who could take over the presidential duties if the president 'was unable to', and as the ICTY was after Karadžić, I accepted the candidacy. However, Karadžić did not want to leave.

He was infected with the power. For him, leaving the position of the president was like separating him from life itself. He told me that he wanted to be president for two mandates and that he hoped to stay forever in the presidency. He loved power. He wanted to rule forever. I only had one month for the pre-election campaign ... But a lot of people were there to listen to my speeches. I told them about the Dayton Peace Agreement and why it was good for us, and about the SDS programme, which was also good; but I also spoke about the illegal trade and criminal activities of some of its staff. I told them, 'Elect me for your president and then we will together bring criminals to courts and put them in jails. We will establish the rule of law. This is what our people deserve and those who lost their lives!'

A roaring filled my ears, pounding like a drumbeat. I pictured Plavšić on the makeshift stage, speaking to the cheerful crowd in front of her. I felt my heart accelerate. For a moment, I felt nauseous. Plavšić blushed, her arms folded across her chest. She had huge support from the Serb people. Karadžić lost the support and trust of his people, and they were ready for change.[73] Plavšić was still seen as a lesser evil than Radovan Karadžić and was backed by the West. While she allowed Bosniaks and Croats to go back to their villages, Karadžić's people had sabotaged any such resettlement effort. The Stabilisation Force (SFOR) at the beginning provided passive support to Plavšić, helping her to secure her personal safety against attacks by pro-Karadžić forces.[74] They started to provide her with more active support, although initially, the international community was wary of associating too closely with Plavšić on account of her well-known role in the Bosnian Serb wartime leadership.[75] However, they knew that if the Dayton Agreement was to be implemented, they needed to find people within the Bosnian Serb leadership willing to follow a more 'moderate' and 'cooperative' path.[76] They saw Plavšić as 'their last chance' of finding a Bosnian Serb who would be ready to modify the fierce nationalist position taken during the war and who could also survive the hostile political climate in the Republika Srpska entity.

Madeleine Albright, who gave testimony in favour of Plavšić, called her 'a fierce Serb nationalist known as the Iron Lady of the Balkans'. She considered Plavšić's views 'extreme'.[77] 'Serb nationalism was a major part of Plavšić's identity, and she was not about to apologize for it'.[78] But Plavšić did not see anything wrong with being an extreme nationalist and confronted Albright when she accused her of nationalism. 'Tell me Madam Albright, do you love your homeland, America?' Albright answered, 'Of course, I do', to which Plavšić replied with another question, 'And would you defend your homeland and its people?' Albright answered in the affirmative and Plavšić had the final say, 'So, you see, the two of us are no different at all'. But the nationalism that Plavšić preaches is extreme. Her concept of a homeland—one in which people must share ancestry, language and culture—is a Serb homeland; one in which there is hardly a place for others except Serbs. And if others are allowed, they must live under Serb rule. Her type of nationalism is both ethnic and expansionist, one that features chauvinism. This kind of nationalism involves a complete dismissal of the right to self-determination of other nations and seeks to exercise power over them. It is a form of nationalism that opposes diversity and the inclusion of others, unless they occupy a subordinate position.

At the beginning of 1996, Karadžić was forced to leave the political scene of Republika Srpska under enormous international pressure. On 25 July 1995, the ICTY filed an initial indictment against him with charges of two counts of genocide, five counts of crimes against humanity and four counts of violations of the laws or customs of war committed by Serb forces during the armed conflict in BiH from 1992 until 1995. Karadžić was alleged to be individually criminally responsible for those crimes, inter alia, through his participation in a number of joint criminal enterprises.[79] He withdrew from political life soon after the indictment was released and went into hiding. He was replaced with Plavšić, who took on the role of acting president for a few months until new elections were scheduled later that year.

> I had to do that. It was the only solution according to our constitution. Karadžić went into hiding. I told him he should surrender, but he didn't want to hear about it. I said the same to Mladić, but he also refused to surrender. I was a bit disappointed with him since I really have a great respect for Mladić. When he was indicted, almost at the same time as Karadžić, I told him that if he wanted good for his people then he needed to withdraw from politics and from his role as the general of the Serb army.[80] He was reluctant. He did not want to. I had to convince him. I pleaded with him that he must do that, that he could not stay in the miliary command of the Republika Srpska as an indictee. After many hours negotiating with him, he finally agreed but did not agree to surrender ... I personally gave him the letter of resignation that he signed in front of me. He did not change the text of the resignation, but he just said, 'If I was asked to do this by one of those two [Karadžić and Krajišnik], I would not do so, but I will do this for you'. We always had respect for each other. He is a man with dignity. We both despised Karadžić. That was our last meeting, the last time I saw him ...

As soon as Plavšić was elected president, she made a political shift and turned her back on her long-term collaborators and mentors, and started to collaborate with the international community. She cut her ties with the SDS and formed her own party, the Serb People's Alliance Party, and elicited Western support for her anti-corruption drive. She changed her tone and became more moderate in her talk about other ethnic groups, whom she welcomed if they were 'ready to accept the Republika Srpska values and defend them with their lives'.[81] Her speeches were about the rule of law, about rooting out corruption and nepotism, about equality and human rights for all.[82] She stated, 'Our [Serb] aim was not an ethnically clean state, but a state in which the rule of law prevails, and in which the rights of all will be in accordance with their obligations'.

Due to such dramatic changes in her politics and tone, she enjoyed support from the international community. Plavšić knew she had no choice but to follow the party line if she was to stay in politics. She believed firmly in the Dayton Accords and decided to follow its provisions, which were extremely opposite to her personal views and wishes; yet she knew that the time had come to play into them if Republika Srpska was to stay an entity. In her opinion, this was the price to be paid: the trade off between ethnic nationalist politics and democracy. The West did not have much to choose from since Karadžić was indicted and already in hiding. As Human Rights Watch observed at the time:

> *The international community's current policy in Republika Srpska of providing political and military support for President Biljana Plavšić is being offered as an alternative to the arrest and transfer of Karadžić to the International Criminal Tribunal for the former Yugoslavia (ICTY) in The Hague.*[83]

They further reported:

> *Plavšić, irrespective of her recent acceptance of the Dayton Agreement, remains an ultra-nationalist, who believes that Serbs and Muslims are biologically different and unable to co-exist, and has described 'ethnic cleansing' as a Western term for a natural phenomenon. She does not regard Karadžić as a war criminal and criticises only his post-war leadership.*[84]

During that time, Plavšić's language became one of inclusion and human rights rather than exclusion and incitement of hatred of 'others'. For that reason, she was perceived as 'a traitor' to those ultra-nationalist Serbs who resented the West and its politics, and who did not want to share their piece of land with other ethnicities. For the next two years until late 1998 when her term was finished and the call for new elections released, she enjoyed support and worked closely with diplomats from all around the world on the implementation of the Dayton Peace Agreement. She told me:

> My role was to keep convincing Serbs that Dayton worked for us—that it gave us the state. We had our piece of land to govern, and in my eyes, Dayton did us a favour. After a long time, we had our piece of land: Serb land with a vast majority of Serbs living in it. We could rule ourselves. Republika Srpska was the first Serb state since 1918, and that was a huge thing. This was a historic moment.

Although Republika Srpska is not a state but one of two entities within the sovereign state of BiH, Plavšić keeps referring to it as such. Her deliberate statements that the Republika Srpska is a state align with the public statements of its officials, especially its president, Milorad Dodik, regarding plans for its secession from BiH. Plavšić has numerous anecdotes from that period of her life. She told me how the (now retired) American diplomat, General Jacques Paul Klein, came to her office one day to show her the newly designed flag of BiH.

> He took it out of his pocket and stretched it across my office desk. I looked at it and had no emotions whatsoever. It was yellow and blue with some stars. I said, 'This is good. I am indifferent towards it. I think other nations will be too. That is a good sign'. I asked him, 'Why do you pity Bosniaks so much? You just look at them as victims and do everything for them'. He said to me, 'Biljana, don't you see what the whole point of it all is?' I asked, 'What?' I was thinking that all the Americans care about is the Middle East, and then it finally became clear to me. He wanted us [Serbs] from one side and the Croats from the other to have control over the Muslims in the middle ... to be kind of a gatekeeper of Europe from their [Muslim] invasion. They used

us as some kind of a buffer zone to prevent the Islamic enclave from spreading ...

Plavšić and her party were not re-elected in the 1998 elections. Around that time, the high representative for BiH, Carlos Westendorp, came to see Plavšić.

> He told me that in the period after the elections, some conditions would need to be fulfilled from the Dayton Peace Agreement. He and his people, together with the newly elected president and his cabinet, would have to cooperate and fulfill their obligations ... I did not understand what he meant so I asked, 'What do you mean? We are fulfilling, more or less, all our obligations from the Agreement'. He said that he meant on actioning the arrests or surrender of Karadžić and Mladić. I just started to pray and cross my chest, praying to God not to give me this job. Two days later, Westendorp came into my office with his delegation to tell me that I had lost the election and that my opponent had got more votes. He was sorry, but he said, 'That can be changed if you want it'. I was totally confused with his offer. 'Is it really possible to do so, to change results? No, I don't want that'. They did not try to push me, but someone said, 'That is not so much a pity for you personally, but it is for Republika Srpska'.

One of her memorable meetings was with Madeleine Albright, the then-US Secretary of State, whom she met in Banjaluka during her presidency.

> After an official meeting with other staff, she [Madeleine Albright] asked if the two of us could have a coffee in my office. She had just delivered her speech, and at the end of it she told me that we must extradite Karadžić. I said to her that I cannot extradite him. I don't want to do so. She gave me some papers with the request for his extradition, and I tore them apart and tossed them in the bin. I told her, 'You should know, Madam Albright, that we have a constitution in my country, and I am not going to breach it. As with all other

constitutions, I believe, and you should know this, we do not extradite our citizens'. There was a silence in the room. A huge tension. Then she suddenly said, all smiles, 'Madam Plavšić, I would love to see your office. Can the two of us go there and you can show me around?' She did a favour to everyone with this suggestion because everyone felt so tense. We went upstairs and ordered ourselves coffees. She told me, 'You know, Biljana, if these were different times, the two of us could be friends'. I replied, 'Friends? No way'. We talked about Karadžić and I told her, 'Why don't you leave him alone? He has just got a grandson, so it is not easy for him to hide all the time'. Albright said, 'You know, maybe we could sweep this under the carpet, but he does not allow us to do so. He seeks attention, he provokes us, he just gave an interview to some Greek newspaper'. I said, 'You see, you could just leave him alone. He can stay in Greece, and you can just forget about him. Can you withdraw that indictment against him?' She said, 'I don't know. I'll have to ask. I will ask Clinton ....' We never met again. She came to testify as a witness in the court [ICTY], and she said about me, 'that woman does not know how to lie'.

After nine years of Plavšić's engagement with state institutions, first as a member of the BiH presidency, then as a member of the Republika Srpska presidency, and then as vice-president of Republika Srpska before finally as its president, her political career was over. She withdrew from all her duties to live a peaceful private life in her apartment in Banjaluka. However, only a year later, in December 2000, she would receive a visit and news that would dramatically change her life.

3

INDICTMENT AND DETENTION

> I am not afraid of the tribunal's secret indictments, because if we take into consideration that more than 20,000 young men died in Republika Srpska and more than 600,000 Serbs were expelled from their homes, what is the significance of some individuals ending up in The Hague?[1]

Just before Christmas 2000, when most of the foreign representatives and ambassadors leave for a winter vacation, Thomas Miller, the former American ambassador in Sarajevo, contacted Plavšić and scheduled a visit. Plavšić thought there was nothing odd about this as almost all of the ambassadors, as well as other representatives of the international community, continued to pay her visits. This was despite the fact that she had lost the elections and her presidency in the autumn of 1998. Still, Plavšić wondered why Miller wanted to see her now, when everyone was going home for the Christmas holidays. Plavšić tells me she was busy and unable to welcome him in the morning. He, however, insisted. He told her that he was in a hurry and said it was 'something extremely important'. So, she suggested he come to her house in the evening.

Miller arrived with another man from his embassy and a female interpreter. Looking through her window, Plavšić raised her brow, clicked with her tongue, and said to me:

> I remember well her [the interpreter's] face, and her eyes full of tears, when Miller asked me, 'Do you know that you are indicted for war crimes by The Hague tribunal? The indictment is sealed'. I was not surprised or confused. I had no fear. It had been a while since I'd raised my endurance threshold pretty high. 'No, I do not know', I calmly answered. However, I was preparing for receiving such news for years, but I never mentioned it to anyone, nor did it affect my behaviour or my determination. Yet, as the time passed, it became the subject of my thoughts more and more. As a result, I was mentally completely ready when it became real.

With a convincing tone, she continued to tell me that she believes the preparation for such news had started in April 1992 at a meeting with the United Nations Protection Forces (UNPROFOR). The Yugoslav People's Army had just withdrawn from Bosnia and Herzegovina (BiH), and Stjepan Kljujić, a former Croat member of the BiH presidency, stood opposite her with two former colonels, Stanislav Čađo and Zdravko Tolimir.[2] Apparently, Kljujić looked her in the eye and said to her, 'Goodbye Ms Plavšić, see you in court for war crimes, where I shall be a witness, and you will stand as the accused'. This meeting, and Kljujić's threat, would be repeated by Plavšić many times during our conversations. She speculated that Kljujić 'knew' then that she was already 'set up by the West' to be accused of war crimes.

> I was amazed by the absurdity of this. How could I be a war criminal if I was still in Sarajevo, and there was still no war in Bosnia? This was the first announcement, and in the meantime, the UN Security Council in 1993 established the Tribunal for the former Yugoslavia, and the first indictments were about to be raised. It was then that I remembered his statement.

INDICTMENT AND DETENTION

This alleged suggestion made by Kljujić was something Plavšić used as evidence that 'it was all prearranged' for her to one day be prosecuted by the Tribunal. It was in those days that, as Plavšić told me, Baščaršija was covered with photos of 'war criminals'—that is, members of the entire leadership of the Serb people in BiH.[3] She was in one of those photos too. Her conclusion was that it was all planned, but Serbs did not know it because they did not practice 'smart politics'.

> What did Serbia do? What kind of information had Milošević received if he received anything at all? Why am I mentioning only him? Because, unfortunately, he was the only one who led the terrible politics. Was there any politics at all, or it was merely survival from one day to another? He was our tragedy. I was his constant opposition.

A month before Miller's visit, something happened in front of Plavšić's home, which she, at the time, did not fully understand. Plavšić was in the apartment on the day but heard nothing. When it was all over, a neighbour told her what had happened. UNPROFOR soldiers, fully armed, surrounded the building in which she lived with other residents. They were trying to break through the building entrance, which was locked. Many passers-by gathered, and the UNPROFOR eventually gave up their efforts. They told the crowd that they had to secure the building because Mladen Ivanić, a Bosnian Serb politician, needed to host someone.[4] They left the area soon after, perhaps wanting to prevent people from panicking.

Having heard nothing, Plavšić was surprised by the call from a UNPROFOR commander apologising for the incident and explaining that it was all about a visit Ivanić was meant to host that day. He explained that one of the American diplomats was to come to the political party premises to meet Ivanić, so they had to secure the whole neighbourhood. However, he did not convince her.

None of this was true, but the apology and deep respect were there. That's how they [the international community] did their business. All lies, but sugar-coated. Just to be ready, I packed the most necessary belongings in my bag and waited for the UNPROFOR to return, but they did not—they postponed it until Christmas. Right after this event, a friend of mine came to my house suggesting I should go into hiding for some time at least. He suggested I should think it over, and together with others, decide what the best course of action would be. First and foremost, his gesture was friendly, and that is something you do not forget. He was a professional, operational agent, and I knew his qualities.[5] But I had made up my mind long ago; the decision was quite in line with my conscience and my principles. No hiding, I am not capable of it. An open life is the best life, and in my life, I did nothing I was ashamed of or needed to hide from, even in those times during the war. I was curious and wanted to know what the Tribunal had against me. I knew I had done nothing wrong, so I wanted to know what they were accusing me of. My hiding would be just an excuse for them to harass the people of Republika Srpska, and we are all familiar with the methods they use to do so. They had become the true masters of this kind of torture. I always remember how our poor priest, Starovlah, ended up with them.[6] Already I was thinking about how we could make that court [the ICTY] meaningless with its judges. It was obvious to everyone that they only prosecute Serbs and are only interested in one side and one story. The court aims for injustice rather than reconciliation.

Plavšić was expecting to be arrested on that day. With a blank look, she continued her recollection of these historic events.

> In 1999, for several months I'd been hearing rumours that the indictment against me had been sealed and that they, *zapadnjaci* [the Westerners], had been waiting for a moment that was right for them to publish it. I heard about it here and there, and it was whispered among some functionaries in my party, that it was not good for the party to be led by someone indicted by the Tribunal. They were impatient,

particularly those who wanted to take over the party, which eventually happened after the election campaign. At the same time, Slobodan Milošević offered me a house in Belgrade, explaining that Banjaluka was a 'small' environment for me.

She looked up at me, clasping her fingers together.

> I remember I was thinking, maybe they [the international community] had given up their usual habit [emphasis on 'usual habit'] of throwing a 70-year-old woman on the ground and placing their boots on her head with their guns cocked, because that is what they did when they arrested and transported many others to The Hague. Much could be written about this, since I was told a lot by those who went through it all. Those images were sent out to the world, but it seems they [the international community] thought it would be too much to do such a thing to me, so they sent Miller to inform me that I had been accused. He also came to notify me about a prosecutor from The Hague who would be coming to visit me in two days' time to personally hand me the indictment. I remained calm and 'kept my cool' because I had already learned that nothing unpleasant should ever surprise me ... I'd survived bad things from my own people, so this could not come as a surprise.

Plavšić reminded me how she'd escaped from the 'Muslim fundamentalists' just when the grenades blasted around her in Sarajevo. She added that 'worst of all', she'd experienced threats and insults from her 'own people' such as from Slobodan Milošević and Radovan Karadžić. Very slowly and calmly, and with a tinge of irony, she said,

> There you go, the Serbs wanted to kill me as well. So, if I experienced and survived all that, there was no need to fear the UNPROFOR, NATO and The Hague. The Tribunal was made up of foreigners who wanted to use trials to put a seal on their [Serbian] politics during the [Bosnian] war. All this went through my mind while Miller, the American ambassador, informed me that I was expected in The Hague

and that I was indicted for war crimes. I looked at him, wondering why he would try at all to alleviate something that could not be alleviated, and I looked at the tears in the eyes of the young woman, the interpreter. I wanted to console her. Deep down, I thought about how unaware they were of my ability to endure much more.

Prosecutor Brenda Hollis arrived from The Hague two days later to officially hand her the indictment. Plavšić's ex-husband, Žarko Banjac, along with his colleague Krstan Simić, arrived from Belgrade and attended the official announcement and delivery of the indictment.

Plavšić said her only goal in her meeting with Hollis was to find out what she could expect from the Tribunal. She was prepared to demand to appear in The Hague only after Orthodox Christmas, which she wanted to spend with her family. She was successful with this request.

The entire conversation during that meeting with Hollis was recorded, but Plavšić does not recall its details. She was more interested in assessing Hollis because Plavšić was convinced she would be the prosecutor in her case, and she wanted to study her and to figure out whether she was 'a professional'. This is how Plavšić thought back then. Little did she know that judging Hollis was done in vain: she was only present during her first appearance in the court. She sighed heavily,

> The indictment could not have been worse: the heaviest indictment possible. It contained terms such as genocide, criminal association and criminal persecution on racial and religious grounds. All of which was done against Serbs in World War II. That is what my lawyers and I concluded after having skimmed through the indictment. Žarko explained that they [the prosecutors] would have to prove all this, and one cannot prove what does not exist. Krstan, already with some experience with the Tribunal, told me I would have to hate them quite a lot to endure all that was awaiting me. But how can I hate? I cannot do that. I still do not hate them.

INDICTMENT AND DETENTION

When Hollis handed Plavšić the indictment, she also announced that the trial would be joint for her and Momčilo Krajišnik.[7] Plavšić claimed that she considered a joint trial improper because 'our positions and the real power were not the same'. Plavšić was disturbed by the thought that for two to three years during the trial she would be tried with Krajišnik, whom she despised. She argued that they did not have the same decision-making powers so they could not be held accountable for the same crimes. 'Krajišnik was the second man to Karadžić and sometimes even the first. Sometimes his word would be the last one. I had been asked nothing'. She pleaded to the court to separate their trials, but the court rejected her plea. Only when Plavšić decided to plead guilty to the count of persecution was her case separated from Krajišnik's.

Once the indictment was unsealed, Plavšić was successful in postponing her appearance before the Tribunal until 10 January 2001 so she could spend the Orthodox Christmas holidays with her family and finish some business. At that time, everyone was preparing for Christmas, going somewhere, or having someone come to visit them, so she hid the news from her friends and colleagues, not wanting to 'spoil all that joy'.

> I thought, nobody will even notice that I am gone since I often spend holidays with my brother in Belgrade. I did not want anyone to feel any moral obligation to hide me somewhere because I did not want that. I only wanted to leave quietly, without hurting anyone, or upsetting them with my departure. And it worked out. My loved ones thought there must have been some mistake in my arrest, even Žarko, who was present at the delivery of the indictment. He knew that an innocent person can be charged, but in the many years of his law practice he did not believe someone innocent could be convicted. It was a sad Christmas for both me and my loved ones, but I consoled myself and them that it could have been worse. We had already seen it: the people

who were taken by surprise, arrested, harassed. At least I was spared from such things.

Plavšić tells me that when the Tribunal was established, it started operating by 'chasing people by using all means.' 'Foreign soldiers', she recounts, 'chased people in their houses, in front of families, on the streets and in public spaces with their arms pressed against their temples, tackling, kicking, being taken somewhere unknown while blindfolded, in pyjamas, without shoes. They even killed some in this process'.[8]

In those three days spent with her family before her departure to The Hague, Plavšić's brother asked her fearfully, 'Is this something that really must be done?' She replied with determination, 'Yes, it is'.

Taken to The Hague

On 9 January 2001, Plavšić was at Mahovljani Airport, Banjaluka. She was accompanied by MT, her long-time and faithful personal driver. While driving towards the airport, MT emotionally offered to testify in her defence: 'I will be your witness'. Plavšić was deeply touched by his offer although she knew she needed witnesses who shared her rank. On her way to the airport, Plavšić was stopped by a UNPROFOR vehicle and handed a letter written by General Jacques Paul Klein expressing his disappointment with her arrest. She told me, 'The letter was full of sympathies, compassion and offers of help, if I was ever in need of any ... Klein's letter was sincere ... others, and there were many, remained silent'. Plavšić was obviously moved by his words, but she said resolutely, 'I knew that only dear God could help me'.

At the airport there was a small group of colleagues waiting to say goodbye to her, which included Prime Minister Milorad

Dodik; the then-Minister of Civil Affairs and Communication Svetozar Mihajlović; and Krstan Simić, the lawyer who would accompany her on her flight. Her last minutes of freedom soon evaporated as she, together with Simić, boarded a modest white plane. The flight 'passed quickly' thanks to Simić, who instructed Plavšić on everything that awaited her in The Hague, from the next-day appearance in court to giving her tips about the Scheveningen Prison.[9] He had experience because as a lawyer he was already engaged in another case before the Tribunal. Plavšić described her thoughts upon arrival in the Netherlands:

> We landed at some military airport. It was my first time in the Netherlands, in the country of tulips. I had studied this country from another perspective. The Netherlands has always been interesting to me and famous for several well-equipped laboratories dealing with plant virology. I always had a plan to visit these institutes in some of my professional roles. Of course, this should be in the month of April when the tulips bloom. Colourful tulips brought enormous wealth to the Netherlands 300 years ago. This flower, over time, has become a true beauty in the hands of seasoned gardeners. The arrival of the tulip from Central Asia to the Netherlands resulted in a huge miracle on the stock market. Their bulbs were measured by the value that is used to measure the value of diamonds today. The irony of this fate was that instead of coming to see a display of tulips, I was here as a war crime indictee before the Tribunal in front of the gates of the famous Scheveningen Prison.

Just less than three hours before, Plavšić had left her friends mourning for her at the airport in Mahovljani. At the Dutch military airport where they landed, the setup was different. Here, Hollis was present again with a few people from the prosecution's administration. There was also a high-ranking police officer wearing white gloves 'as if he was going to a parade'. Next to him was another police officer holding a tray covered with a white cloth, and in the middle of the tray, there were handcuffs. Plavšić's memory of her official incarceration is powerful:

> The first one [police officer] read something in Dutch, then the translator translated it into Serbian. It was a statement outlining that I had been a prisoner of their country since I put my foot on Dutch ground. The man in the uniform informed me that I was being deprived of freedom. He read the text. I heard the translation, but my attention was directed to the tray with the white cloth. I saw the handcuffs, but also my head cut off like the severed head of St John; I was just surprised to see what was on the tray, the handcuffs, my head, St John's head. I cannot understand why they wanted to handcuff my hands. Was that truly necessary when I came to them on my own? They wanted to humiliate me. The handcuffs in my case held no real significance, but represented a symbol of humiliation.
>
> This was a real arrest, not like the one in Vienna or the one at the Belgrade airport when I was interrogated by Milošević's police following the instructions of Radovan Karadžić. Can a normal mind understand this, and can some connection exist between these events? My god, what was going on, and what else was going to happen to one peaceful person, the aggrieved, a university professor, who, as Dodik once said in an interview, 'wouldn't hurt a fly'? I am a person who never ever raised her hand against anyone. I mourned everyone's evil fate and never reconciled with my inability to help everyone in need.

It was at this moment that Plavšić fully became aware of the situation in which she found herself: the indictment was there, the cuffs were there, she was 'the prisoner of the International Criminal Tribunal for the former Yugoslavia'. She said goodbye to Simić before being taken to a military base surrounded by policemen in civilian clothes. She spent the night there, and the next morning, before going to the court, a young police officer 'kindly offered' her a thirty-minute drive through The Hague. He wanted her to get some sense of the location of the city where she would be detained. In a short time, after being driven from one end to the other, and then to the coast, she could see and feel 'the connection of this country with the sea, and how these people had created land from the sea'.

> I admired the people who created such a beautiful land, because everything here, including the soil I stood on, was the work of the human brain and hand. On the other hand, God has given everything to some, and yet they cannot make a thing. I thought about this while talking to this pleasant man. The time was slowly running out as the time and place approached where I would spend my days and nights with those who would govern my destiny. The ride was over, the conversation stopped, and suddenly everything became very serious. He apologised and handcuffed me, tightening the cuffs. Suddenly I had to scratch my ears, my hair falling over my face. I had to put it behind my ears. I could not breathe normally, as if the handcuffs clamped my lungs and not my hands. I took a deep breath but there was no air. I recognised what it was all about; it is just like the fear of a small space; it's claustrophobia, manifesting itself for the first time in a serious form, which followed me through the prison cells to the present day.

Handcuffed, Plavšić was picked up from this 'tour' by three female guards who took her to the back entrance of the court, which in 1994 and 1995 established its offices within the Aegon Insurance Building in The Hague. At that time, the building was still partially occupied by Aegon. The court's detention facilities were situated in the suburb of Scheveningen, three kilometres away from The Hague. These three female guards would accompany her each time she went to the court. Plavšić was the only female prisoner, at the age of 71. They walked her down the long hallways to the elevator, and eventually they entered a small room where the accused waits to enter the courtroom. The room had no windows. It was empty with only three wooden boards fixed to the wall, two chairs and a small table. There was a toilet in there too, with no curtains or door.

> Well, for the purpose of this room one does not need anything else, but I still think that one windowpane would have eased the anxiety that was now boiling. But that was probably what was expected: for the anxiety to grow and for you to then enter the arena—the courtroom. I had never been in any courtroom before; I had only seen it in the movies. But now I was the one to participate in its function, and I was just 'a cog' in that machine. The machine existed because of me and the others who were placed behind those bars of the Scheveningen Prison. My people [Serbs] made up the majority of the 'machine cogs'.

Once Plavšić was settled in the chair, one of the guards passed her a cigarette from her bag.

> While smoking, I was thinking that most humans are perfectly adaptable, and I am in that majority. I started thinking of the whole situation as a biologist, and my profession helped me to get through the situation that I now found myself in. Cigarettes helped me, biology as well, but still defiance helped the most, and fatigue a bit too; there were too many impressions, mostly negative, in such a short time since the plane had landed in the Netherlands. Yet the most striking image was the tray with the white cloth and handcuffs, on which I imagined my head, and the head of St John. I suddenly lost interest in whatever was supposed to come next.

With this train of thought, having prayed, and holding a small icon of Bogorodica Trojeručica, Plavšić was taken to the courtroom.[10]

> I remember 10 January 2001 very well. It was the first time I had been in a courtroom, and in my thoughts, I was with my parents, wondering if they could see this thing going on, what was happening to their child. They were proud of me in every way, and now, with no false modesty, I could tell, they had a reason. That is what came to my mind in the courtroom that day.

INDICTMENT AND DETENTION

Once in the courtroom, Plavšić was greeted by her lawyer, Krstan Simić, and she repeated to him what she had to say. She told me, 'It was all pure formality, but this was a necessary part of the show, whose end would be unknown for maybe two to three years'. There followed a series of standard questions and answers that Simić had taught her how to answer. Back then, she said she did not feel she was guilty of any of the charges.

> It was all terrible, that place, people, reality ... I prayed to God and my dead parents: they did not raise me for this. But who would know that patriotism is a war crime? Not for the others [Croats and Bosniaks], but for Serbs, yes. This is what was going through my head. Once they finished talking, I just said, 'Your Honour, I have read the indictment, and I do not feel guilty on any count of the indictment'. It was all over in forty-five minutes. Afterwards, I was talking to Krstan when I saw her [Carla Del Ponte] slowly approaching. I saw her for the first time as she walked straight towards me and held out her hand. As she was much shorter than me, and I was standing on a step, the only thing I saw was that straw-yellow hair, which resembled a cheap wig, but it was not a wig. Politely, which is somehow unnecessary in this situation, she suggested that the two of us have a coffee in her office. I agreed, provided that Krstan, my lawyer, joined me. She left after ten minutes, and Krstan and I were escorted to her office. We met several staff as we passed through, and finally we entered her very modest office. I noticed nothing except a few pictures that I would normally gladly look at, but there was no opportunity to do so, and my attention was focused on one person who, whenever she appeared, enacted her authority.

Plavšić's first encounter with the ICTY's chief prosecutor, Carla Del Ponte, has stayed etched in her memory to this day. Plavšić told me that she studied her as they engaged in conversation, as they drank coffee, and as the two of them smoked. Plavšić scoffed,

> We only had the same cigarettes in common ... white Marlboros. She tried to bribe me by saying that she would supply me with original

American-made Marlboro Golds while I was in detention. She thought I would sell myself for a box of cigarettes. I told her, 'No, thank you, my Marlboros are just fine'.

This mutual 'sin'—smoking—was a topic of conversation between them for a short period. Plavšić was drawn to Del Ponte's facial expressions, which she described as a 'combination of curiosity and domination'. Plavšić dipped her chin, her eyes widening.

> Her [Del Ponte's] look expressed a sort of pleasure while watching her prey. Prosecutor Hollis had a face that evoked austerity and calmness without a single trace of Del Ponte's 'bestial' look. Carla offered me her Marlboro cigarettes, saying they were original. I took one but continued smoking my own, which was also quite good. In the conversation, she informed Krstan that it would not be possible for him to represent me since he was already appointed in another case as a defence lawyer. Everything but this last bit of information was completely insignificant. When we left the office, we both wondered what this call for coffee meant. But eight years later, an answer came from her book, from Carla Del Ponte herself. As we talked about some ordinary things, I was analysing her face, looking for the dominant trait of this woman, because as a *lovac* ['hunter'], she was thinking about what tactics she could use against her 'prey'—me.[11] My initial feeling was that she was a professionally ambitious woman who would crush everything that stood in her way. That feeling was confirmed when three years later, I read an interview her ex-husband gave about her, and he emphasised that this was her main character trait. During our first encounter, although the conversation was insignificant, I noticed her face strongly revealing her emotions. I left her office with some new cognitions of a woman whom I was to confront for a long period of time. After this conversation—which I still do not know whether it was a part of the court's procedure, or whether Del Ponte, being impatient as she is, wanted to get to know her 'victim' better, which is probable—they took me back to that tiny room without windows. Soon after that they took me to Scheveningen. And this is how my prison days began.

Carla Del Ponte also describes her encounter with Plavšić in her book. Plavšić copy-pasted the paragraph from Del Ponte's book into the diary she wrote while in prison. This is what Del Ponte wrote about their meeting:

> *She tried to talk to me woman to woman. Dressed in a stiff tweed skirt, like a proper British lady, she informed me that she was a doctor of biology and proceeded to describe the superiority of Serbian people. Her nonsense was nauseating, and I brought the meeting to an end. I wanted to seek a life imprisonment against her.*[12]

The animosity between these two women remained until the end.

Taken into Detention

Around noon, the meeting with Del Ponte was over, and Plavšić was to be taken into detention. She told me she became suddenly curious to 'enter behind that solid gate and high walls into the building that is already known to everyone ... its inhabitants mostly members of my country'. She had to hand over all of her personal belongings at the entrance. Between two drags of cigarettes, she added, 'New faces ... new guards led me through some halls before we reached our destination—that is, my cell. I did not meet anyone from my floor; it was lunchtime, and everyone was locked up.' The prison warden of 'the most famous prison' arrived to greet Plavšić. A smile stretched across her face as she recalled, 'I really could have almost completely forgotten where I was, as if it was some sort of celebration. He was so friendly and wonderful'. Plavšić's experience with the prison administration and the staff was positive during her short stay in Scheveningen Prison. She said, 'I may not be qualified to talk about the professionalism of the staff there, but one year is still enough time for some evaluation'.

During her stay, the demographics of the prison changed a few times; new people would come, some would leave, but her initial positive impression did not change. Plavšić befriended Dragoljub Prcać, who came not long after she did.[13] Prcać was a deputy commander of the notorious Omarska prison camp during the war in BiH and was detained on 5 March 2000. He was convicted of crimes against humanity and violations of the laws or customs of war and sentenced to five years imprisonment. General Radislav Krstić, to whom she was close in age, was already there. Krstić was a Bosnian Serb deputy commander and later chief of staff of the Drina Corps of the army of Republika Srpska from October 1994 until 12 July 1995.[14] He was arrested on 2 December 1998. Krstić was convicted of aiding and abetting genocide, crimes against humanity and violations of the laws or customs of war. He was sentenced to thirty-five years imprisonment. Krstić was later moved to another floor where most of the military personnel were, and Plavšić 'missed him'. The two of them became close while awaiting their trials.

> When I arrived on that first day, my neighbours—martyrs from the same floor—came to greet me. Everyone from my floor arrived carrying gifts—coffee, sugar, cookies, sodas—as is the custom in our culture when coming to pay a visit to someone. They were Dragoljub Prcać from Prijedor, Mario Ćerkez from Vitez, Dario Kordić, Goran Jelisić and Esad Landžo. In that period, this was the composition of the inmates from the first floor of the prison unit in Scheveningen.

For about ten days, while drinking coffee and going for one-hour recreational walks in the detention yard, Plavšić listened to their stories and experiences with the court and detention; according to her, they 'were selfless in sharing them'. Her new fellow inmates were aware of the importance of these first encounters that would make the beginning of her prison life easier. Everything was discussed, but certainly what was most discussed was, according

President Biljana Plavšić and Javier Solana, the NATO Secretary General, meeting Plavšić's president's cabinet. Banjaluka, 19 December 1997. © Ranko Cukovic

President Biljana Plavšić holds up three fingers in the Serbian nationalist salute at a rally. Banjaluka, 18 November 1997.
© Ranko Cukovic

President Biljana Plavšić's rally in support of her political party. Prijedor, 7 August 1997. © Ranko Cukovic

President Biljana Plavšić's rally in support of her political party. Doboj, 20 July 1997. © Ranko Cukovic

President Biljana Plavšić with Bill Clinton, the US president, Jacques Paul Klein, the head of UNMIBH, and Miloš Prica, chief of the president's cabinet, Sarajevo, 22 December 1997. © Ranko Cukovic

Vice-President Biljana Plavšić with Manojlo Milovanović, Colonel-General of the Army of Republika Srpska, and Ljubiša 'Mauzer' Savić, the commandant of the paramilitary 'Panthers Guard' unit, from Bijeljina. Vranovača, near Brčko, the demarcation line bewteen the Serb and Bosnian armies, 17 April 1995.

© Ranko Cukovic

The president Biljana Plavšić praying at the liturgy in the Cathedral of Christ the Saviour, a Serbian Orthodox church in Banjaluka.
© Ranko Cukovic

Biljana Plavšić strolling in her local park, September 2019.
© Olivera Simić

Biljana Plavšić going through her archives, March 2019.
© Olivera Simić

Biljana Plavšić reading the daily newspaper *Politika*, November 2018.
© Olivera Simić

Biljana Plavšić in her living room. Belgrade, October 2019.
© Olivera Simić

to Plavšić, 'the interrogators [prosecutors and judges]'. However, they never discussed the reasons they were in prison, 'which was normal', Plavšić guessed. But there was one person she did not want to meet—the Bosnian Muslim commander, Naser Orić.[15]

> One of the Serb detainees told me one day, 'I want to introduce you to Naser Orić, he is a nice guy'. Nice guy? My goodness how can he say that about a man who committed atrocities in his region. I said that I did not want to meet him.

The composition of fellow prisoners on her floor changed over time; some were moved to other floors, and new defendants came in. There was enough space for them all because, according to Plavšić, 'Everything was planned in advance: how many defendants, and to which ethnic groups they belonged. Two thirds were Serbs, and the rest were Croats and Muslims'. Plavšić told me that relationships among the detainees of all ethnicities were very good.

> Those relationships among detainees were strange. It is a phenomenon that deserves special research—a whole institute of psychiatrists are needed to delve into it! I am not sure if I even understand why I did not want to meet Orić, as if other Muslims there were better than him ... no, they were not, but still I did not want to have anything to do with Orić.

Plavšić believed that the shared sense of suffering and isolation brought inmates from various ethnic groups closer together, fostering mutual understanding and trust, so their different ethnic origins became less significant. If tensions or frictions existed among any of the defendants, they were based on other reasons. Plavšić gave examples:

> There were small and big differences in the status of the families of defendants. Where they came from and their upbringing made a

difference—whether they were from urban or rural families. Some were also working on improving themselves. So, on this basis, people were making friendships; for example, Serb Goran Jelisić[16] and mujahideen[17] commandant Amir Kubura.[18] These two were hanging out a lot and had no respect for anyone there. They were rude and arrogant. In a long talk with Jelisić, I concluded that his values were upside down. He was proud of the things normal people would be ashamed of and vice versa. What is crazy for us was normal to him. I was sincerely sorry for his parents, and I asked him where his parents and teachers were during his childhood, and he replied, full of himself, 'I would pretend to go to school, but I did not really go to school, but you know, I was doing stuff around the school'. This was enough for me to understand that his childhood, and what he did in his youth, made sense of his later actions for which he was prosecuted before the court. I wanted to find out more, especially about the beginning of the war, so I asked him, 'Was there someone superior to you in your unit, to whom you were accountable to?' His nice face turned into a grimace of an offended man and he said to me, 'What is wrong with you? Me, to be subordinated to someone? I was subordinated to no one. If you were my boss there, or Radovan [Karadžić], and ordered me to stop killing, I would kill you too'. This was the end of our conversation, and I thought that if we [Serbs] had just three more people like this man, it was unavoidable that what happened would happen. And there were more of these men. Someone supported them, someone whose hands stayed clean, someone who refused to obey the rule of law. He was the lord of life and death. And maybe this was the connection between him and Kubura.[19]

One morning in the first few months of my imprisonment, the guard opened my cell door and all I could see was the tip of his black boot, inching forward as it slowly pushed a black box into my cell … it was full of evidence against me, 800 pages or so. I was given these documents so I could prepare my defence. I was nauseated from going through them—texts, copies of official orders, the crimes that we [Serbs] committed. I was disappointed … It was unfortunate but there it was ... I knew about some of these crimes; I recognised two names in these files. Serbs told me about these crimes, and many trials were already ongoing. Many of the allegations had already been proved by the court. I tried to prevent some crimes but could not. Batko was one of them. He was killing even some Serbs in Grbavica in the parts of Sarajevo under Serb control. When I learned of these events, I immediately requested to talk to the Minister of Police and the Minister of Justice, but they did nothing to prevent his crimes. Batko was a crazy man.

Veselin Vlahović, a former Bosnian Serb paramilitary dubbed 'Batko' and the 'Monster of Grbavica', was convicted on 29 March 2013 for inflicting a reign of terror on Sarajevo civilians, Bosniaks and Croats during the Bosnian War. He killed a famous Bosnian handball player, Goran Čengić, whose mother was a Serb and father a Bosniak. Goran wanted to protect his Bosniak neighbour Husnija Ćerimagić from Batko, but he killed them both in the end.[20] In her memoirs, Plavšić writes in detail how she tried to prevent Batko's killings in Sarajevo once she found out about them, but the Serbs, the police and the judiciary did not want to act on her pleas. She also personally knew the Čengic family.

Plavšić was pleased when two young women, originally from the former Yugoslavia, were employed as interpreters at The Hague's detention centre. They would regularly appear on her floor to share some news 'from the world beyond the prison walls'. Their presence brought some optimism among prisoners. Plavšić told me how this was important, because the mood among prisoners was often melancholic, and as time went by, more hopeless. Half smiling, Plavšić lit a cigarette and recalled,

> We followed their pregnancies, and celebrated the births of their children. However, someone I want to single out, someone who is not only a noble human but also a professional who helped me endure the experience of facing prison conditions in my late age, was prison

psychiatrist Vera Popović.²¹ We used to hang out. She came at the right time to encourage, to rejoice, to interpret many new experiences in the prison so I could understand myself and others around me. I was very pleased to hear very positive thoughts from my fellow prisoners about my Vera. Those were my first prison experiences.

Plavšić's issue with claustrophobia was solved to her satisfaction. She complained during her first morning in detention that she could not sleep in the locked cell without windows. The guards never again locked her up in the cell, and she never felt the urge to get out of it like she felt during those initial two or three evenings. She used every opportunity to be outside in the air as much as possible, and took regular prison walks. But she spent most of the time in her cell, which she called 'the cage'. She was amused, dropping her head to chuckle, 'We called it Annan's cage because I was told it was a gift from Kofi Annan, Secretary-General of the United Nations'.²² After a few weeks in detention, Plavšić decided to complain about her prison conditions since she was the only woman among men.

> I wrote a letter and requested a bigger cell in which I should have my own toilet so I don't have to share the one with men. I explained to them that I am the only woman detained, and due to my claustrophobia and my private needs, I deserved to have more space. The administration of the jail accepted my complaint, and they knocked down the wall that separated my cell from the one next to me, merging those two cells into one. That was done efficiently and with no comment from their side, and I was really thankful for that.

Although the food 'was nothing special', Plavšić said with her eyes on me, 'It wasn't bad either. I was never picky or gave significance to it in terms of enjoyment'. But the meals were not enough for the men, so they always cooked for themselves. Dragoljub Prcać was the 'head chef' as well as Mario Čerkez. She told me,

INDICTMENT AND DETENTION

I did not cook my own meals. I made potato pie once, but since there was no oven, I baked it on the plate, and it wasn't bad at all. Sometimes there were waffles too. We took turns in making coffee, and I knew when it was my turn to make coffee for everyone. We used to spend time together and drink coffee, but one spends a lot of time alone.

Plavšić spent time walking with and talking to Esad Landžo.[23] She had heard his name before but had never met him until Scheveningen. Landžo told her about his young, ruined life and how he had trouble sleeping because of his criminal actions. Plavšić explained how 'his victims followed him in his dreams, but he thought that if they continued coming into his dreams and bothering him, God would have mercy on him'. Landžo also told Plavšić that 'if this all did not happen to him', he would never have met her and had a chance for 'long talks with a university professor'.

> I later understood the deeper meaning of what he was telling me because if this had not happened to me, my whole life would have passed, and I would never have known what the bottom of life looks like, and I would go to another world with superficial knowledge about its existence.

In 2001, Orthodox and Catholic Easter were celebrated on the same day. There were dyed eggs on the table since a few days earlier all the inmates from her floor were collecting onion skins and colouring the eggs. Plavšić told me they cooked a decent meal considering the prison conditions. The guards joined in the festivities too. A holiday atmosphere was created far from homes and families, but as Plavšić noted, 'surely each one of us mourned that our families were not with with us'.

On this occasion, a Dutch guard, who was pleasantly surprised at how they organised the celebrations, told Plavšić that Dutch people 'were losing the importance of the holidays and that the churches were being rented out for different purposes as less and less people were interested in coming to mass'.²⁴

The daily communication between prisoners through the corridors, and the time spent in the courtyard during walks, was changed due to the arrival of Slobodan Milošević in the late hours of 28 June 2001.

> We had all noticed that the arrival of someone high-ranking was being prepared. It was particularly obvious on our floor, which suggested that Sloba would be my neighbour.²⁵ They closed the door in the middle of the hallway and pasted some paper to the glass, which was a sign that he would be kept in isolation. And that's how it was for a couple of days.

The day after he arrived, Plavšić saw Milošević from the common room window that could not be opened, walking around 'the cage like some mighty beast'. She recalled the journalist Aleksandar Tijanić calling him a 'Bengal tiger'.²⁶

> This was the way in which Tijanić showed that he respected him [Slobodan Milošević] and thought of him as powerful. In the common room with everyone present, I described Milošević 'like a Bengal tiger in a cage'. Everyone nodded, and someone said, 'Yes, that's him now'. And I thought about his power, our last freedom encounter and his unsuccessful attempt to destroy me physically, my courage to resist him and his successful campaign of destroying my party. He organised the whole programme and the people who were doing it for him. I forgave him for everything he did to me, but never for what he did to the Serbian people.

The day before this gathering, Plavšić was sitting in a detention telephone booth. She noticed someone was slowly tearing down the paper covering the glass door in the hallway. Milošević's face appeared; he waved at her. She waved back at him. Plavšić laughed at the memory and took a cigarette from the pack sitting on the coffee table next to her.

> I was talking to my brother on the phone when Milošević's face showed up through that paper hole. I told my brother I was waving to Milošević as they had brought him here.

Milošević's isolation only lasted for a few days. The prison warden spoke to Plavšić explaining that his isolation would end, but he told her that they should not talk or be in the common room at the same time or talk during their regular walks, and that there would be guards who would stop any collaboration between them.

> It was then that I said for the first time what I repeated many times later, which everyone found unbelievable, or did not want to believe. I did not talk to him during the entire [Bosnian] war when I perhaps needed to, so why should I now? That is true ... all my meetings and conversations with him were only after the war ended. Milošević laughed. I told him this in the presence of the others, the first time when we were all in the living room. Still, we did talk to each other during our regular prison walks. He told me everything. Lots of things. He asked me, 'How could you be in the company of such men?' I answered, 'You were in their company, not me. They were coming to you all the time'.

While in the common room, Drago Prcać made waffles and coffees, and Plavšić told Milošević, 'You go out and you will get your waffles in the hall'. Everyone laughed. Shortly after the 'waffles' story, Plavšić was released to await her trial under house arrest. She was away from Scheveningen for almost a year. While in her home in Belgrade, from time to time Plavšić watched the broadcast of the trials from the Tribunal. One day, she turned on the TV and saw there was a broadcast of Milošević's trial. The prosecutor, Geoffrey Nice, asked him, 'Regarding ethnic cleansing, the thing that Ms Plavšić said in an interview about Eastern Bosnia, that Muslims should be evicted, did it come true?'[27] Milošević's response was, 'Well, I said before that she should have been excluded from political and social life'. Plavšić stared into space for a moment before drawing on her cigarette again, squinting due to the smoke.

Months went by, and Plavšić was back in The Hague. In the meantime, the demographics changed again on her floor. Some of her former fellow inmates were still there, like Prcać, whom she befriended. There was also Jelisić awaiting his transfer to a prison in Italy to serve his sentence. Milošević was in the same cell on the same floor.

> I would sometimes peek into his cell and could see a small red book lying on the floor near the door. It looked as though he was kicking it around. I asked one of the detainees who sometimes cleaned his cell what was that red book about and he told me it was a Bible he got as a gift from Metropolitan Amfilohije, who came to visit him in the prison. Milošević was a godless man who hated the church and its clergy. What kind of man was he with no respect for the Orthodox Church and its clergy?

The rigour in the control of their contacts was slightly eased, and one day during the prisoners' one hour of recreational walking, Milošević told Plavšić what Nice had asked him in the courtroom. Without asking him how he replied, Milošević told her, 'And I answered him: Ms Plavšić is a true intellectual, she would never say that'.

> Sloba must have forgotten that the trial was broadcast live, which I did not follow, but by chance that day I turned on the TV at that particular moment, and I heard his comment. He never changed his opinion about me. It was hard for me not to tell him that I watched the trial and that I knew what he said about me. I felt sorry for him. If he was in his White Palace residence, sitting on his huge armchair, I would tell

him the whole truth, that he was lying, but in these prison conditions where we were both left without any rights, two people deprived of liberty, I forgave him for everything.

Responding to the Indictment

In the spring of 2001, once she returned to The Hague from her house detention in Belgrade, Plavšić read her indictment in detail as she had only skimmed it briefly before her first appearance at the Tribunal. In the silence of her prison cell, she could finally read it 'slowly and in peace' and, for the first time, clearly see what the prosecution had accused her of. Plavšić wondered what they believed she 'did during the war', and wanted to see 'what [her] fault was'; 'what crime have I done to be accused by them?'. She thought that the court made some mistake since they lacked information about her activities during the Bosnian War.

> I know I'm not capable of doing any harm, let alone a crime. During the war, I was in such a position that I was part of the presidency and a command, so I was judged by my command responsibility. As a member of the presidency from 6 July 1992, I was in charge of humanitarian affairs and contacts with UNPROFOR. So, what was my fault? That is what I was really interested to find out.

Plavšić approached this matter 'as some sort of scientific research', distancing herself, as she said, 'as much as possible from my emotions or some of my hidden desires, as if someone had given me this text [indictment] seeking my opinion, implying that I am not an expert in the field. As a scientist, I was seeking the truth. Is there any at all?'

The war crimes indictment covers the period from July 1991 to the end of December 1992. The war in Bosnia started in April 1992, so Plavšić wondered 'what kind of war crimes could have happened in Bosnia's peacetime'.

My indictment was from mid-1991 until the end of 1992. The war had not yet started in Bosnia and Herzegovina in mid-1991, and I asked myself what kind of war crime I could commit when there was no war in Bosnia at that time. There was a war in Croatia, but not in Bosnia, and my indictment refers to Bosnia, right? The war started in 1992, sometime in April, and soon after, I, as a representative of the Serb people in the presidency of Bosnia and Herzegovina and as an elected representative of Serbs at those multiparty elections, gave my resignation, as did Dr Koljević, who was the second representative of Serbs. I did not have a chance to say that publicly in the courtroom. If the presiding judge was not interested in what I had to say, he just said, 'it is not relevant', and then pressed a button and turned off my mic. The good lawyers, when they analyse the work of that court, will conclude it was all one terrible shame. The good lawyers will tell you that the establishment of that court was completely irregular. The court was not established by the General Assembly of the UN.

Plavšić does not consider warmongering as something relevant to be counted and used against her. The fact that her speeches incited hatred and a witch hunt against Bosniaks and Croats was, to her, 'nothing but a patriotic call' to protect the Serbs. She considers only physical acts of violence as relevant features of war crimes; 'who said what is irrelevant,' she claims. She leaned towards me and said, perplexed,

> The crimes were only committed from March 1992, starting with the murder of the Serb groom's father in Sarajevo[28] and the massacre of Serbs in Sijekovac on 26 March and in Kupres.[29] And these crimes were perpetrated by the Muslim-Croat coalition against the Serbs, and the war had not yet begun. Who created this deliberate 'mistake', and why? Maybe someone has an explanation for this, but I do not have one to this day.

The indictment lists the names in the following order: Slobodan Milošević, Radovan Karadžić, Ratko Mladić, Momcilo Krajišnik,

INDICTMENT AND DETENTION

Nikola Koljević and Biljana Plavšić. 'From a formal point of view, without any analysis, the order may be correct', Plavšić told me.

> My role was minor, which is why I was listed last on the indictment. Still, the content, spanning over fifty pages, covers all the war crimes typical of the conflict, which they classified as inter-ethnic. My horrible indictment was copied and pasted, since it was the same as the ones for Karadžić, Krajišnik and Mladić. They were all the same.

Plavšić, for the first time, learnt about the indictment terminology, especially the 'joint criminal enterprise'. She only later found out that this mode of liability was borrowed from the Nuremberg and Tokyo trials. She remembers stopping when she came across this term to wonder about it. As she moved through the text, she realised that the term runs throughout the entire indictment. She concluded that it must mean 'something very important to them'. Plavšić's eyes swivelled towards the bookshelf pressed against the wall. At this point Plavšić stood up from her chair, shuffled towards her bookshelf and stretched up on her toes. She picked out a book. She turned it over in her hands and flipped it open, flicking through its pages.

> If you read Carla Del Ponte's book, she says that they could not write indictments for leadership because there was no direct accountability on their behalf because they did not kill anyone directly. She said the ICTY statute worked well for direct perpetrators of the crimes, whom she calls 'the lower-ranking trigger-pullers' but that these provisions did not work well for the senior political figures who committed crimes.[30] And then Del Ponte went on to explain that she and her colleagues analysed the Nuremberg process and there was one term established there called a 'joint criminal enterprise'. That crime did not exist in our law. I consulted lawyers here. My husband was an attorney, and he consulted lawyers in Belgrade and those around the world. They invented this term in the Nuremberg process so they could accuse Nazi leadership and now ours. I cannot remember how many of them were

sentenced to death. Seven of them were sentenced to imprisonment, one being Albert Speer who was Adolf Hitler's chief architect and during the war the Minister of Armaments and War Production for the Third Reich. Speer went into the Nazi concentration camps that held Jews and Serbs, but most of them Jews. He judged their health and condition: whether they could work ten days in factories for armaments, and of course, if not they would kill them. Imagine ... that was what Speer did, and he was sentenced to twenty years imprisonment. And me, what did I do? I had a contract that I was responsible for humanitarian work, care for refugees, contacts with religious representatives and for securing safe passing of humanitarian convoys. I took part in the presidency meetings, but I did not have command responsibility. At the time of promulgating judgement, when the prosecutor spoke, and then the defence and judges, the prosecutor said, 'She did not directly do it' ... you know, those crimes they listed. As I said to you, all indictments were the same; they just changed the names on them. The judge said, 'She did not have command responsibility', and in that room I wanted to shout spontaneously, 'So, why are you prosecuting me then? Why did you accuse me?' But they added this, 'You knew, or you should have known about crimes'. The truth is I did not know, but I agree that I 'should have known'. Serbs did the same things as others, but who started first? Serbs did not. And they [the judges] never made the link with 1941. There were crimes, [she paused here] but believe me, I did not know at that time about them. I received instructions about my duties, and I only performed them [and nothing else]. It was important to me that humanitarian convoys passed through regardless of whether they were going into Serb or Muslim villages or towns. I made every effort [to carry out this work] and also fought for the latter ones [meaning Muslims].[31]

Plavšić rested the book in her lap for a moment, staring ahead before continuing.

> I tried to relate it to an actual wartime situation to help them grasp the nature of the undertaking I shared with others. First, I never even

INDICTMENT AND DETENTION

met Milošević during the war to receive instructions directly about the 'enterprise', nor indirectly through Karadžić and Krajišnik, who regularly visited him. I do not know whether they participated in the undertaking and received orders. I know nothing because I was not there. And yet, as Serb leaders, we were all accused of the same crimes. I have heard from people who knew Milošević well that he was a 'zero strategist'. Later, I saw it for myself. Even the post-war violence within Serbian countries is the best evidence of his strategic incapacity. Karadžić too was unable to organise anything except for the thugs who were already organised by themselves.

I am not an expert on military issues, so when it comes to Mladić, I guess that's why I was excluded from those considerations. But I wonder what kind of undertaking can be made when Mladić, the commander of the general staff, was, by the nature of his rank, unable to take orders? He can only give orders. Krajišnik was the only one capable of any undertaking. And now, finally, me ... my obligations from 6 July 1992 explicitly stated: humanitarian activities related to the consequences of war, contact with an international staff solely related to humanitarian issues and not to war. And that is how it was. So how is it possible this is a joint undertaking if only one of us did something? How on earth did they come up with this term?

Plavšić decided to consult some experts. She talked to Banjac on the phone and during his visit about her indictment. He then consulted with several of his colleagues in Belgrade and told Plavšić that such a formulation did not exist for criminal offences under international law. She remembers reading an interview in the *NIN* weekly magazine with, according to Plavšić, a 'world-renowned' lawyer, and they interpreted the newly established term on two pages.[32]

> I remember it saying that under that formulation, 'a joint criminal enterprise', the leadership, presidents and vice-presidents of many states could be accused. And what did it look like in practice? The made-up term did the work because those of us who were accused on

that basis got decades of imprisonment. I am still unable to accept the fact that only one side of the conflict was being judged. My conviction then, when I voluntarily surrendered to the Tribunal, is the same as nowadays, but I did not want to hide, to go underground. That would be disgraceful for my character, dignity, and for my conviction that someone who holds a leadership position, especially in those times of war, must be ready to bear all the bad things the position carries, even loss of life. It is all normal to me since I have always considered that anything that happens to others can happen to me as well. I never distinguished myself from others. And when misfortune comes, and I see the Tribunal as a misfortune, then one needs to be brave, face it with dignity, defend oneself against it. And of course, always pray to God that this misfortune does not go beyond the limits of human endurance. Well, just like that, and with such a mindset, on 10 January 2001, I got on a plane and flew to The Hague to face my fate.

Pleading Guilty

Plavšić straightened her back in the armchair and took a deep breath. She raised her head and glanced at me. Her gaze was hard, her eyes moist, her face tight.

> I have suffered. I went through a lot of things. I was in The Hague for a relatively short time. Altogether one year. I saw people who were going to the courtroom—one of them was ten years younger than me. One day they brought him out from the courtroom on a stretcher. He had very high blood pressure but needed to be 'fit' [she used this word in English originally] by the next day to continue the hearings. I remember saying to myself, 'they will bring me out dead from that courtroom' because there were so many fake witnesses to my accusations, and they would be giving false statements, and that would go on for three to four years. For example, I remember one witness said that I went to Bileća [town in BiH] with Mladić every seven days by helicopter. Me?! What nonsense!

INDICTMENT AND DETENTION

Plavšić's eyes grew wide, and her open palm flew towards her chest. Her cheeks blushed.

> That man [witness], who was apparently in Bileća, could have seen me only once during the war when the parliament of Republika Srpska was held there, and then obviously never again. So, I was supposed to go through the torture of listening to the fake witnesses like this one ... and I also knew that all these trials were planned long before the war broke out in Bosnia. When I gave my resignation as the representative of the Serbian people in May 1992, I was told by one of my colleagues that I will be accused one day of war crimes. Also, one of my neighbours in Sarajevo told me, 'Your photos have been pinned up all over the Baščaršija and it says beneath them, "a war criminal"'. At that time, no one knew that the court [ICTY] would be formed; it was only later that the court was established, but that meant that everything was planned in advance. It was even determined in advance who would be accused. And Kljujić, who was also a member of the presidency, knew it as it was all prepared by the West. They had a plan to destroy Yugoslavia and to set up the Tribunal to prosecute us. It was all premediated.

Her hands were trembling as she fished a cigarette out of the pack. She puffed a few times to catch the flame.

> When I was in Belgrade in house detention, Patriarch Pavle came to visit me.[33] A holy man. I asked him what shall I do, how I should act? My lawyers were pressing me to admit guilt, otherwise I would not avoid trial, which would go for several years ... I am old, I had no time for that, but I struggled to confess guilt for something I had not done. I had done nothing wrong. I wanted to protect my people from the repetition of 1941 when Serbs were slaughtered in masses. I asked His Holiness Patriarch Pavle what I should do, how I can confess something before this terrible court and people in it. He answered, 'God is there too. He will listen to you'. And that was it. The decision was made: I will plead guilty for something I had not done.

She leant her head back and closed her eyes for a moment. As a deeply religious person, Plavšić took the words of Patriach Pavle as sacred and made the decision to plead guilty out of respect for him, believing that his advice was supreme. Plavšić told me several times that her meeting with him was groundbreaking and helped her to make her decision. She finally felt blessed and in peace, ready to move forward with her case. On 2 October 2002, Plavšić pleaded guilty to one count: persecution. She stated: 'I have now come to the belief and accepted the fact that many thousands of innocent people were the victims of an organised, systematic effort to remove Muslims and Croats from the territory claimed by Serbs'.[34] After the plea bargain, the ICTY cut down their original indictment of Plavšić to one count of persecution, namely, for:

> *acting individually and in concert with others in a joint criminal enterprise, planned, instigated, ordered and aided and abetted persecutions of the Bosnian Muslim, Bosnian Croat and other non-Serb populations of 37 municipalities in Bosnia and Herzegovina [during the period between 1 July 1991 and 30 December 1992].*[35]

'Persecution' is a broad charge, and in Plavšić's case, encompassed a range of charges from property destruction and discrimination in hiring, to deportations, rape and murder.[36]

In her book, Carla Del Ponte described her surprise when she heard that Plavšić wanted to admit guilt for the crime of persecution but not genocide. Del Ponte saw this as 'a fantastic opportunity', hoping that Plavšić would testify against her former colleagues. She described Plavšić:

> *as a close associate of Radovan Karadžić and Momčilo Krajišnik she had participated at the highest political levels in the campaign to dismember Bosnia and Herzegovina and ethnically cleanse large swaths of its territory. She had sat in the presence of Slobodan Milošević. She had heard discussions*

between Karadžić and Mladić … I wanted her to be a key witness against Milošević, Karadžić, Krajišnik, and other accused Serbian and Bosnian Serb leaders.[37]

Plavšić negotiated about pleading guilty with the ICTY prosecutors Alan Tiger and Mark Harman. Del Ponte agreed to accept Plavšić's plea for crimes against humanity and to drop the charges on the genocide count. Del Ponte later admitted that she made a mistake in not asking Plavšić to commit to testifying against the other indictees in a written form. Del Ponte said that at the time she thought it was enough that Plavšić orally promised her that she would do so, but she 'cheated on her'.[38]

However, Plavšić insisted, 'I never promised anything to her or anyone else from the Prosecutor's office, which is evident from my judgement that is available to everyone. If I promised her something, even if only verbally, I would do what I said'.

I asked her if it is true that she did not want to cooperate with the Prosecutor's office. Plavšić wiped something from her brow with her wrist, catching my eye, suddenly grim.

> Now, look, you have my indictment, you can find it on the internet; then you will see that the Prosecutor's office, when they processed the indictment, complained to the court chamber that I did not cooperate with them, and they asked for twenty-five years. That fact should be taken as a negative point, because in all indictments you have positive and negative points. In mine, there were lots of positive ones. First, I did everything in my power to implement the Dayton Peace Agreement. Madeleine Albright said publicly in the courtroom that the Dayton Agreement would never have been adopted if it wasn't for me. She said, 'This person does not know how to lie'. You know, I am telling this in my own words, but you look at it for yourself to see. Carl Bildt said the same. To me, these were positive points that were taken into account at the time of pronouncement of my sentence. The prosecution asked that negative points be added because I did not cooperate with them, and they got this answer from the court chamber: 'The cooperation

with the prosecutor brings positive points [stressing each of these words in a high-pitched voice]—but non-cooperation does not bring negative points'. And that has been written in the judgement.

I looked at her in silence as I waited for her to continue. She cleared her throat and took a sip of water.

> I agreed to admit to guilt of one of the counts, the one on ethnic cleansing, just so they had to reformulate their indictment. I was not interested in how many years of imprisonment I might get. My only condition was that I didn't want to defend myself of their other accusations. The prosecutors did not like it, and they asked the court to give me a higher sentence, but the president of the court, Judge Meron, stated that non-cooperation with the prosecutor's office does not bring negative points and cooperation brings positive points.[39] So basically, Meron told them that they couldn't force me to be a witness in other trials. When the prosecutors asked that I testify in the case of Milošević, I said to them, 'We made an agreement: I did not ask for a lower sentence because I admitted guilt, and you accepted that I did not want to testify'. Still, they flew me to The Hague from Sweden against my will. Carla Del Ponte, God protect us from her, ordered that. When they failed in convincing me to testify in the Milošević case, they returned me to the prison in Sweden.[40]

I still wanted to know more about the plea bargain. 'Can you tell me when you made a plea bargain—' I was not allowed to finish my sentence. Plavšić abruptly interrupted me, obviously annoyed with the term 'plea bargain'.

> No! I did not make a 'bargain' ... Look, what is a bargain? We bargain in a marketplace, right? I will give you this, and you will give me that, right? It was nothing like that. They [the prosecutors] told me, 'You can get life imprisonment', and I did not at all raise a question about the longevity of the sentence. I did not care. They thought they would frighten me with that. They thought I would do whatever they asked me to do to get a lesser sentence. They thought they would scare me.

INDICTMENT AND DETENTION

But what was it worth, my old life? I didn't care how much they would give me. I told them that I won't be a witness in anyone's trial. If they call that a 'bargain', there you go. The only thing from all these things they have written [in the indictment] that I could confess to was that I was indifferent to ethnic cleansing because that was true. These people who were 'ethnically cleansed' were not killed, right? When people are killed then that it is terrible. Because I left my home with a few bags and a sick mother in her 90s, I did not pay attention to it ... In the end, I told them I had reasons why I would admit, out of all those things they had written against me, only this one: that I was indifferent when Sadako Ogata, a witness in my case, said to the court, 'I warned her [Plavšić] that there are cases of ethnic cleansing'.[41] She was, as far as I can remember, the only representative of the international community who explicitly told me that Serbs were committing ethnic cleansing. I think it was in late August 1992. I asked Mrs Ogata to explain what 'ethnic cleansing' means. I had never heard anything of that kind before so I had to think about what it actually implied, and maybe I could have investigated it, but I did not. I failed to do so. I was too indifferent about it all. And after that, because I had never heard of such a thing before, I simply refuted those allegations. Maybe I should have enquired, regardless of the fact that I did not have to believe Mrs Ogata. If I had enquired, I would have been informed, just as I was informed about the events that had taken place at Grbavica in Sarajevo. But I did not do it. I denied it and said, 'No, no. That's not happening in our territory'.[42]

But, you know, when only in one day in Pale, I could see fifty obituaries for Serb people killed in the war, when thousands of people were fleeing on a daily basis, then you think what matters most is life and those who are living, so I did not pay attention to the phenomenon [ethnic cleansing] they invented.[43] As far as my priorities were concerned at the time, in that situation, ethnic cleansing, as they call it, came second place. On reflection, I should have paid attention, but I simply did not. I always thought of myself. I was kicked out of Sarajevo, and many people were migrating from one part of Bosnia to another ... it was a war. Everybody was going somewhere carrying their personal belongings. People were fleeing their homes because they wanted to stay alive and not be killed or tortured. I always tried to inspire optimism in refugees, to cheer them up by saying that I was a refugee myself, and I would tell them that I am happy that I am alive and that we should all be happy that we are alive. This is what I honestly believed, and still believe. The fact that you have lost your house is not the most concerning thing at that point. They [the ICTY] call this natural phenomenon 'ethnic cleansing', and I call it *seobe* (migration) and displacement. They know nothing about this phenomenon in our history. They just call various forms of leaving houses and places of residence 'ethnic cleansing' but cannot understand it. In that courtroom [ICTY], no one knew better than me what that means in practice! My Plavšić family was cleansed from Sarajevo in 1941, and I was in 1992. Serbs have been many times displaced throughout their history ... The Serbs were expelled from their homes in this war, and they expelled, because of that, others from their homes. In the same basket of 'ethnic cleansing' they added the forced fleeing from homes because of the danger of the close proximity of war and fighting; fleeing because in war 'each bird flies to its flock'; fleeing under pressure from leaders like Izetbegović, who ordered the Muslim population to leave Trebinje. So, it can really be called systematic persecution—ethnic cleansing—under the threat of those in power. But, because of their lack of knowledge about such complex phenomena which exist in every war, they promulgate decade-long punishments and ruin justice principles.[44] So, their idea of ethnic cleansing was happening throughout the whole territory of BiH, not just territory under Serb control. Serbs did not leave their houses just for fun!

I responded, as carefully as I could, 'So, you admitted that you knew about ethnic cleansing and persecutions?' I noticed a slight smile at my question, and then suddenly her face became still. Plavšić paused and stared down at the coffee cup on the little silver tray sitting next to her.

You know what they say, 'each bird flies to its flock' when times are difficult. I left Sarajevo where I had spent my whole life ... I had to leave it in twenty minutes, and I never regretted that ... I never felt sad, I was only happy when I realised that we all stayed alive ... who cares about home? It is important that families are alive. So, no, I don't see anything strange about the fact that in war you run for your life and leave your home behind. That is how it is. It's normal in war. I witnessed Serbs fleeing Goražde. One hundred thousand Serbs from Sarajevo had to leave. I could see what was happening on the ground. But, why were Muslims fleeing Pale? Nobody was forcing them to leave. Their Serb neighbours were truly sorry that they were leaving.[45] There were lots of rumours that Izetbegović's party told them to leave so it looked like Serbs forced them to flee.[46]

However, the narrative that 'nobody was forcing them to leave' does not hold up. Plavšić herself, as co-president of the Serb leadership, was convicted of persecution on political, racial and religious grounds in thirty-seven municipalities in BiH, including Pale. She pleaded guilty to that count, but it is evident that she did so for reasons other than genuine acceptance of guilt for ethnic cleansing. Prosecutors at the Tribunal also established this crime during the trial of Ratko Mladić in The Hague, showing that in the spring of 1992, the Serb authorities expelled Bosniaks from Pale.[47] Some were detained in five detention facilities under harsh conditions. In some of them, they were severely beaten, sometimes to death.[48] Broadly speaking, civilians who found themselves as a minority population in Serb-occupied regions feared for their lives if they stayed. They were often first expelled from their workplaces and verbally threatened by the political elites in power. Many civilians were killed because they believed nothing would happen to them and chose not to leave their homes. In Banjaluka, my hometown, among many killings, one that remains imprinted in my mind is the murder of the well-known Čivljak merchant family in August 1995. I was in town at the time. The Čivljak family were my neighbours and known to everyone who lived there.

Skender Čivljak, an Albanian Catholic, disappeared for several days and was later found dead on the banks of a river. His wife, Azra, a Bosniak, was shot in their apartment. Their sixteen-year-old nephew, who was staying with them at the time, was killed too. Azra was killed while searching for them, unaware that they had already been murdered. No one was ever held accountable for their deaths. Radoslav Brđanin was held accountable and prosecuted before the ICTY for the complete evacuation, or ethnic cleansing, of nearly all Bosniaks and Croats from the so-called Autonomous Region of Krajina, where he served as President. Banjaluka, where the Čivljak family was murdered, belonged to this region. Brđanin's position enabled him to facilitate the ethnic cleansing by putting all of the instruments of state power (media, central administration, housing, health service, police, legal system, means of production and employment) in the hands of the governing bodies and those persons committed to an ethnically pure Serb state.

I still remember watching him on TV as he spoke to the press in 1992, saying, 'Everything will be all right when we get rid of the vermin [meaning Bosniaks and Croats] that has bred here', and 'We will make soap from children of mixed marriages'. I remember my childhood best friend and her sister—both children of a Serb mother and Croat father—deciding that if they have to end up as soap, one would be Palmolive and the other Fa. My friend put those soaps on the TV in the living room. When her mother asked, 'What are these for?' she replied, 'When someone comes to visit you, you can tell them these were my daughters. Your friends may show you framed photos of their children—you show them these instead'. We laughed and made dark jokes about these fascist statements out of fear and shock. When Brđanin died soon after being released from prison in 2022, the president of Republika Srpska, Milorad Dodik, stated,

> I was deeply shaken by the news of the death of Radoslav Brđanin, a great patriot who sacrificed most of his life for the freedom and survival of the Serbian people in this region. Brđanin will be remembered with special distinction in the history of the Serbian people, who have lost a sincere and true patriot with his passing.[49]

A man responsible for mass murder was publicly mourned by the political elites in Republika Srpska, who continue to deny any of the war crimes committed by Serbs. In the Banjaluka municipality, as many as eighty-one Catholic churches were destroyed, and all sixteen mosques were demolished.[50] Croats and Bosniaks were killed, abused, persecuted, dismissed from their jobs, expelled from their apartments and homes, sent to perform forced labour and imprisoned. My parents' best friends at the time, a Bosniak family, were beaten up, sent to perform forced labour and spent time in jail on false accusations of espionage. I personally knew many families who had to leave to survive and also ones like the Čivljak's who did not have a chance to leave or trusted that nothing could happen to them, just to end up ditched in a canal or killed in their own home. The once multinational Banjaluka became an almost ethnically pure city. Banjaluka is an example of what was happening to citizens who found themselves an ethnic minority in the towns where the ethnic majority ruled. Serbs were also displaced from the towns and villages where they were a minority, such as Zenica,[51] Bugojno[52] and Konjic.[53]

At the time when Plavšić publicly stated remorse for her role in crimes committed against non-Serbs, such a move was seen as extraordinary and significant, since she was the first high-ranking Serbian politician to admit guilt.[54] She told me all of these backdoor negotiations around her plea bargain some twenty years later in 2022. Plavšić's act of remorse was praised by the ICTY and a number of victims, as well as the international community.[55] On 17 December 2002, Plavšić was sentenced to eleven years' imprisonment. Once convicted, she was sent to Sweden to serve the remainder of her sentence, as the time she spent in The Hague detention centre and under house arrest was deducted, which amounted to nine years and two months left to be served. After consultations with her lawyer, Plavšić decided to serve her sentence in Hinseberg Prison, the largest women's prison in Sweden, which hosts mainly, according to Plavšić, drug dealers and former prostitutes, some of whom were convicted of murder and manslaughter.

> It seemed the most humane one [Hinseberg Prison]. My lawyer also suggested I should go to Sweden since they are well-known for their very good prison system. I trusted this advice, but I made a mistake. I regret that I decided to spend my jail time there.

4

IN JAIL

Biljana Plavšić spent much time talking about her prison experiences from 2003 to 2009. She was transferred to Sweden's Hinseberg Prison for women after spending ten months in The Hague detention unit. Locked up far away from the public, the stories of international war criminals' imprisoned lives remain largely hidden. We know little about how they spend their time once transferred to local prisons scattered across western Europe.[1] Except for a few anecdotes reported by journalists, it is rare that we hear about a war criminal's incarceration firsthand. Eric Stover, for example, in his book *The Witness*, wrote that Plavšić, while serving her sentence in Hinseberg, enjoyed 'plush suites with color TV, sauna, horseback riding, solarium, and salsa dancing lessons'.[2] Similarly, one of the BBC journalists stated that 'facilities at Hinseberg include a sauna and horse-riding paddock'.[3] Some reported that in this high-security prison, together with the 'sauna and solarium', there was also a basketball court and a gym with workout bikes and step machines. To summarise, it was described by reporters as 'the jail known to staff and inmates as "the castle"'.[4]

Plavšić was aware of these descriptions of her jail environment while serving her sentence. She read newspapers and watched TV. 'I laughed when I read all of these ... I would be the luckiest woman in the world if these were true. But it was all lie'. She said this with sharp anger. 'Nothing even came close to such descriptions. We had no sauna, no gym. Nonsense'.

Plavšić's stories may illuminate our imagination as to what may have been the experiences of convicted war criminals while serving their sentences. When talking about this time in her life, I could see the mixture of emotions she experienced: grief, anger and bewilderment.

It was as early as the second day of my first visit to her Belgrade apartment that I asked Plavšić to tell me about her time in prison. When I arrived that morning, she had been preparing a black Turkish coffee as one would typically prepare in the region to welcome guests. She greeted me on the doorstep with her usual hug and bright smile, and then rushed to the kitchen and reached for a pot on the stove. The water in it was boiling. I shut the door behind me and took my shoes off. I walked into the living room where we spent most of our time together.

Plavšić soon brought in two cups of coffee on a silver tray. She placed my cup on the mid-sized chestnut oval table in front of me and another cup on her small coffee table next to her red velvet armchair, in which she was always sitting. I took out a notepad from my backpack, a pen and voice recorder, and placed them next to the coffee cup. I turned my cell phone to silent and put it on the table. I took a sip of coffee and sat up straight. Plavšić paused for a moment and took a deep breath before speaking.

> In Hinseberg, I lived in a terrible environment. There were all kinds of people there [in prison]. There were some who would commit a crime before the winter, only to spend the winter in the prison—to warm themselves up. One of them told me, 'Every autumn I do something so

I can spend winter here'. That woman was homeless; she was sleeping somewhere under a bridge. The rest of the prison population were also from similar environments.

Plavšić paused again and looked thoughtful. She took a sip of coffee and sat very still. Colour was rising in her cheeks, and she was clenching her jaw. She stared at me for a moment then continued.

> I often say that if I had not come to such an environment, I would not know what the bottom of life looked like. And it is incomprehensible that I gained this experience in my seventy-third year of life. At the beginning it was somewhat interesting. For example, there was one gypsy woman. I imagine that she was *naša* [ours], but she lived in France.[5] I asked her, 'Why are you here?' She was surprised by my question. 'I was stealing, and the elders made me look like a twelve-year-old because I was tiny and so I would have an easier pass with the police. They also wrote a paper saying that I was twelve years old'. And this was my environment. Not like [Albert] Speer, who had been surrounded by educated people like him. They [Nazis] were criminals, but they were not thrown among murderers, drug users and petty criminals who mistreated them. Although, I know from his [Speer's] memoir that for years they were not allowed to communicate with each other, still ....[6]

But Plavšić seemed to forget that the Nazis were also murderers, accused of killings, deportation and persecution—just as she was. In comparison to Speer, in the Hague detention unit she freely communicated with other detainees from the former Yugoslavia. She fell silent for a few moments, then stroked her throat and turned her head to meet my gaze. Her tone had an edge.

> It was terrible, but then every time you tried to say something about it, to complain, they [the prison management] would reply, 'In Sweden, everyone is the same'. I wrote a letter to the government of Sweden and

said that I couldn't be equal, no way. I told them who I was. I was a scientist, a university professor for thirty years, the vice-president, and then president for eight years. Even if I had two more lives, I couldn't be equal with those criminals.

Plavšić said this firmly, raising her chin proudly. I swallowed hard. She seemed totally divorced from reality. She did not think poorly of herself for even a second, but lived in an imaginary world where she still reigned. Her words strikingly echoed the self-aggrandisement of other narcissistic leaders. Augusto Pinochet, the dictator of Chile, while under arrest in the UK, snapped at the medical doctor who asked him whether he understood why he had been detained. He said, 'I was President for seventeen years, head of the Army for twenty-five, they are treating me like a common criminal, I am not a common criminal'.[7] Like Pinochet, Plavšić was in complete denial of any guilt. I heard the ticking of the clock that was sitting on the bookshelf on my left side. I racked my brain and remembered the letter she mentioned having written. Some segments of it were published online in the Serbian language.[8] I turned my gaze back to Plavšić, whose lips were now slightly pursed, as if she read my thoughts and wasn't sure if she should continue.

She explained to me how she came about writing to the Ministry of Justice of Sweden. Her letter was her reply to two letters she received from them. She was asked to explain her relationship with Dr Miloš Prica and Miroslav Michael Djordjevich, who sent a letter of support for Plavšić to the Ministry. Dr Prica, cardiologist-turned-politician, was the former chief of Plavšić's presidential cabinet. When Plavšić was serving her jail time in Sweden, he was working with the Ministry of External Affairs as a representative of Bosnia and Herzegovina (BiH) to the United Nations. Miroslav Michael Djordjevich, an American international banker of Serbian origin, founded the Serbian

IN JAIL

Unity Congress in the US.⁹ They were both strong supporters of Plavšić and even lobbied for her release. After receiving letters from Prica and Djordjevich, the Swedish government sent a letter to Plavšić asking her to explain her relationship with these two men. Plavšić told me that the Swedish government also wanted to know what her treatment was like in prison.

She asked me eagerly whether I wanted her to read me that letter. I said, 'Of course, if you would like to'. She hurriedly went to her study to fetch it. I could hear her going through some papers. Plavšić then walked into the room holding a couple of handwritten pages. She held them up, waggling the papers with a confident nod, as if telling me, 'Here it is, I found it'. And then she slowly sat back in her armchair, straightening up her solid shoulders while pressing her glasses closer to her eyes. Plavšić was still; her eyes became narrower as she brought the papers closer to her face. She coughed and started reading:

> *I would like to thank you for your letter from the 25 December and 16 November 2006, in which you are asking for my opinion with respect to the letters that your institution received from Dr Miloš Prica and Mr Michael Djordjevich. My first knowledge about these letters came from the Swedish media because they published them. I thought they must be fictional, made up by some journalist who keeps asking me to give him [an] interview. Your letter explained this situation. Dr Miloš Prica and Michael Djordjevich are my friends who are concerned with good reason whether I will, having in mind my age and health condition, survive a difficult prison environment. I am in my 77th year of life, the age in which even in freedom, every day brings uncomfortable health surprises, which cannot be considered in the conditions in which I now live. The constant stress I am exposed to causes high blood pressure and other problems. I have been asking myself for years: what has happened to me and how did I end up in prison to serve a long-term sentence among prostitutes, murderers, drug abusers, drug dealers, thieves, petty criminals, cheaters, who individually and together with their families through generations, professionally do criminal activities and return*

to the same prison many times? Their psyche is totally adaptable to their work, which is evident in my daily communications with them. All the methods that are used in Hinseberg towards this clientele are used towards me too. For example, stripping off the prisoners' clothes to become barenaked and then searching their bodies and clothes after every visit. On my complaint about this method, the prison management, with pride and sadism, replied ...

Plavšić paused, looked me in the eye, and raised her voice to emphasise each of the following words.

... everyone is the same here. However, we are not all the same. I have to explain this to you.

She turned to me as if in doubt, 'Do you want me to continue reading?' I forced my shoulders back and nodded. My throat tightened as I crossed my legs. 'Yes, of course', I muttered. She looked down at her notes, swallowed hard, adjusted her glasses, and tucked some loose hair behind her right ear. Plavšić read more of her letter, her eyes darting back and forth between my eyes and the words. She kept reading while running her finger down the page.

I was born and raised in the notable family of Dr Svetislav Plavšić, the world-renowned scientist. My schooling lasted for over twenty years and my education is still ongoing. I received my Master's degree, a PhD, and specialised in several renowned institutes worldwide. I was a Fulbright's scholar [sic], a professor at the University, the dean of the Faculty of Natural Sciences, a world-renowned scientist, a respectable citizen of my homeland Yugoslavia that was destroyed by a new-world order. It is for this and for my clear anti-communist attitude, and my family background, that I was elected in the first democratic elections in 1990, as a member of the presidency of Bosnia and Herzegovina, and later as a member of the presidency of Republic of Srpska.

When the war started in Bosnia, and it was not started by the Serbs, I remained with my people. During the war, some other non-elected people

IN JAIL

took the power and made decisions, and I did humanitarian work. I was aware of the significance of this work in a civil war where half of the population lacked food and a roof over their heads. I knew what that felt like, since in May 1992 I ran away from Sarajevo with my mother, who was 90 years old, and my brother and sister-in-law, from the wild Islamic fundamentalists, leaving all that was acquired over generations, saving my bare life. What I had to know in the war that was related to my work was: if the roads were free and secure for the passage of humanitarian convoys, if there was enough room in collective accommodation for refugees, if the sick and wounded had medical attendance, if the sick were provided with medicines ... I regularly visited hospitals with the most severely injured, taking care of the accommodation of their families ... I did not have the power to decide, command, nor had I official information about actions in the field.

Despite all this, I was convicted for all the evil that happened, regardless of whether I had the knowledge or the power to influence the events. Shortly before coming to Hinseberg, the media in Sweden announced that Biljana Plavšić, a war criminal, shall serve her sentence in the Hinseberg jail. Some journalists did their best to represent me as a beast in human form. Slavenka Drakulić, a journalist of Yugoslavian origin, particularly stood out. She should be held accountable for her disgusting, false information. However, she was not the only one portraying me in such a manner.

Furthermore, I am different from other prisoners at least in two aspects: my origin and my education, as well as having had a public announcement of the criminal act before my arrival to the prison. The consequences of these announcements and the journalistic misrepresentation of my personality were too harsh, and I still feel them today. There are many prisoners of Islamic origin who were born in Sweden. One was from Tunisia, and the other from Iraq. I received continuous threats. With shorter breaks, they were in my section for a year and constantly threatened me with Al-Qaeda, saying that they were about to kill me because 'Allah is great'. They got instructions from their bosses and made my life horrible in other ways too. I warned my guard who is a Muslim, and two other guards from my country, who were Muslims too, about the threats I received. One told me that they [the Muslim prisoners] were both young, which is true, and that they didn't know what they were saying, which is not true.

On October 4, 2004, I warned the principal, Mr Longberg, in writing about ongoing threats, but I received no reply. The torture continued. On November 25, the insult happened again outside the building, but then, apart from the threats about Al-Qaeda, they shouted in Arabic, gesticulating in the same way they do in Islamic countries, and it was all directed to me. Wishing to escape from them, I started to run. I tripped, fell on the concrete and broke my arm. That happened on Friday, and only on Tuesday they took me to a hospital where they found a fracture in my arm and put a plaster on it. The days went by and the tortures continued without any reactions from the guards and management of the jail. It was clear to me that someone in this jail supported it. The journalists found out what was going on and asked one of the guards—whose name I don't know, but he often comes to Hinseberg—what happened. He said there were no threats, and nobody had broken an arm. In this way, he confuted both the doctors and the hospital in Orebro and said a horrible lie.

In September and October 2003, air of an unusual smell was pumped into my room at night under a very strong pressure. It would start at 7.15 pm and continue until 7.15 am. During the first few days it was low intensity, but it grew later on. So, at night my room looked like a gas chamber in which I struggled to survive until the morning. That air caused redness and strong itching of my eyes and nose mucosa and gradually went down to my lungs, leading to a cough and in the end, bleeding. Night guards only confirmed the presence of a strong air in the room ... they would take me out for some air for about fifteen minutes ... nothing improved.

One night, the blood from my lungs ran like water from the tap. I was immediately transported to a hospital in Orebro. They returned me in the morning and the same thing happened over the next two days but in a much more drastic form, and then I was kept in hospital for eight days. The tests for possible infections were negative. In the end, I explained to the doctor what was happening in my room at night [the strange air]. This excellent doctor, and a good man, Dr Lennart Nicholl, was flabbergasted and told me that the strange air was the cause of my bleeding, combined with my weak immune system that was on a lower limit.

IN JAIL

The prison doctor was asked to undertake some measures to help me breathe normally. She came to my cell to tell me she was not a doctor for ventilation. That was all she did. That was her medical help ... and the night suffocation continued as before.

Then I wrote an open letter to the public that was published in its entirety on November 17 and 18 in Belgrade, and the day after some parts of it appeared in the Swedish press as well. On that same day in the evening, the ventilation in my room, after more than forty-five days of suffocation, was normal—and it never happened again.

It all happened during the period when the prosecution in The Hague asked me to be their witness in the Milošević case. Two times, two men came to Hinseberg to pay me a visit. It was in December 2003 when they took me to The Hague so I could be interrogated by Prosecutor Carla Del Ponte for two days. They wanted to hear from me what they needed to pursue the case, but I don't know how to lie and accuse someone falsely. During the war, Milošević did not contact the person who dealt with humanitarian problems in the war and that was me.

The prosecutor sent me back to the prison, informing the Trial Chamber that I was not a credible witness. Can you imagine from this letter the terror I was going through, which was much, much harder than my own trial? According to legal regulations, after two years spent in prison, I am entitled to stay out of the jail for four hours with someone who will escort me. In June 2005, I addressed that request to the jail management, and they forwarded it to some higher level where my request was rejected. I was informed about it in writing, with the explanation that there are many Muslims in Orebro who might protest.

I was puzzled, not only for being rejected, but by the explanation. Reading the letters written by Mr Djordjevich and Dr Prica, I saw that they are familiar with the conditions here, which is difficult for me to bear. But many important details are unknown to them, and this is why I am informing you about them because you asked me about my time in jail. Comparing my case to the Nazis' cases in the middle of the last century, I came to the conclusion that in the latter period there was more respect for those who were imprisoned (memoirs of Albert Speer, author Gitta Sereny).

> They served their sentences in their own countries, not among drug addicts, criminals, prostitutes, and their dignity was not humiliated like mine, and I am still degraded in this Swedish jail. That is the worst that could happen to me and that is why my sentence is not eleven years, but much, much longer. I am not used to begging for myself, but is it possible, according to your laws and judicial practice, and considering my age and how ill I am, that I am entitled to mercy, and to make it possible for me to be free at the end of my life?
>
> Biljana Plavšić, Hinseberg, 27 November 2006

Plavšić sighed and dropped the papers into her lap. Her face fell. She poured herself some water and took a few sips. I prompted her to continue by asking whether anyone replied to her letter. She was sitting still in her armchair, leaning forward, her eyes fixed on the floor. She shook her head with a gesture of helplessness and shrugged her shoulders. 'They did nothing, although I told them that I felt as if my prison cell was a gas chamber'. Plavšić sniffed a few times and raised her eyebrows. Looking troubled, she leaned back in her armchair, as if to establish the greatest possible distance between herself and that memory. She began to fidget with her napkin, pressing one corner of it against the left side of her forehead and wiping off a non-existent something. Meanwhile, she tried to catch my eye. I was thinking how, in her eyes, she was never anything less than a professor. She seemed genuinely bewildered and disappointed that people dared not treat her as such. I wanted to change the topic and asked her how she occupied herself in the Hinseberg jail.

> I read a lot. I read books written by internationals who worked in Bosnia during the war, some of whom I personally met. For example, General MacKenzie, a chief of UNPROFOR, sent me a copy of his book with a dedication and his signature. General Michel Rose's, Martin Bell's, Carla Del Ponte's, Lord Owen's and many others. I could not bring any of my personal belongings in there. They took it all,

> snatched my stuff from me. One book helped me a lot, a book by Jerotić, called *Duhovni razgovori*.[10] And then they wanted to take my books, because apparently, I could have only four in my cell. If I wanted to read a specific book, I would need to write an application to them to allow me to read that book, and they would give it to me. Can you believe that?

Plavšić rolled her eyes in bewilderment, clearly distressed. 'Totally crazy! I told them that reading, for me, is of the same importance as the wool to those prisoners who knit sweaters, or whatever'. She looked around the living room as if she had never been there. She was so embroiled in her story, obviously travelling through time—back in her prison cell talking to the manager. I felt chills down my spine. Still looking agitated, she took a sip of water and continued.

> One day, the new manager of the prison came to visit me. He entered my room and saw the books scattered all over the floor. He counted them, and I had 150 titles [books] in my cell. I collected them over the years. People brought them to me, sending them to me via mail and so on. He told me, 'You must throw these books out in the next twenty minutes and can keep only five'. I just looked at him and said, 'If they bother you, you take them, but you need to know that these books are my life; now go ahead and take them'. He said, 'I will be back in twenty minutes to take them if you do not take them out yourself'. I just sat back and continued with my reading. He came back after twenty minutes and said, 'You did not return them'. And I replied, 'No, I don't have any intention to do so. I won't take my life myself. If you want to take it by taking my books, that is your problem'. He left the cell and did not return.

She lifted her chin and smiled, obviously proud of this small 'victory'. Plavšić still speaks with a Sarajevan accent, but she now mixes it with Serbian accents.

> I read a lot there—for example, a book by Speer, Hitler's architect, which was almost 600 pages long.[11] I was interested in comparing the treatment of prisoners now and back then. Back then there was only one humanitarian organisation, the International Red Cross in Geneva. Since then, and when we were in jail, there have been thousands of humanitarian organisations. Only the Red Cross came to visit me a few times. In Spandau, those who were convicted, those seven men, were detained in a nice building from the Middle Ages, which was adapted to become a prison.[12] They were in their own country, wearing their own clothes, hearing their own language. Speer wrote that his wife was knitting him a jumper, and so on. And they put me in one room that was two and a half metres by one metre. When I arrived, they told me to take off my clothes, and two of them entered the room with gloves on their hands. I thought they were going to strangle me. Why did they bring me here? They threw some synthetic clothes at me. I had to take off all my clothes and stay naked, to be searched. It was a horror ... that examination ...

She looked down at her feet for a moment, shuffled her slippers, and then continued.

> Why did I read Speer's book? To compare the treatment of Hitler's ministers and ours—my treatment. His family visited him. The prison gave him a part of the park in Spandau so he could occupy himself there, growing his own fruits and the like. Friends visited him, and you know he was imprisoned in Germany. And us ... our families could not afford to visit us, we could not speak to our countrymen, we lived in isolation ... to serve our sentence in our country was unimaginable ... And also, what is very important: Jews could not be employed by the prison detaining the Nazi war criminals. And I had a female Muslim guard from Gradiška who did everything in her power to insult me during my imprisonment.[13] She enjoyed humiliating me. The other guard was a Croatian man, and he was a good man I have to say ... To protect myself, I managed to spiritually rise above her and the rest, as

if I was watching this all happening to someone else. I succeeded in creating some distance from such acts in order to keep my sanity.

Plavšić mentioned Speer several times, telling me about his time in prison and made comparisons. She was fascinated with the treatment of Nazi war criminals and read all the books she could get hold of that discussed their trials, sentencing and prison experience. I, on the other hand, was fascinated with her fascination with Nazis. She kept comparing their treatment with hers and that of her peers. I was not sure whether she realised that by comparing herself to the Nazis, she was effectively making their crimes relevant to hers. Why compare yourself to Nazis if you don't believe there are similarities in your crimes and theirs—and that, therefore, your treatment should be similar to theirs? Why else make such a comparison? I said nothing but asked her to tell me a bit more about how she ended up serving her time in Sweden. Her smile disappeared, the lines in her face deepened. She gripped the edge of her seat, suddenly visibly disturbed, her eyes targeting me like a hawk.

> My attorney asked the administration of the Swedish prisons to check their rule books—how prisoners lived there and what sort of treatment they offered. Based on this information, I concluded that I could handle such treatment. However, it was said, for example, with respect to the TV, that the BBC, CNN and other non-Swedish TV programmes could be watched. But when I got there, I could watch only Swedish channels. I did not know or learn Swedish. They also said in the rule book you could practise your religion. So, I asked for some food, to prepare myself for the big Orthodox fast. I asked just for a few greens, vegetables.

Plavšić looked me in the eye. 'You know how they replied?' I shook my head. She quickly responded, 'Their reply was, "It is not true that Christians fast, only Muslims fast"'. She waved a dismissive hand in the air and opened her mouth while rolling her eyes upwards. With her head tilting to one side, she looked as if transported back in time, still in disbelief about their response to her request.

> When I asked to take Holy Communion, it was a drama. They said alcohol is banned in prison, but for taking Communion only a small spoon of wine was needed. About that small spoon of wine, there was discussion by the Swedish prison management. It is all lies in their rule books, all lies. Because there was no BBC channel in the prison, one of 'our' [Serb] men, who lived in Sweden, said that he would personally help, so the whole prison could get these channels.[14] The management of the prison rejected his offer, but one month later we got the BBC because I wrote to them and told them: 'Your rule book is a pure lie, in comparison to this reality'.

Plavšić shuffled, looked down, and slowly got up from her armchair. I came to realise that she spent a lot of time in prison writing all sorts of complaints to the administration. She was persistent and occasionally successful in her various requests. Taking three steps to pick up her purse sitting on the desk, she fished out an unopened pack of cigarettes and tore off the cellophane wrapper. Plavšić took a deep breath before taking a cigarette from the pack and putting it between her thin, red-coloured lips. She then grabbed the lighter from the table and lit the cigarette. Plavšić returned to her armchair, exhaled the smoke and looked at me. Only then did I notice the moisture glistening in her eyes. I could see she struggled. She wanted to explore her past, but at the same time it was obvious, as she once told me, that while doing so, she 'was sacrificing her peace of mind'. Cigarette smoke lingered in the air and its odour filled the space between us. I averted my eyes from Plavšić for a moment. I took a sip of coffee. I checked my audio recording volume. I was nervous the battery may run out in the middle of our conversation.

I then asked her if she had visits from 'our' people in Sweden, and if she often received letters from her friends and family. Her mood changed, and a bleary smile appeared on her pale face. She shrugged her shoulders right up to her ears. Her eyes narrowed a little as she drew on her cigarette.

> Yes, of course ... those visits meant a lot to me. The priest, Rafailović, often came to visit me in Hinseberg. He travelled by car for more than 200 kilometres to pay me a Sunday visit. He also prompted the rest of the clergy to come and visit me. For example, Bishop Vladika from Sweden came, but also bishops from Serbia came when they visited the Orthodox churches in Sweden. But thanks to the priest Rafailović, I could write my memoirs. He supplied me with paper and pen so I could write. Once I finished my writing and gave him my handwritten pages, he organised their publication as a book with a printing house in Banjaluka. He is an extraordinary man whom I could fully trust.
>
> I had visits from the president of the government of Republika Srpska, and representatives from the Serbian embassy. Carl Bildt came a few times, as well as some other friends. But for them it was not pleasant when they had to take their clothes off, and for me that examination was horrible. Every visit was traumatic. It was of course great, and I loved visits, but they were totally overshadowed by those horrible procedures. I received more than 150 letters, but I only kept a letter from His Holiness, Patriarch Pavle of Serbia, who wrote to me after my verdict and congratulated me. That is a wonderful letter, and I read it many times over in prison.

Her lips curled into a sad smile, and then her eyes lit up for a moment.

> Many of these letters were from the people who wanted my signature on my portrait photograph, which they would send to me in an envelope. I had many such requests. I received these requests from all around the world. These did not mean much to me but still ... they were indicative that the world does not think the same as the Tribunal.

Plavšić's face was now joyful, and her eyes widened while an arc of smoke followed the sweep of her arm. I felt warmth creep up my neck as I tried to cover up my surprise by her revelation. She continued to tell me that such requests are ongoing.

> The other day, I was entering my building on my way back from a morning walk, and I saw the man who worked in the local news agency where I buy a newspaper every day coming towards me with one of those letters. I asked, 'What is this?' He said, 'Two men came, some Czech people, and they asked me to give this to you'. The letter was open, and inside there was my photo with a request that I sign it, and a note to say that they would come tomorrow to collect it. So, it has been ongoing for a long time, to this day. With their requests, some have also sent a group photo of eminent people from around the world whose signature they acquired. I remember Hajle Selasije and others were there.[15] They were collecting photos of presidents from around the world. I think they sent me those so I could see why they needed my photo too. They always referred to me with the highest distinctions: 'Madam ex-President' or 'The President' or 'Ex-Vice-President' or 'Respectful Doctor'. In these envelopes there was always a letter, a reply-paid envelope, my photo, and they wrote a bit about themselves.

Plavšić was obviously amused when talking about these anecdotes. She stood up and led me to her small guest room to show me the collection of such letters that she carefully kept in a special leather folder. She sat down, her back straight, her knees together, and rested the folder in her lap. I sat next to her. She grabbed a bunch of letters and put them on the small oval table in front of us. I went through some of these letters, and they were as Plavšić described them to me: a photo of her accompanied with a short letter kindly asking her to sign the photo and return it to the address that was written on a pre-paid envelope. She said she never replied to such requests.

> I stopped counting how many such requests I received and how many requests I received for interviews. Hundreds, perhaps? Maybe because I was the only woman prosecuted by the Tribunal. These all went through the manager of the prison and through censorship. They explained to me why they had to open each letter, apparently because of drugs. There is a method where you can glue drugs to paper, so they had to check if the letters contained some chemicals.

Going through her files, I was amazed when reading people's requests for Plavšić's signature. I had to make an effort not to let my face betray my bewilderment. They indeed honoured her with the highest courtesy and pleaded for her autograph. Plavšić's unique position brought her fame: the only woman prosecuted by the ICTY, the ex-president, the oldest prisoner, a professor and dean of a university, now prosecuted for crimes against humanity.

These requests also fed her confidence that she had done nothing wrong, and that she was someone people should admire rather than despise. Yes, she is an intelligent woman, who can talk about literature and the arts. She is well-travelled, and a highly accomplished, sought-after academic who—even while in prison—reportedly received an invitation by the Royal Swedish Academy of Science to give a lecture. Plavšić replied to the Academy, saying that she would love to do so but she was in prison, and they must have been aware of that fact. And as such, she had no means of preparing a lecture since she had no access to the scholarly literature from her cell. I was dumbfounded. I could hardly believe what I was hearing. If I had not seen that invitation myself, I don't know if I would have believed her. But I saw their request, and I have the original invitation in my files. Still, upon closer inspection, I realised that it could not possibly be truthful. Plavšić, however, took it seriously, and responded to it. The letter was then translated into English and Swedish and sent as her reply to the invitation.[16]

While she was going through her letters, I now understood why Plavšić believed she had done nothing wrong when she was surrounded by such continuous attention and admiration. I wondered whether someone on the streets of Örebro, where the prison was located, would have recognised her, which the prison management thought possible. Her eyebrows arched, and she looked out of the window for a moment. A car sped by. Birds chirped. But then, she turned around and looked me in the eye.

> In their rule book, I think it was stated that after two years, prisoners had the right to go out to the closest city, and that was Orebro, but they had to be accompanied by the guards. I saw how other female prisoners were glad to be able to use that right. For the occasion, they gave them their own clothes, and although it was not pleasant to be followed by the police officers, who were in civilian clothes, it did not matter, as they were going out, could see people, do some window shopping. However, every prisoner had that right, except me. They told me, read to me, that I had a right to do this, but when the time came, you know what they said?

She stretched out her arms, her hands trembling and her mouth quivering. Her eyes were now wide open. She did not blink.

> I asked them why I couldn't exercise this right when they said we were all equals there. I got an answer, not a written one, but the manager of the prison just told me, 'Because that would hurt the feelings of the Muslim population in the city'. These were his words exactly. They were afraid that Muslims would make some public outcry. I was the only prisoner who was not allowed to go outside of the prison to the city. I was surprised. How can a country such as Sweden abandon exercising human rights promulgated by itself because it was afraid of protests by the Muslims?

Plavšić shook her head and paused for a moment. She then turned her eyes away, seemingly still perplexed about this. Plavšić took a deep breath. I asked, 'So, you could not ever leave the prison in the time you served your sentence in Sweden?' She continued to shake her head without looking at me and clenched the arm of her chair with one hand. Clearing her throat, Plavšić placed her elbows on either side of her armchair and formed a tent with her fingers. She leaned over to me and was silent for a moment. Then she ran the tip of her tongue across her lower lip.

> No, not even once in those seven years I was there. From the beginning, everything was unique for me. First, I was the only woman convicted in The Hague, the oldest detainee there and in Sweden. You know, they said that when a convicted person is 73 or 74 years old, they would release her or him from the prison. Whether they would have returned me to my country, I don't know, but they were supposed to be more tolerant towards elderly prisoners, as they said so. Across all Swedish prisons, I was the oldest female prisoner. I was twice in Sweden during the war to collect humanitarian aid for our soldiers, our amputees. Who could have thought back than that I would come for a third time to Sweden as a detainee, and that the priest Vlada would visit me regularly and share my concerns and suffering ...

She said this in one breath, disdainfully. She then scoffed, her face strained and grim. I took a deep breath and searched for a way to continue our conversation. I shifted my weight in the chair. 'Was there anything positive and nice that happened to you during that time?' I asked her. She was evasive. She skirted my questions.

Plavšić closed her eyes for a moment; her head was resting deep within her shoulders, as though it was heavier than usual. She placed both forearms—palms down, fingers spread—on her thighs.

> The only positive thing is that I saved my sanity. I did not allow them to drive me crazy, to crush my spirit. In the Middle Ages, and during totalitarian systems, they beat you. Here, these were beatings of the

soul, mental beatings. But I did not go crazy, thank God. When I saw what their aim was, I was stronger, and prepared to survive that ordeal. Only God could give me strength to rise above all of that. In that incident with the books, I had a feeling that I was watching all of that from somewhere above me. The same happened when I got out from my cell one morning and those Muslim women made a movement with their hands as if to cut my throat. I controlled myself and was just thinking 'whatever'.

I was interested in the famous interview she gave while imprisoned, in which she withdrew her admission of guilt, stating that she did nothing wrong and had admitted to the crime just to get a lesser sentence. I asked her to tell me more about it. Namely, two years into her sentence, Plavšić began to publicly renounce her plea of guilt and her statement of remorse. She did so in the interview she gave to a local TV station in Banjaluka, but the one that hit the headlines and shook the international and local community was the one written by Margaretha Nordgren, the Swedish journalist, in the magazine *Vi*.

> Let me tell you this. I don't know if you know that woman, the Croatian journalist, whose husband is in Sweden. Her name is Slavenka Drakulić. She asked me many times for an interview, but I refused her each time. She published a book where she stated how I held myself very proudly during the trial, and how it was almost as if I put 'them' [judges] on trial. Maybe I did look like that, and she questioned me, 'Who are you to act so dignified?' She wrote some other nonsense in that book of hers. God protect me from her.[17] Then a female journalist from Sweden asked for an interview.[18] I forget her name [it was Margaretha Nordgren], and that is the interview you mention. She brought a cake for my birthday in Hinseberg. However, they did not allow anything into the prison, neither food nor clothes, nothing. Nordgren and Drakulić premeditated all of this. The prison managers refused to bring that cake to me so they must have eaten it. However, before that, they took a photo of the cake and brought it

to me, together with her [Nordgren's] letter, a heartbroken letter you know, about how she came to see me, how she drove—I don't know how far from Stockholm—to bring me a cake and congratulate me on my birthday.

She looked at me for quite a while as though searching for words. Plavšić shook her head a little, and her hand trembled as she poked strands of white hair behind her ear.

Maybe one month after this, she sent her request again, and said that she wanted to see me. And what I could do? So, I agreed. I, however, made a condition that I did not want to give any interview. So, everything that she wrote, she made up.

Plavšić said this in a low voice, looking sad. According to Nordgren, Plavšić stated: 'I sacrificed myself. I have done nothing wrong. I pleaded guilty to crimes against humanity so I could bargain for other charges. If I hadn't, the trial would have lasted three ... three and a half years. Considering my age, that wasn't an acceptable option'.[19] I asked Plavšić why she revoked her remorse publicly. She laughed, her cheeks wobbling:

I found it very funny, the term remorse. That was not remorse, please, not at all. I was never remorseful. I admitted guilt for what they call 'ethnic cleansing'. They [the prosecutors] succeeded in extracting that [admission] from me. But it is only me who did it. I was the only one who accepted individual responsibility, and no one else has done that except me. No one. I followed those hearings occasionally on TV, and no one accepted their own accountability. If there was any luck, they would all surrender and say, 'Let's go all of us, we will stand before that court and tell what happened. Leave the people, leave Republika Srpska alone, we are guilty.'

This infamous interview caused shockwaves among scholars, policymakers, people in ex-Yugoslavia and beyond.[20] It hit the local and international community like a bombshell. Carla Del

Ponte wrote to the court asking for a re-trial.[21] Victims felt betrayed. The judges and prosecutors felt tricked and ridiculed by Plavšić. Del Ponte argued that such abdication should put Plavšić in violation of her plea, but the ICTY judges refused to permit the prosecutor to raise the charges against her. Plavšić's plea agreement dropped seven counts 'without prejudice', which means that a violation of the plea agreement could permit the prosecutor to bring these charges again without running afoul of 'double jeopardy' provisions that do not permit multiple judicial dispositions of the same case.[22] In her memoirs, Del Ponte states that she was 'taken in' by the 'apologetic' Plavšić, and then nearly in the same breath recounts that upon meeting the 'tweed-dressed' Plavšić in her office, she found her 'determined, unflinching nationalism nauseating'.[23]

Miroslav Lazanski, a well-known Serbian political analyst who visited Plavšić in Hinseberg, replied to the article written by Nordgren and wholeheartedly defended Plavšić, claiming that the interview was made up.[24]

> The journalists from the *Politika* newspaper asked me for [an] interview, I think fifty times, but I said no. It was my principle not to give any interviews. I received between 120 and 140 requests for interviews while I was in prison. I received lots of requests from researchers, and academics too, and because I did not reply to them, they tried in various ways to get me.

Plavšić showed me some of these requests sent to her by various local and international journalists and scholars; some of them I knew. They were well-renowned in the fields of politics and law. She kept those together with her admirers' letters, folded documents and newspaper clippings, all neatly piled into folders. She frowned while peering closer at one of her documents. Plavšić leant forward, looking up at me:

IN JAIL

If it was not for your aunt and uncle, I would not talk to you either. I have only recently given a few interviews to local media. Did you know that I had helicopters flying above the prison during our break times when I was doing my one-hour prison walk? They were flying as low as possible to take photos of me. The journalists from the magazine *Nacional*, from Zagreb, did this and then interviewed other convicted women in the prison but reported they talked to me. They also took a photo of a fellow female's prison cell, and they said it was mine. I could not defend myself from such things. But that interview with that woman who brought the cake [Nordgren] was an introduction to what would follow. One other journalist from *Večernje Novosti* came to visit me, and he asked several times for an interview.[25] I have never seen him in my life, and he published 'an interview' with me! He made it all up! My brother went into that journalist's head office and told them that it was horrible what that man, their employee, had done. He faked the whole thing. When the manager of the prison found out about that 'interview', he questioned all the guards to find out who let that man into the prison to 'talk to me'. They interrogated me, and I said, 'I don't know that man at all. I have never seen him'. And they said, 'But he describes everything, the prison and other stuff'. They suspected that he had bribed someone to let him in. The night guards, the day guards ... everyone wondered, how could this happen? He made trouble not only for me, but for the prison staff too. The management of the Swedish prisons was alarmed. The office gave the statement that he was never in the prison because he could not enter without permission.

Two years after I'd left the prison, Miroslav Michael Djordjevich invited me to the launch of his new book. The event was held in the aviation club in Belgrade. Lots of people were there, and many of them came to greet me, of course, and the flashlights from cameras were everywhere. As Djordjevich told me jokingly later, 'You were the main person there, not me'.

Plavšić told me this with a smirk, obviously amused and proud of herself.

One short man with grey hair introduced himself, and I realised he was the man who fabricated the interview. I told him, 'Ah, you are the one who publishes fabricated interviews'. I then turned around and said in front of everyone present, 'People, this journalist is a liar'. And I told everyone about how he fabricated the interview with me. If he had any honour, he would have disappeared from that launch. When the book launch was over, he found me, apologised, and asked me for an interview. Unbelievable! You see what kind of people I had to deal with.

She paused to light another cigarette, coughed and raised her arm to cover her mouth. She stretched to grab some water, swallowed a few gulps and then continued.

Another journalist, I even have his photo, was a journalist from the Vatican. Since I am religious, he was hoping that I would agree to an interview, but I stuck to my principle, 'no, no and no', and the prison manager told him so. I did not personally reply to anyone, but because such a man was asking, I asked the manager to please reply to him and tell him that I did not give any interviews.

One week passed. It was Sunday. No one was there from the administration office, and from the building in which my cell was, on the ground level, I could see a path that led to the park. I came closer to the window and looked more carefully. I saw one of the directors (who lived in Orebro and almost never showed up in the prison) with a small chubby man. Fifteen minutes later, the guard came in and said, 'Could you please come to the office? The director is looking for you, he comes only sometimes'. The director said, 'The journalist from the Vatican is here'. I told him, 'I said I didn't want to meet with him'. He said, 'What shall I do? Please receive him. I will bring him in'. So, I agreed. The director then sat with us in the room the whole time. I said to the journalist, 'We have a witness here. Please, this is not an interview and I only agreed to see you because you are already here, and because the director begged me. We can have a chat, have a coffee, if they make us one, but I am not giving you an interview'. And you know what? We talked for a long time. He did not publish anything about what we talked about. I asked some people to check, and they confirmed. You know what his suggestion was? He told me, 'You are a believer, and not only journalists know that, but the Vatican knows it too. The Vatican would like to help you. I would like to bring you a poster of the pope to put up in your cell'. I made a joke and told him, 'I would stick up a poster of the ex-pope, not this one'. But he was determined. 'I will bring the pope's poster for you to put in your room'. I looked at him and said, 'You know that I have a photo of His Holiness Patriarch Pavle on my table. He is our patriarch. The same as what the pope is for Catholics'. He replied, 'You know that the Vatican would help you to be freed'. Imagine that! I laughed.

She pushed her hair back from her face, and her eyes widened; she was grinning. Her hands flew to her face in disbelief.

He wrote to me later to ask if I would agree to do an interview for a famous women's magazine in Italy. I said, 'No, you came the last time, and not because I invited you, and you created a situation in which I had to receive you'. I had so many offers for interviews, from Rome, Washington and who knows where else. The prison manager had a lot of extra work because of me. You know, prisoners from other blocks would come to my block and say they heard that there was an ex-president prisoner amongst them.

Plavšić said this with warmth, laughing, obviously entertained for a moment by these memories. However, she quickly put on her serious face again and said that it was not fair that she was the only prisoner whose identity and crimes were revealed to other prisoners. 'They put me in danger. Muslim prisoners and guards used every chance to humiliate me', she said sullenly.

I fiddled with my pen and then told Plavšić about how significant her so-called interview with Nordgren was in the academic world, and how lots of people referred to that infamous article where Plavšić reportedly said that she was not guilty for the crimes ascribed to her. Plavšić was visibly stressed, disappointed and surprised by what I told her. She swallowed and raised her eyebrows while muttering, 'unbelievable'.

> You know what one man told me? He visited me in prison. He was a journalist and writer in Sweden. I have some of his books here with me. He visited me and wrote some fantastic things about me. He told me, 'When you decided to pick Sweden to serve your sentence, it meant you had no idea about Swedes'. They sent all those nicely written prison regulations to me and my attorney, and after reading them I elected Sweden, but the reality was terrifying. The ICTY has no problem with lying, and that one court from which you'd expect justice gives so much injustice and untruth and uses this to punish someone over a decade-long punishment. You know, crimes happened [during the Bosnian War] of course, but they cannot be all one-sided; all three warring factions were implicated. What kind of reconciliation is the Tribunal talking about if prosecuting only one side? Serbs. The work and procedures of The Hague tribunal needed to be studied. Also, the judges needed to be examined. When I arrived there [in The Hague], I heard from others who were already there that the only real judge was the one who was presiding.[26] From a professional judge you expect the truth and justice, no matter the cost, even if that costs one's life. They told me about Judge Meir, an Englishman who died during the trial of Milošević. He was the one who signed my judgment too. He was the one who refused the request of prosecutors for a higher sentence because I refused to act as a witness in other cases. He told them, 'She admitted her guilt under the condition not to be a witness in other cases. The judges must judge correctly'.

In 2009, with two thirds of her sentence served, the ICTY chambers ruled on Plavšić's early release.[27] The court elaborated on its decision:

> *Plavšić appears to have demonstrated substantial evidence of rehabilitation and has accepted responsibility for her crime ... She has participated in the*

institution's walks and she also occupied herself by cooking and baking ... [She has] exhibited good behavior in prison.[28]

There was no mention of her public renunciation of her statement of guilt nor of her refusal to voluntarily cooperate with the ICTY in other cases.[29] Reactions to Plavšić's early release were strong and mixed. The news outraged the Bosniak victims' associations in the region. Hundreds of victims gathered to protest the ICTY decision to grant Plavšić early release. 'They [the Tribunal] don't think about the blood of so many of our children, whom we are still digging out of mass graves,' said Kada Hotić, a mother who spent two decades searching for a son who went missing in the 1995 Srebrenica genocide. 'Nobody feels sorry for them, but they feel sorry for Plavšić, who spent her prison days very comfortably, writing books, and memoirs,' Hotić said.[30] Hotić lost her son, husband and two brothers in the genocide.

But while Bosniaks were outraged by Plavšić's release, Bosnian Serbs celebrated. Republika Srpska Prime Minister Milorad Dodik travelled to Sweden, where Plavšić was detained, to visit her and make arrangements for her safe return home. On 27 October 2009, Plavšić flew back to Serbia as a free woman, despite her lack of rehabilitation and repentance. Plavšić never changed her position that she did nothing wrong and that she was 'the victim of an international conspiracy against her and other Serbs'. She entered and exited the prison with the same conviction.

5

OUT OF JAIL

After spending seven years in prison, Plavšić was free. She told me about the moment she left her prison cell for good.

> Around 4 am, the female prison manager came in. She opened my cell and said, 'You are free today'. I left some food, bits and pieces, and some books in front of my cell. I tiptoed through the hallway upon my exit of the prison. They did this very early, probably to avoid other prisoners and their reactions. That is how I finally stepped into freedom again.

After leaving her cell that morning, Plavšić was driven by car to another building where representatives of the Republika Srpska government were waiting to pick her up and fly her to a long-awaited freedom. The prime minister of Republika Srpska, Milorad Dodik, organised her trip home, and she was flown in on the Republika Srpska government's plane. Together with a delegation of ministers, he welcomed her at Belgrade airport. The police and military security had a heavy presence to ensure she safely arrived at her family residence in the Belgrade suburb of Vračar. From the airport she was driven in a black limousine, hidden behind its dark tinted windows. She was followed by the Serbian state police officers who escorted her to her brother's unit located in the same neighbourhood as her current two-bedroom apartment. Plavšić was welcomed by curious neighbours and other onlookers who wished to celebrate this special occasion with her.

Her family was not on the street but waited for her in the apartment. Journalists gathered around the car with their cameras ready. Plavšić stepped down from the limousine in her long, brown fur coat while a group of journalists circled around her, wanting to grab a glimpse and take a photo of an ex-president turned war criminal who was beaming as she looked up at her brother's home. The arrival of Plavšić was directly broadcast that day across the Serbian media.

Dodik took Plavšić by the hand and led her to the entrance of her family's building. Elegant and dramatic, with a smile mixed with tears, she hurried inside to meet with her brother and sister-in-law, whom she had not seen in all those years. The traditional orchestra of accordionists were playing on the street that afternoon and welcomed her with the song *'Nema raja bez rodnog kraja'* ['There is no heaven without homeland'].[1]

Before disappearing through the building entrance, Plavšić gave a brief statement to journalists, saying, 'I don't know what to tell you ... after nine years I will be free. I don't know what it will look like, but we will figure something out, I promise you.' Dodik, her former colleague and friend, added, 'Ms Biljana Plavšić is free, according to all laws: worldly ones and those of God. I said what I think about her punishment in the past. It was unjust, but now that is totally irrelevant, especially for her who needs to forget it as soon as possible, as we her friends need to forget it too'.[2] After this, still holding hands, Dodik gently ushered Plavšić into the building, away from the crowds.

Plavšić decided to settle in Belgrade rather than Banjaluka, where she'd lived before being taken to The Hague. She told me, her voice barely more than a whisper, 'I wanted to be closer to my brother and sister-in-law'. I asked her how she had imagined her homecoming after all those years spent in jail. Plavšić's face lit up. She lit a cigarette and sucked on it. She squinted, lifted her chin with satisfaction, and released a cloud of smoke from her mouth. 'To be honest, I did not think what it would all look like. I wanted to see my brother, my sister-in-law, my friends'. She paused and sighed, then turned to me. Her eyes bore into me. Her chin quivered, and she cried for a moment, the words catching in her throat.

> I was so pleasantly surprised by how people welcomed me. I never found out who organised the musicians for me. I was just told it was for my 'happy new beginning'... But not only then did people welcome me ... Even today people stop me on the street to greet me. They may want to take a photo with me, or some just say when passing by when they see me, 'Today is my lucky day'... Oh, my people. And all those official welcomes were great too. I never had any problems with the people. I was, in fact, surprised to see how people embraced me, accepted me. I cannot tell you enough about their hospitality. For example, before you came to visit me today, I went for a walk. A young man was walking with his daughter and a dog, and he stopped in front of me and said, 'You don't have a clue what kind of authority you are for us. We love you; we respect you. We wish you all the best'. He just simply said that and walked away. And then two hours later a lady stopped and said, 'You don't know me, but I know you. You are our hero'. I feel uncomfortable to talk about this, but this is how Belgrade have accepted me. And these are common, ordinary people, not politicians. Because of the people, I entered into politics; because of the people, I accepted individual responsibility. As I said many times: an indictment refers to me and not to the Serb people, and the guilt is mine and only mine.

After she settled into her apartment, for the next two to three years she enjoyed Serbian police protection. They policed her building and followed her on her outings. Plavšić touched her forehead and told me she did not particularly enjoy that attention. Her eyes dropped to the floor. Then she looked back at me. Her eyebrows shot up.

> They [undercover policemen] would follow me everywhere. I often asked them to keep a distance from me. I did not like them being in my footsteps all the time. I was irritated a lot with it, but that was their job and I did not want to interfere with it. If they thought that is the way it should be, then fine, but I asked if they could be more discrete. One woman, a neighbour, told me one day when she met me on the street, 'You know, I saw you this week several times and a young man was following you all the time'.

Plavšić smiled and sipped her coffee, adding, 'She [the neighbour] could not get what it was all about'. She slowly inhaled and then exhaled a cloud of cigarette smoke, watching it dissipate as she was immersed in her thoughts.

Plavšić lives alone and has her daily routine. For years, her morning exercise has consisted of long walks around the nearby Orthodox Church of Saint Sava, which she mentioned in her plea bargain speech. She watches TV news and shows, reads daily newspapers, smokes a packet of cigarettes a day and drinks a few cups of strong black coffee with milk. She talks on the phone to her family and friends each day and occasionally to local journalists. With restricted mobility and no internet connection in the apartment, Plavšić's life revolves around this daily routine. She is still sought after by journalists to comment on politics in Serbia and Bosnia and Herzegovina (BiH) or to give her opinion about high-profile war criminals such as Radovan Karadžić or Ratko Mladić. She is fond of Mladić and thinks of him as 'a modern Serbian hero'.

> He is a man of his word. You could always trust him. He loves his people and he is a good man. He saved Muslim villages from hunger.

OUT OF JAIL

> The only thing I don't approve of is that he went into hiding once he was indicted for war crimes. He should not have done that. He is not a coward. No, he really should not have done that. I also never understood what he was doing in Srebrenica. The army was waiting for him on the Western front. I was wondering: Where is Mladić? Why is he not going to Bihać on the front? Soldiers were waiting for him. I was there too on the Bihać front bringing cigarettes to the soldiers.

Plavšić seemed genuinely puzzled with Mladić's decision to go with the army to Srebrenica rather than Bihać. She told me many times that he was not supposed to be there. Still, she never admitted knowing about the plans to commit genocide in Srebrenica, and she would not refer to the crime as such. For the past several years, Plavšić has had a cleaning lady who comes once a week. Until December 2022, she could still go herself to a local store to buy her daily groceries, visit her sister-in-law or a doctor. During one of her walks, she tripped and fell, hurting herself badly. Since then, her mobility has been restricted, and she hardly goes out anymore. Her sister-in-law died recently, which was another big blow for Plavšić. 'I just wait to die. I've lost all my friends and family, and I know my time is coming. I am tired of life, and I really want to die and finish with it'.

Plavšić receives regular visits from her former colleagues and friends. She still opens her home to journalists if they want to record her audio-visually. They often report on her hospitality and warm welcome.

During my visit to Belgrade and our extensive talks, I followed Plavšić on her walks before her fall to see her daily routine for myself. I witnessed people greeting her on the street. Some of them were beaming from happiness and would often give her flattering comments. I also accompanied her to the doctor for a scheduled medical check-up. The doctors in her local medical centre all knew her. There were a lot of people waiting in the queue for their turn to see the doctor, but as soon as one of the nurses saw her, she hurried up through the crowd and took her by the hand, saying, 'Madam Plavšić, come this way'. Plavšić jumped the queue with the nurse and went straight into the doctor's office. No one said a word. People in the waiting room made a space for her and the nurse to pass as swiftly as possible. Plavšić's acceptance of being picked out by the nurse from the long line of 'her people', who may have been waiting for hours to see the doctor, seemed to be against her 'democratic' principles that she claimed to live by. This was a blatant demonstration of her sense of entitlement.

Ten years after she was released from prison, I only witnessed the utmost respect and admiration for her from people around her. She is well-known in the neighbourhood in which she has been living since her release in 2009. In March 2021, Plavšić was diagnosed with COVID-19 and spent two weeks in hospital in intensive care where everyone treated her 'with respect and care'. After recovering and leaving the Belgrade hospital, it took her several weeks to recover. Still in relatively good health, Plavšić claims she inherited this from her mother, who died when she was 94, around the same age as Plavšić at the time of this book's publication.

In 2010, a few months after her release, Plavšić visited Banjaluka, the city she lived in during and after the war. Her former presidential office was there too. During her visit, she gave several interviews to the local media about her case and plea bargain, which has been the topic that always preoccupied local and international media and scholars. However, between 2011 and 2016, Plavšić largely withdrew from public life and has hardly appeared in the media, refusing numerous calls for interviews by journalists and researchers. As she stated, 'I did not want my peace to be disturbed'. However, in the last few years, she has appeared in the local media a few times. Most of her interviews have been similar.[3] Journalists usually want to know whether she is remorseful, how she spent her time in prison, what she thinks of Karadžić and Mladić, and how she escaped from Sarajevo. I listened to all the publicly available interviews with her and could not find any difference in her account to me. Her opinions about the Bosnian Muslim population, the Bosnian War and possibilities of reconciliation have not changed over the past thirty years.

Plavšić sucked in air through her teeth and smoothed down her pastel green silk blouse. Shuddering, she jabbed her finger on the coffee table and raised her voice:

> As fire and water, we cannot live with Muslims. When we lived together before the war, it was barely a happy life. During the first multinational elections, I spoke about the express pressure cooker: when the pressure works, the food cooks well, but if the lid does not function well, then steam and all the ingredients pop out. And that was what Tito did to people in ex-Yugoslavia: put the lid on the pressure cooker which eventually exploded.[4] So, it is all good if you don't change the pressure. But as soon as pressure changes everything goes to hell. During Tito's time I was warned by the Communist Party not to speak about him and his tactics that were functioning as an express pot. Only with iron discipline and instilling fear could the Communists dictate. If you are disobedient, you go to prison. That is how they enforced the slogan of 'brotherhood and unity'. The multi-ethnic joint life was unnatural and under pressure. It had to blow up somewhere. No, we [Serbs] cannot live together with them [Muslims]. We can live next to each other as we live now, and that's it.
>
> We had a lot of mixed marriages in Yugoslavia. The brother of my sister-in-law was married to a Muslim woman. They studied in Ljubljana and met there. She was from Mostar. It was terrible for his family when he brought her into his home. She lied to him that she was pregnant. She was a cheater, a terrible woman. The father of my sister-in-law was humiliated by his neighbours. They would greet him with 'As-salamu alaykum Serb'.[5] He felt humiliated as if they were stabbing

him in the heart. And that Muslim woman was the daughter of a man who in 1941 was transporting dead Serbs into the mass graves. And of course, that man was also a Communist Party member. My goodness! That woman hated me. All Muslims joined the Communist Party and then later on, Alija's Islamic Party. Muslims have no identity. They have two faces. They are Serbs but won't ever admit that.

She shook her head and let the words hang over us. An icy jolt ran through my body. I pressed my fingertips on the corner of my eyes, unable to open them for a moment. I wanted to say something, but the words got stuck in my throat. Plavšić's hand shook a little when she returned her cup to its saucer. She then pressed her fingers to her chin. I watched her profile, the wrinkles in her cheek moving and changing with every puff she made with her cigarette. She looked away, sipped her coffee, and began again. She cleared her throat. After nine years of serving her prison sentence and almost a decade since she was released, Plavšić still holds the same views she had during wartime and afterwards.

> The court failed to bring justice and reconciliation ... The Hague Tribunal produced ten times more hatred among Muslims, Croats and Serbs than there was before. The key goal of The Hague Tribunal—reconciliation—they failed to achieve.

We held each other's eyes while sitting in silence. Her body tightened like a wind-up toy. She grimaced, and drew heavily on her cigarette. Leaving her cigarette for a moment, she wiped her reading glasses on the tail of her blouse. She looked up, squinting at the sound of a plane flying low. Putting her glasses back on, she looked for her cup. Plavšić shuddered, threads of memories tugging at her. I asked her if she could return to those times whether she would enter politics again. She picked up a cigarette, and after a few puffs said,

OUT OF JAIL

I entered politics because as a child during World War II I was young but still mature enough to understand that only Serbs were getting killed. Bosnia and Herzegovina was a part of the Independent State of Croatia... [Here she starts talking about the 1990s war]. They first killed Serbs at the peripheries, villages, then *starog svata* [the bridegroom] in Sarajevo... 'What else do we need to do to you?' asked one of my Muslim colleagues at the time. He was a friend of mine until then. In other words, what else did they need to do to Serbs so we could see what has been prepared for us. I thanked him for telling me that. 1941 was in preparation. I was very much aware of that, and I entered politics only because of that, and the only goal Serbs had during the 1990s war was to avoid 1941. Muslims wanted to take all of Bosnia and Herzegovina as theirs. And Croats wanted western Bosnia to fulfill their desires for that part of Bosnia ... We [Serbs] only entered into the war to prevent 1941, and I think that we fulfilled our goal. Many people have died, a lot, but not even close to the 900,000 or one million who were killed during World War II. I think in this last war there were around 30,000 victims. That is success! We Serbs, with only that aim, to prevent 1941, organised ourselves, and we achieved that goal, not 100 per cent, but a very significant part of it ... and Muslims who entered into the war to take Bosnia for themselves were thinking Christians can be here, but they will be only second-class citizens; that we will be as we were during the Turkish time—*raja*, slaves ... only under that condition could they somehow live with us ... They are Serbs who took Islam and they will always want to do everything to destroy Serbs ... and Croats wanted to enlarge *lijepu njihovu domovinu* [their beautiful homeland][6] so we had to fight to not be slaughtered as sheep as we were in World War II in Jasenovac and elsewhere.[7] This time we did well ... we defended ourselves and won our state.[8]

She paused and stubbed out her cigarette into a cracked crystal glass ashtray. I tried not to appear disturbed by her ranting, so I averted my eyes and stared out the window, feeling the breeze on my face. My head reeled. A bitter taste stuck to my tongue.

I thought about the war, and my neighbour with whom I grew up, Predrag, who was killed at the very end of it, in October 1995. His mother told me that he was sitting on the crest of the hill when a grenade hit his neck. He died on the spot. Predrag was 22, perhaps daydreaming at that very moment about the war ending soon and finally reuniting with his fiancée and enjoying their freedom together. I thought about my aunt and uncle, and wondered why I was sitting with Plavšić in her living room. I stretched my legs out and crossed them at my ankles to regain composure. As mentioned before, Plavšić often blurred her memories and stories from 1941 with 1991 and the beginning of the dissolution of Yugoslavia. Plavšić is, however, not the only one who speaks about 'the continuation' or 'repetition' of 1941, and the thinking that Serbs and Jews were the greatest victims in the Balkans during World War II.[9]

I pressed more and asked if she would do something differently if she had that time again; whether she thinks that ethnic cleansing could be avoided during war. Plavšić sucked air through her teeth, and then let out a heavy, drawn-out sigh. She stared at the wall in front of her. Then my stomach lurches. Three minutes passed. I dug my fingernails into my palms. Eventually, she tilted her head and said:

> No, that could not be avoided. You know, one institution [the ICTY] bases its work on the wrong premise/assumption, and they draw wrong conclusions from it. All honourable lawyers, historians, scientists and analysts categorise this as a civil war, but they [the ICTY] started from the assumption that Serbia was aggressive to Bosnia, and that we, Serbs from Bosnia, helped in that aggression. So, when the premises are not true, all conclusions drawn from them are not true either. If the war qualified as a civil war, then they should not have had the right to prosecute only Serbs. The court was established without a legal basis. My husband knew that, he wanted to defend me, but he was half blind

although his brain worked perfectly; he was a fantastic criminal lawyer. Bob Pavich defended me; he was not a criminal lawyer but a business lawyer. I cannot say anything against him, he did his job honourably. The court was not established properly. The UN General Assembly should have established it, but that did not happen. The appointment of judges was purely a political exercise. The ICTY offered them big salaries; they were all international. They wrote laws for that court, and they accepted those among themselves. If they did not like some provisions, they just simply changed them during the process or added something. If someone could analyse these things, I can imagine what could come out of it. So, from the beginning, something was not right.

Plavšić was furrowing her eyebrows, her eyes full of scorn. '*Možete li vi to da zamislite?*' ['Can you believe it?'] This expression was repeated by Plavšić many times during our conversations. To this day, she has expressed bewilderment, and could not understand or accept many of the ICTY arguments and conclusions. Plavšić was very invested in proving to me the illegality of the Tribunal. Almost three years after this conversation, she sent me a message through my aunt one day in July 2020 to call her because she wanted to tell me 'something'. She never, in all those years we kept in touch, asked for my phone number or email address or any sort of personal contact detail. It was always me who had to initiate the contact and call if I wanted to talk to her. Although I often reported to my aunt and uncle about being in touch with Plavšić, only that one time did she use my aunt as 'a middle woman' to send me a message. So, I was surprised and excited. For a split second, I naively imagined that Plavšić, to whom I had spoken recently just three days after she turned 90, realised that the time had come to confess her remorse that she had buried deep down. I called her, sensing the urgency of her need to speak to me. My stomach tightened as I asked her what it was all about. She seemed excited and blurted out, 'Did you know that a group of experts have written a book and even made a TV documentary about the illegality of the Tribunal?'

I was dumbstruck. She went on to explain that she'd watched the TV show and was excited to learn that there are 'experts working to prove the illegality of the court'. I promised I would find the show on the internet and see it for myself. And I did. It was one of the shows run by the Serbian media who found an ultra-right Serbian teacher working in Mexico who apparently wrote a book about the 'illegality' of the Tribunal.

Plavšić spent a lot of time analysing documents that contained her charges and questioning the legality of the court. She adjusted her glasses, shuffled the papers in her lap and sighed.

> During the court's work, there were so many changes to the statute articles; you know, when they do not like something, they would just say *bis*; for example, bis 47 ... that is an addendum to the article, and they make these changes between themselves. When you bring laws here in our country, they go through parliamentary procedure. For example, if the government suggests changes to the provisions, they have to go through a procedure, but there, the court did not go through any procedure. When the modification of some provisions suited them, they simply changed them. So, the court was irregular from its beginning, and I talk only about formalities ... I am not a lawyer. So, you can imagine what expert lawyers think of it all. Naser Orić and his mates killed 3,200 Serb civilians in Srebrenica and walked free, and me, a woman who only did humanitarian work, a biologist, was sentenced to eleven years. That is ridiculous. And Srebrenica happened because Serbs had enough of Orić's rampage killings in the region, and they did not want to put up with it anymore. I had an idea of forming a special commission on Srebrenica that would bring together all relevant experts in the field to do the research based on facts and evidence, and once and for all establish whether that was genocide or not. I made a list of arguments why what happened in Srebrenica could not qualify as genocide and how it is impossible to compare it

with the Holocaust. Serbs saved their women and children; they gave them food and shelter. They safely removed them from Srebrenica before the massacre happened. But my initiative for establishing such a commission was not of interest to the government in Republika Srpska.

She held me in her gaze while rubbing her brow—a habit to ease her discomfort, perhaps. The room spun. My stomach had knotted. The hair on my neck prickled. Nothing has changed her views; she did not recognise the ICTY as a court of law, so its facts and evidence were to Plavšić irrelevant and untruthful. Despite the enormity of it all, I was once again convinced that nothing could change her views, and that any attempt at intervention on my part would mean the end of our conversation. It was emotionally excruciating to accept this fact and to keep going. Plavšić was pale, exasperated with herself. Her mouth dropped open. I asked her if she had any intention to write a third book.

> The publisher of the first two memoirs wrote on the back cover of the book that he expected a third book. It would be logical that I write that third book, and I should have written it a long time ago, when I was released. I started to write it, and I think I have half of it, but it has been tough for me because during that time, leaving The Hague and all of it was extremely difficult, and I knew I would have to go through that again if I was to write about it. So, I thought to myself, 'Okay, if I had to do that, why now? For whom should I write it?' The people [Serbs] do not need me anymore. Poor people ... You know, the people need to reach a certain standard and then be interested in something. As long as they are digging through the garbage bins, my book is not of interest, and for me, writing and recalling all that trauma is a torturous exercise.

'Trauma' here refers to Plavšić's time in prison, which she believed was undeserved. Plavšić never received a formal offer to publish the third book. Not from her former publisher or other publishers. Her memoirs were not translated into other languages. There were efforts by the Orthodox priests in Sweden to translate them but to no avail. Plavšić, however, told me that she saw copies of her book translated into English during her hearings. According to her, the ICTY judges and prosecutors all had them on their desks. Her lips and cheeks sagged. She tilted her head without looking at me.

> I saw copies of my first memoir in English in the court. I don't know who translated them ... The books were popular among my people. One journalist sent me a letter after she'd read my books. She said, 'I want to tell you about something that will make you happy. I saw a man going with his small pot to get a lunch in a social kitchen because he had no money for lunch. In his cheap plastic bag, I saw your book'. That's what she told me. People still ask me for copies of my books, if I have them, but there are no books anymore. You know what 'they' did? They burned down the printing house. The Serbs did it. Those I chased, such as Karadžić, and those who said I was a traitor because they were mentioned in my books, all of them. My third book was meant to be about the Tribunal. I felt terrible when I heard that they burned down the publishing house of my publisher. Terrible. The publisher told me that he sent one or two copies to all the libraries in Republika Srpska. It is impossible to find them. People would stop me on the street to ask me about them. I have only one copy.

I told her that I didn't have the second book of her memoirs written in prison. She got up from her chair and fetched the copy from the bookshelf. 'Here it is for you. I don't need it anymore. You need it since you write about my life'. I said that there was no need and that I would find it in a second-hand bookshop somewhere. Plavšić twisted her face, waved me off and changed the subject.

> Our individual interests cannot be put before the interests of the people. I took the guilt upon myself and took it from my people and

OUT OF JAIL

was convicted. I did not want to be an obstacle to my people. I am the only one who did it; the guilt is mine and only mine. I did not accuse anyone else. No one else did it, except me. Those who were in command were hiding, making fools of themselves, protecting themselves with fake identities, and once they were caught, they made comments referring [Plavšić was sarcastic now] to 'their people'. No, an indictment is individual; it is in your name, not the parliament's or the government of Republika Srpska's.

Regarding Karadžić's judgement, that he was guilty of genocide in Srebrenica, Plavšić commented in the Serbian media, 'If that was genocide then the army would kill women and children. I saw they were saving them instead'.[10] For Plavšić, killing men was legitimate since they were 'soldiers pretending to be civilians. In war, enemies become your legitimate target'. Plavšić still holds a strong, racial view of Bosnian Muslims. She narrowed her eyes, frowning.

> They [Muslims] have political victims organisations—for example, the Mothers of Srebrenica, who gained public recognition through the tragedy of their own people. Evil happened in Srebrenica, but not genocide—that was not genocide. If the killing of one million Serbs in World War II was not a genocide, then Srebrenica cannot be either. And if the 3,200 Serbs slaughtered by Naser Orić is not genocide, then Srebrenica is not either. And it was not 8,000 people that were killed by Serbs. In their [Srebrenica genocide victims'] graves under tabuts [the burial site], there are many Serbs they [Muslims] killed themselves and then brought their dead bodies and buried them there. Everyone manipulates these victims. They [Muslims] are not afraid of God, but they like to pray to him five times a day.

Denying genocide and even celebrating it is not something unique to Plavšić. Once again, she aligns herself with the nationalist views of Serb politicians in Republika Srpska and Serbia. Her disdain for Muslims has never waned. Almost thirty years ago, in

1996 during the BiH elections after which she became president of Republika Srpska, she shouted to the crowds, telling them, 'You heroic people, you showed the world we can never live with them [the Muslims], even in peace!'[11]

EPILOGUE

Plavšić raised her eyes from the document lying open in her lap and blinked. I kept my eyes fixed on her as I opened my mouth to ask the next question. Plavšić turned her head and gazed out the window. I felt a chill go down my spine. 'So, you don't run away from the fact that Serbs committed crimes too?' Plavšić took one last drag of her cigarette before stubbing it out in her ashtray.

> Of course they did, but the crimes against Serbs were horrible and I only mentioned to you some villages, and not the pits in Herzegovina full of dead Serb bodies, some of them still not recovered from World War II, and now mixed with dead Serbs from this war ... and many other terrible crimes committed against Serbs. I know that in war everyone suffers, but I was crying only for Serbs and their destiny ... Also, Serbs did not have private prisons like Muslims. Those who conducted politics on behalf of my people said nothing to me. And so, as if I was blindfolded, I went through the war without any information about what was decided during those negotiations regarding the future of our country. Everything was hidden from me. Some things should not have happened, but I found out about them only after the war.
>
> I had no idea that Serbs were capable of committing evil, that they could hate. I was preoccupied with crimes against Serbs and was

trying to collect information and data about these crimes and raise awareness about them in the international media. But no one cared. They'd already decided in advance who will be victim and who will be perpetrator. I was naive in believing that the world would see what had been done to Serb people. But they did not care. They just cared about crimes committed by Serbs, not against Serbs. If I knew about crimes committed by Serbs during the war, I would have done something, tried to prevent them, to ask for accountability like I tried when I found out about crimes in Grbavica by Batko. I never got information about Serb army crimes, although I was a member of the presidency. No one ever shared any information about such crimes with me. I found out about it in The Hague detention unit when one of the prison guards pushed a box of papers with his black boot into my cell. These papers were evidence against me, and they contained pages and pages about crimes committed by Serb troops. I was dumbfounded to discover that my people could commit such crimes.

Plavšić looked like dropping, her eyes wide. I asked, 'How would you like Serbian people to think of you? How would you like to be remembered?' Her face crumpled. Silence stretched between us for a minute or two. Then she shook her head, smiled up at me and spoke in her raspy smoker's voice.

> I have never been concerned about what other people will think [of me] because I can freely say that I am a moral and ethical person. As one of my nephews told me, 'Aunt, people like you have died off'. He wanted to say [she laughs] that I am a dinosaur, that it is my time to go. As a professor and later a member of the presidency and the president, I lived a modest life ... You know, it never occurred to me that I should have more. Each job that I did outside of politics, and in politics, was because Serb people were in danger and that '41 could be repeated. This is why I jumped from a professorship into politics without any experience. I felt an urge to prevent the mass slaughter of Serbs from repeating itself again. But our fight continues in peace time. The war never really ended, it has just been fought now with

EPILOGUE

other means. The Serb fight to preserve our survival and independence continues, but peacefully.

I continued to probe. 'Is reconciliation possible between Serbs, Croats and Bosniaks?' Plavšić cocked her head, looking puzzled, her arms stiff at her sides.

> With respect to reconciliation, that's very weak, poor ... I studied [the] Dayton [Agreement] day and night and saw that it was good for Serbs, but also for all residents of Bosnia and Herzegovina. You know, if someone thinks that Bosnia and Herzegovina needs to be a Muslim state, they are against Dayton. We live with our former enemies in the creation called Bosnia and Herzegovina, and we have to accept that. While I was in detention, fifty-eight institutions in our exclusive jurisdiction were transferred from Republika Srpska to Bosnia and Herzegovina's jurisdiction. I am not happy about it. It could not have been transferred if some Serbs did not allow it; they were just interested to have money in their own pockets. You know, I have been disappointed a lot ... Some Serbs care a lot about war profiteering ... Four days ago, it was the anniversary of establishing our motherland Republika Srpska, which has now existed for thirty-three years. It's lasted longer than the Kingdom of Serb, Croats and Slovenes. And it will last with God's will ... They often accused us Serbs of wanting to establish the Great Serbia, which is nonsense because we just wanted what belonged to us. But if they need to use some prefix, it is better that they use 'great' rather than 'small' Serbia [she giggles]. They have their Great Britain, and no one questions Britain about it. So, what would be wrong with having Great Serbia?

I asked, 'Have you been approached to testify in Karadžić's case?' Plavšić glanced at me, her voice confident. She tilted forward. I put down my coffee cup. I sipped my water, then gulped.

> Four and a half years after I returned from jail to Belgrade, the attorneys who defended Karadžić came to me. I was not sure if he sent them to me or they came on their own. They begged me to testify in his

defence, and I told them, first, that the only condition under which I admitted guilt was that they would not use me as a witness in other trials; and second, I asked them how I could testify in defence of a man who said he would kill me. Of course, I did not agree, and they kind of understood that and left me alone.

I asked, 'Do you still get invitations for interviews?' Her shoulder muscles slackened, her voice firm. She poured more coffee into her cup.

> Recently I gave a few interviews to local media ... Milorad Marić pursued me to do two TV shows with him ... and there is no censorship on the things I have been telling you.[1] You can tell it all. I am telling you the truth. You can publish everything I have said. I make no limitations. I am 94. My legs are giving up on me a bit, but my brain and memory work well. The last interview I gave was in November 2023. The journalists from Banjaluka came to my unit to record a TV show for the anniversary of Republika Srpska that will be marked on 9 January 2024. They come every year to ask me to say something in honour of our Republika, which I helped found. I always gladly accept these invitations.

On our last day together, I held my breath and asked her a final question. 'Do you have any remorse for your policies and actions after all these years?' She did not answer right away. Her eyes glazed over. There were many times during our seven years of conversations that I hoped that Plavšić would break down and apologise, maybe even shed a tear for the crimes of which she was accused. Naively, I hoped she would confess to me.

'Do I have remorse?' She raised her voice and looked at me. She was silent for a moment, our eyes locked. My heart was beating faster. My fingers trembled. Plavšić inhaled sharply.

> If I contributed, even a little, towards Serbian people not experiencing another 1941, and I did, then I don't feel remorse, I have no regrets.

EPILOGUE

I understand my role as a victim for my people, and that's why I never had remorse. On the contrary. If I contributed even a little to preventing Alija Izetbegović's dream—that Bosnia and Herzegovina, as he said in one interview, becomes *Islamska džamahirija* [an Islamic state]—from coming true, from becoming reality, then no, I don't have remorse. Highly ranked foreigners confirmed that if it was not for me, the Dayton Agreement would not have been implemented, although I was called a traitor and could have lost my head because of it! In one article that I read somewhere, it was written that I created a democratic revolution, and I did. I am proud of it. I dismantled dictators from the Serb Democratic Party, the party that would have destroyed Republika Srpska. So, I have no regrets. On the contrary. As time passed, it became more obvious that we were creating Republika Srpska, and we were right. We have our own state, the first Serbian state since 1918. The creation of Republika Srpska was a historical moment in the true sense of the word. As I said many times during my presidency, Republika Srpska is our precious gem that we need to protect with all our might. Too many lives have fallen for it ... I did the right thing and would do it again. My conscience is clear, I sleep peacefully. I am happy that something I worked for with all my heart is successful and lasting. And I wish for it to last forever.

She paused, letting the meaning of her words sink in. Heat had risen to her cheeks. Plavšić stroked her hair, straightened her back, and buttoned the top of her pastel green blouse. She pulled out a cigarette from her pack and placed it between her lips. As she flicked the lighter, she stared hard at me. Biljana Plavšić took me in for a long time before she declared, 'No, there is nothing to regret. I had to protect my people'. I remained silent; there was nothing left to say. Plavšić was, and remained, unrepentant.

***

Biljana Plavšić is an unremorseful perpetrator who has never changed her convictions. She is not a pathological individual but rather an ultranationalist whose public posture and wartime expressions were, as some scholars argued, nearing proto-clerical fascism. Plavšić not only feels a lack of guilt about her actions, but remains utterly convinced of their righteousness until the end. So, what might her views tell us about mass atrocity trials, the law and sentencing? And what about extreme ideologies, the absence of rehabilitation and a lack of remorse? Perhaps nothing that we don't already know and that Hannah Arendt hasn't already told us: that criminal proceedings are inadequate and insufficient to fully address mass atrocities and their perpetrators. Once again, the law itself has proven incapable of changing the hearts and minds of those who hold extreme views. But the question remains: is that even what the law is supposed to do?

Still, this is not to say that Plavšić's experiences are irrelevant or that there is nothing to learn from them. Despite many years that have passed since she was sentenced, regrettably, this book is timelier than one might imagine. At the very least, Plavšić serves as a symbolic reminder that someone can be cultured and worldly, polished and intelligent, yet 'still commit acts of startling brutality'.[2] Or, in other words, she may serve as a prompt, as Philippe Sands writes, for 'how decent people with good families and fine educations could become embroiled in terrible things, or turn a blind eye to them'.[3] Plavšić's appearance and background stand in sharp contrast to the words she spoke and the actions she unleashed and fervently supported.

Plavšić was prosecuted before the first tribunal created by the United Nations since Nuremberg and Tokyo. In the 1990s, after fifty years of stillness, crimes against humanity and genocide were back on the agenda, and Plavšić was one of the key figures to be indicted for such crimes.[4] This book also arrives at a moment when warfare is no longer confined to distant hotspots but is unfolding in our very neighbourhoods. Waging wars has become increasingly normalised internationally, while the restraints of the international law system have weakened, spiralling towards its utter impotence in preventing, halting and punishing violence. In such a new world (dis)order, one in which the concept of civilian protection is strained to the point of obsolescence, and where the far right is being revived and even celebrated, Plavšić's case seems particularly relevant. Her strong nationalistic views and narcissistic personality traits are not anomalies in this era, where the discourse of globalism has diminished and been replaced by a discourse of nationalism that leaves no room for the 'other'. Nationalist identity has become a central signifier and mobiliser worldwide, with racist, anti-immigrant, and anti-Muslim views gaining ground. These are the views that Plavšić holds dearly. For her, there was never any doubt that she needed to fight solely for her ethnic group, while the rest were unwelcome and needed to leave, or risk annihilation.

As radical views become increasingly normalised in the West, we might benefit from a deeper insight into Plavšić's reflections that, unfortunately, now resonate internationally more than they did in the 1990s. Back then, she appeared as a relic of a dark past; today, she would find herself in fine company with some of the most powerful world leaders, such as the American president, Donald Trump, who publicly incited the forcible displacement of Palestinians, an international crime that amounts to ethnic cleansing.[5] Similarly to Plavšić, Trump believes that ethnic cleansing is an acceptable solution to end a war, and he is far from alone in that worldview, which is rapidly becoming the new mainstream. In these troubling times, international law seems to have taken a back seat, while double standards and hypocrisy continue to prevail.

Plavšić's case may thus serve as a cautionary tale for both our present and our future. She is a highly intelligent and articulate woman, a once well-established scientist and former president. She was not someone who merely followed orders, but rather someone who gave them: a high-ranking perpetrator who preached extremist views. This makes her story especially pertinent, as we are witnessing a rise in female participation in extremist ideologies around the world, most of which reinforce and perpetuate patriarchal systems. A wave of reactionary women have been taking leading roles in populist and far-right circles across the Western world. Female populists such as Giorgia Meloni, leader of the far-right Brothers of Italy party, who speaks out against 'global elites', evokes fascist rhetoric, and clings to Mussolini-era slogans like 'God, homeland, family'.[6]

Beyond formal party leadership positions, women have also taken on leading roles as far-right influencers, particularly in the US and Canada, where figures such as Lauren Southern, Lana Lokteff and Tara McCarthy have all cultivated large online followings for their radical ideology.[7] There is a thin line between thinking, preaching and ultimately unleashing radical ideology in action, as the case of Plavšić shows us. Her story may serve as a forewarning of what can eventually happen when radical views are freely propagated with impunity. They may result in mass atrocity and genocide.

The fact that Plavšić received hundreds of letters from people from all walks of life across the globe only reinforced her belief that she had done nothing wrong. However, it was also telling, and deeply troubling, that some people still regarded her with admiration and even idolisation. In many of these letters, she was referred to as 'Madam Plavšić' or 'President Plavšić'. Indeed, who is Biljana Plavšić? Madam, Professor, President or War Criminal convicted for horrendous crimes? Or can she be all of them at once? The seemingly mundane yet significant question of how I should refer to her became one of the many contentious issues I faced with some of my relatives, who struggled with me calling her a war criminal.

***

EPILOGUE

Plavšić is the primary source that informed this book. I seized the opportunity to work with her 'in the flesh'—to observe and engage with her over many days, weeks, months and years. I had access to a research subject in a way that is rarely available. I also gained access to her massive private archive, which contained hundreds of letters, newspaper clippings, original wartime documents and even a handwritten set of three notebooks—diaries she wrote in prison. I also conducted desk and archival research into other characters surrounding her and the events in which she was implicated. With some, like Esad Landžo, a hands-on perpetrator, I conducted extensive interviews; his reflections on the time he spent in The Hague detention unit helped me better understand Plavšić's experiences.[8] I had to introduce myself to Plavšić, persuade her to speak with me and gradually build trust. This meant returning repeatedly to Belgrade or picking up the phone to call her. These conversations were extensive, and building trust was essential because she would not share anything unless she felt her words were being treated with respect.

I could neither challenge her frequently nor be rude, nor would I have wanted to. Seeing her as the 'other' would make us the same. I needed to give her plenty of space and respect her time; after all, she is of a delicate age. I believe it is important to explain to the reader not only what I discovered, but also how I went about finding it. This book was also a personal journey, driven by my family histories and my own experiences with war, witnessing firsthand Plavšić's rise to power, eventual presidency and later on her fall, imprisonment and release. Plavšić's story is intimately connected to my family, particularly my aunt, who played an important role in my life. And the writing of this book has further complicated my relationship with some of my relatives, who sympathise with war criminals such as Plavšić.

I believe that the book, besides detailing the case study of Plavšić, raises a broader set of questions as to how societies treat convicted war criminals once they are released. What does Plavšić's story tell us about the legacy of war crime trials? How is it possible that a person convicted of war crimes and crimes again humanity is publicly celebrated? What does this say about the times we live in, when the world can observe such celebrations with impunity? Can Plavšić, after serving her sentence, publicly deny the crimes for which she was convicted? Can she be held accountable for stripping victims of their victimhood after serving her sentence? Is her case an example of impunity following accountability?

With this book, I also hope to spark a discussion about the rehabilitation and reintegration of war criminals, an issue that has so far attracted little interest from international courts. The Plavšić case is a stark example of failed rehabilitation but successful reintegration, a paradox we have seen with other Balkan war criminals. Those who denied their crimes, such as Plavšić, were successfully reintegrated into their ethnic communities, while those who admitted their crimes were shunned. This, along with her genuine lack of remorse, may also help explain why Plavšić changed her mind and retracted her confession. She realised quickly that admitting to crimes would not do her any good within her Serb community, for whom she immediately became a 'traitor'.

As a scholar, I was deeply concerned about potential consequences of telling her story, specifically the risk of inadvertently empowering the very forces we are trying to resist: extreme nationalism, historical revisionism, the 'othering' and dehumanisation of victims. The challenge was immense, but my scholarly curiosity to uncover untold aspects of her life ultimately prevailed. Did she tell me the truth? Yes, she told me her version of the truth, perhaps carefully constructed to protect herself from the horrors in which she was directly implicated. Plavšić has a reputation for being strong-willed, formidable

EPILOGUE

and authoritarian. While she clearly wanted to present herself in the best possible light and sustain the self-image of being a 'good person', it was also evident that she did not even attempt to pretend that she saw non-Serbs as fully human.[9] Any sign of moral conscience or empathy for these victims and their humanity was strikingly absent, both in her narrative and in her physical presence. She saw 'other' victims only as a threat to her and her own people's existence. Her own sense of victimhood never diminished.

I was aware that Plavšić had a strong incentive to present herself in the best possible light; she was given the opportunity to tell her story on her own terms, and over an extended period of time. Notably, on a number of extremely significant occasions, she chose to go off the record. Each time she did so, she fixed me with a gimlet eye and said, 'Of course you cannot write this, but ...' Her assumption of my personal and professional integrity in these matters was total. I absorbed the weight of what was spoken but deliberately left unwritten.

This work in general, and this part of it in particular—where the interlocutor, who happens to be a war criminal, places unconditional trust in the researcher—raises significant ethical questions. Throughout the research process, I was continuously torn between my professional ethics and personal morality. Do we, as scholars, have an ethical responsibility towards our subjects, even when that subject is a convicted war criminal? Did I betray Plavšić's trust by portraying her in ways she might not approve of, despite the hospitality she extended to me? Would she have ever given me access to her story, her private space and her personal archive had she known how I would represent her? Do war criminals have a right to privacy and confidentiality? Should we, as researchers, respect their wish not to have certain things documented when they tell us something off the record? Does it make any difference if they are remorseful? I continue to ponder these questions. While I do not claim to have definitive answers, I believe it is important to raise them and discuss them openly with colleagues.

As with any other qualitative work, I had to decide which conversations should be included in the manuscript and which should be left out. The choices I made may not have been perfect, but they were necessary. It would have been impossible to condense hundreds of hours of conversations into a single book. Some material was omitted simply due to the volume of text that could not fit into a standard monograph, while other parts were excluded based on my (not easily made) decision to honour Plavšić's request to keep certain things off the record.

I could have written this book in many ways, but I chose to let Plavšić speak and rarely challenged her views. I did not do so to excuse or justify her actions, but to allow her to speak freely—fully aware of the methodological and ethical pitfalls of this approach. The very genre of biography inherently humanises its subject. This is inevitable; by recounting her life story and offering insight into why she acted the way she did, the narrative provides an explanation—though not an excuse—for those actions. I am not the first to engage with a perpetrator of atrocity in this way, or to reflect on their words and thoughts.

Time and again, however, such journalistic and scholarly work has provoked visceral reactions. Gitta Sereny was once accused of 'growing too close' to her subjects, including Franz Stangl, commandant of the Nazi extermination camps Sobibor and Treblinka. On the last day she spent with him, she made him soup. She later reflected, 'I had to ask myself whether there was something morally wrong with what I had done. But, it was a pragmatic thing. I needed him for another day'.[10] Her simple but powerful statement captures my own sentiment: I needed Plavšić for another day.

EPILOGUE

During the course of my work on this book, I was often asked why I did not confront Plavšić, why I did not tell her she was wrong. I understand these questions. There were many moments, while listening to her, when I felt compelled to interrupt and disagree. But confronting Plavšić, challenging her statements or actions directly, would have ended our conversations. And there would not have been 'another day' with Plavšić. Still, avoiding open confrontation or expressing humanity towards a perpetrator puts the researcher at risk of being accused of sympathising wih him or her. Gitta Sereny, because of her work with Albert Speer, was accused by some of being a 'Nazi sympathizer'[11] simply because she dared to admit that she 'grew to like her subject'[12]— an admission that, for readers committed to moral absolutes, was unforgivable. The act of humanising a war criminal is something many find repulsive and unpalatable. Yet Sereny was not the only one accused of 'growing too close' to her research subject. Jessica Stern was faulted for being 'attracted to' and even 'falling in love' with her research subject, Radovan Karadžić.[13] I asked Stern for her comments on such accusations. She seemed bewildered.

> Oh my goodness, that was pretty funny. He certainly doesn't think I fell in love with him—he's furious with me. Of course, I saw him as entirely human, not a devil, but I thought all readers would understand that I was repulsed by him. I was utterly devastated that I was so misunderstood. We will never understand why terrorists and violent nationalists rise if we don't study how they appeal to their followers. I was trying to show the nature of his appeal, but that doesn't mean that I found his arguments persuasive. I assumed that Serb nationalists would go after me, certainly not Bosnian Muslims. I tried to be fair to him, just as I've tried to be fair to all the terrorists I've written about, but I strongly condemn their crimes.

Pumla Gobodo-Madikizela was also asked by her curious readers, 'Are you in love with him?' 'Are you fascinated with him?'—

him being Eugene de Kock, one of apartheid's most brutal covert police operatives, whom she interviewed extensively. She wrote how it was 'interesting to see that some people struggled with... the fact that I could be talking to him at all...' Someone else even commented, 'He [de Kock] must be a very good-looking man'.[14] Gobodo-Madikizela found such suggestions to be nothing but an easy way out of engaging in serious dialogue.

> Casting my professional interest in de Kock in terms of a romantic motive ('in love with him' or as something mysterious ('She's so fascinated with him!') makes it too easy for my listeners to distance themselves from the reality of interacting with the man. It allows them to dismiss my work as something unnatural, something kinky. It allows them to set it aside—to set *me* aside—as an exception...There is a charming madness to it. It closes off the possibility of any serious dialogue on the real subject...Connecting on a human level with a monster therefore comes to be a profoundly frightening prospect, for ultimately, it forces us to confront the potential for evil within ourselves.[15]

Over all these years of writing about Plavšić, I have come to accept that, no matter how I wrote this book, I would always be at risk of being accused of sympathising with her. There seems to be one common experience among researchers studying perpetrators: they are either persistently accused of sympathising with their subjects or find themselves endlessly defending their work as an intellectual enquiry rather than admiration for mass atrocities, or both. In some circles, including academic ones, there remains a continuous and stubborn lack of understanding as to why researchers talk to and listen to perpetrators. Many times, I have heard, as have my colleagues, about the need to make repetitive claims about why it is important to listen to what perpetrators have to say—like I am doing now—rather than outright dismissing them as 'evil'. Understanding the motivations of perpetrators who participate in mass atrocities is essential, as such knowledge may contribute to preventing future occurrences.[16]

Similar accusations were directed at me for my work with Plavšić even before the book was printed and published. The very idea of such a book sparked controversy, and I was peppered with questions like, 'Why would you give a microphone to Plavšić?' Indeed, why give Plavšić the platform? Why allow her to present her views in a largely unmediated way, to tell her story from her perspective at all? What is to be gained by doing so? For one thing, there are new accounts and insights that Plavšić had never previously shared in public. For example, we previously knew little or nothing about her time in detention and later in prison. We also had limited information about her negotiations with the Office of the Prosecutor or her post-sentence life. How and why she made the decision to enter a plea bargain was also largely unknown.

I anticipated that reactions to my research and the book would be polarising, and that I would risk critique—perhaps even demonisation—for some parts of it. I have found myself in that position several times before. This is part of the paradox in which scholars from the Balkans, or those who research the region, often find themselves: no matter how they write, how intellectually and ethically rigorous they are or which method they use, they may still be accused of being either traitors or nationalists. I was warned that some Serbs would not appreciate me calling Plavšić a war criminal. Indeed, I was asked by some, 'How dare you call her a war criminal when she is the President?' One of the people who raised this question was my own father. I also anticipate criticism from segments of the Serbian public who may claim that I effectively betrayed Plavšić, who trusted me with her story and access to her private archive.

But, at the same time, being an insider and from the same ethnic group as Plavšić made me, *by default*, an easy target for accusations of siding with her camp, too. I was warned that I may be eviscerated by Bosniak victims or victims' advocates and scholars. These warnings came from different places—some out of genuine concern for how I would cope with the criticism, and others in the form of cautionary remarks like 'I hope you won't be another Serb apologist,' meaning coming across as a sympathiser of Plavšić. During all of this time, while being exposed to such comments from various actors, I began to wonder: how does one defend against such accusations, comments, suggestions or warnings? Would I have protected myself from such reactions if I had written on every page of the manuscript that Plavšić was an 'evil woman' or a 'monster', and that I was utterly repulsed by her actions?

***

A few years ago, I presented my then ongoing work with Plavšić at the University of Sarajevo, engaging with a full theatre of undergraduate and Master's students. They were interested in her reflections, but mostly in who she was in her everyday life. At the very end of the exchange, one female student asked me, 'If Plavšić was not a war criminal, what would you think of her?' I found this question to be the most interesting. I paused, thinking about how to reply, and decided to be honest. I told her that I would consider Plavšić a single-minded, yet smart, cultured, well-mannered and well-travelled person with a decent sense of humour. And this is similar to how Hannah Arendt described Eichmann, the perpetrator of mass atrocities: as 'neither perverted nor sadistic' but 'terrifyingly normal', the kind of person you would never expect to 'hurt a fly', let alone commit horrific crimes.[17] Or to put it simply, a person like us.

EPILOGUE

It is a paradox that this book may likely face criticism from all three constituent groups in Bosnia and Herzegovina: Serbs, Bosniaks and Croats. Each may cherry-pick aspects they dislike for political, emotional or other reasons—things they wish I could have portrayed differently or omitted all together. That part does not concern me as much. What does concern me is retraumatisation of victims, those who lost everything at the hands of the very ideology that Plavšić continues to ardently glorify. They have always been on my mind, and I have been deeply concerned about how this work may affect them. To them, and only to them, I can try to explain that the purpose of my book was not to relive these terrible crimes, but to understand how they could happen in the first place.

Uğur Ümit Üngör suggests that many people find the study of mass violence and its perpetrators repulsive, and react with strong, condemnatory emotions.[18] This is why conducting empirical work with perpetrators—meeting and spending time with them in person—is both extremely challenging and often met with strong discouragement. It is extraordinary yet still largely thankless work that may haunt researchers in many ways: psychologically, morally, ethically and in terms of the risk of strong public condemnation.

Similarly to Gobodo-Madikizela, Üngör suggests that moralistic approaches to perpetrators and mass atrocities 'do not add anything substantial to our understanding of it'.[19] Experts in mass violence have argued that to understand the dynamics behind it—the actual processes that lead people to participate in atrocities—we need to study perpetrators. And this is what I did; I studied one of the most notorious female perpetrators, Biljana Plavšić, one of the highest-ranking war criminals and the only woman prosecuted by the International Criminal Tribunal for the Former Yugoslavia. She told me her version of the war in Bosnia and Herzegovina: what led her to take part in it, why some events happened, according to her and how. Plavšić was seeking to justify behaviour that I thought was not justifiable. I am convinced that the data and narrative I (re)produced, shaped by years of conversations with her, no matter how we may judge it now, constitutes a unique historical account that will be studied for years to come. It is data that can inform and potentially reshape our understanding of the devastating events of the 1990s.

This book is my contribution to scholarship more broadly, and specifically to the field of perpetrator studies, which seeks to explore perpetrators' motives, decision-making processes, and the broader dynamics of perpetration within the context of large-scale violence and war. There is no doubt that genocide and crimes against humanity are morally repugnant. However, when we approach the study of those who commit such acts primarily through moral condemnation rather than analytical enquiry, we risk hindering our understanding of both perpetrators and their motivations. Such an approach also obscures, and may even prevent, the adoption of a comprehensive, empirically driven methodology, which remains rarely utilised in the field.

It is not easy to let this book go to print with a light heart. I would much prefer that none of the above had happened, that I had met Plavšić merely as a resentful, single-minded person at a family gathering, ruminating on the margins. However, her views became central to the shaping of historical events; hence, it is our responsibility to try to understand how they developed, but also how they fell on so many receptive ears.

Olivera Simić, Brisbane, 8 September 2025

ANNEX I

JUDICIAL DOCUMENTS

Monday, 16 December 2002

[Sentencing Hearing]

[Open session]

[The accused entered court]

MS. DEL PONTE: Thank you, Mr. President. Before I proceed with my introductory remarks, there is a short procedural point that might best be dealt with at the outset. Today's hearing is in a public session, but a key document, the factual basis for the plea of guilty, was filed confidentially by the parties on 30 September. There is now no reason for that document to remain under seal, and it would facilitate today's proceeding, which I understand are to be broadcast live in the former Yugoslavia, if a document were now made public. And therefore ask the Chamber to order that the status of that document be changed so that it can be referred to without difficulty. I only seek the immediate unsealing of that particular document; others should remain confidential until the end of the hearing.

[Trial Chamber confers]

JUDGE MAY: The document will be unsealed.

MS. DEL PONTE: Thank you, Mr. President.

Your Honours, sentencing hearings are, by their nature, public events central to the criminal justice. It is by open process in the Court that the members of society learn about the nature of crimes committed and the responsibility of individuals for them. It is often a painful process, but it is a necessary one. I believe that today's hearing is of unusual importance in bringing to light what occurred during the conflict in Bosnia and Herzegovina. It is the first time in this Tribunal that a senior figure in the former Yugoslavia indicted in a top leadership role has admitted responsibility for horrific crimes committed during the conflict in Bosnia and Herzegovina.

Mrs. Plavsic has pled guilty to count 3 of the indictment, which is a comprehensive charge of crimes against humanity comprising persecution and ethnic cleansing, crimes which resulted in untold suffering for many thousands of innocent victims. Many of those who survived will bear the scars for the rest of their lives, and I wish to stress that there is nothing in the nature of a plea of guilty which in any way alters the seriousness of the crimes

ANNEX I

themselves. They are of the utmost gravity and are fully detailed in the relevant schedules to the indictment. In my submission, the gravity of the crimes should be the Chamber's primary consideration when determining sentence. Leaders have a duty to protect all citizens of a country, and crimes committed against people who deserve protection are all the more serious as a result. Nevertheless, it is of enormous significance that

Mrs. Plavsic accept before this Chamber that horrendous crimes were committed in Bosnia-Herzegovina and that she acknowledge her own individual criminal responsibility for them. Her position stands in sharp contrast to that of other leaders of the period, who either continue to deny that crimes occurred or who try to keep themselves beyond the reach of international justice.

Your Honours, we should not forget that this Tribunal is ultimately itself an instrument of peace. Reconciliation in the Balkans will not be achieved so long as denial persists. The plea of guilty by Mrs. Plavsic rests upon the acceptance of two inescapable truths: First, that the massive crimes set out in count 3 of the indictment did take place as they are described; and second, that in playing the role she did, she bears criminal responsibility. Unless those stark truths are confronted honestly, as they are in these proceedings (supported of course by other findings in the jurisprudence of the International Tribunal) there can surely be little hope for true reconciliation in society in the former Yugoslavia.

I do not suggest that the plea of guilty by Mrs. Plavsic should compel instant forgiveness from victims or indeed from the Chamber. The crimes are too serious for that. In her plea of guilty, and certainly in her dealings with my office, the accused has not sought to gain personal advantage or to evade responsibility for what she herself has done. But the fact of the plea in itself must be an important step towards reconciliation in Bosnia and Herzegovina. It must help to break down revisionism and denial, and I hope that it will compel others to face up to the reality of what happened during the conflict.

Your Honours, the Chamber will hear more on these aspects of the plea from eminent witnesses called to give evidence in the course of the next two days, as it will hear more on the crimes themselves and the role played by Mrs. Plavsic.

Thank you very much, Mr. President.

ANNEX I

Biljana Plavšić Guilty Plea Statement

17 December 2002 (extract from transcript of hearing)

[Interpretation] Mr. President, Your Honours, Madam Prosecutor, Counsel: I'm thankful to have this opportunity to speak today. Nearly two years ago, I came before this Tribunal, having been charged with participating in crimes against other human beings, and even against humanity itself. I came for two reasons: To confront these charges and to spare my people, for it was clear that they would pay the price of any refusal to come. I have now had time to examine these charges and, together with my lawyers, conduct our own investigation and evaluation. I have now come to the belief and accept the fact that many thousands of innocent people were the victims of an organised, systematic effort to remove Muslims and Croats from the territory claimed by Serbs.

At the time, I easily convinced myself that this was a matter of survival and self-defence. In fact, it was more. Our leadership, of which I was a necessary part, led an effort which victimised countless innocent people. Explanations of self-defence and survival offer no justification. By the end, it was said, even among our own people, that in this war we had lost our nobility of character. The obvious questions become, if this truth is now self-evident, why did I not see it earlier? And how could our leaders and those who followed have committed such acts? The answer to both questions is, I believe, fear, a blinding fear that led to an obsession, especially for those of us for whom the Second World War was a living memory, that Serbs would never again allow themselves to become victims. In this, we in the leadership violated the most basic duty of every human being, the duty to restrain oneself and to respect the human dignity of others. We were committed to do whatever was necessary to prevail.

Although I was repeatedly informed of allegations of cruel and inhuman conduct against non-Serbs, I refused to accept them or even to investigate. In fact, I immersed myself in addressing the suffering of the war's innocent Serb victims. This daily work confirmed in my mind that we were in a struggle for our very survival and that in this struggle, the international community was our enemy, and so I simply denied these charges, making no effort to investigate. I remained secure in my belief that Serbs were not capable of such acts. In this obsession of ours to never again become victims, we had allowed ourselves to become victimisers.

You have heard, both yesterday and today, the litany of suffering that this produced. I have accepted responsibility for my part in this. This responsibility is mine and mine alone. It does not extend to other leaders who have a right to defend themselves. It certainly should not extend to our Serbian people, who have already paid a terrible price for our leadership. The knowledge that I am responsible for such human suffering and for soiling the character of my people will always be with me.

There is a justice which demands a life for each innocent life, a death for each wrongful death. It is, of course, not possible for me to meet the demands of such justice. I can only do what is in my power and hope that it will be of some benefit, that having come to the truth, to speak it, and to accept responsibility. This will, I hope, help the Muslim, Croat, and even Serb innocent victims not to be overtaken with bitterness, which often becomes hatred and is in the end self-destructive.

As for my own people, I have referred today to their character. I think it, therefore, important to explain what I'm speaking of. There now stands in the centre of Belgrade a great domed church, still under construction, the construction begun in 1935. Our people have persevered in building this church as a monument to a man who more than any other formed the character of the Serbian people. That man was the great St. Sava. The path he followed was marked by self-restraint and respect for all others. A great diplomat who gained the respect of his people and the world around him, a man whose character has become deeply ingrained in the Serbian people.

ANNEX I

It is the path and example of St. Sava that the great Serbian leaders have followed, even in our own times, demonstrating a noble endurance and dignity, even in the most difficult circumstances. One need only point to Bishop Artemije Radosavljević, who to this very day is a voice crying out for justice in what has become for Serbs the wilderness of Kosovo. Tragically, our leaders, including myself, abandoned this path in the last war. I think it is clear that I have separated myself from those leaders, but too late. Yet, this leadership, without shame, continues to seek the loyalty and support of our people. It is done by provoking fear and speaking half-truths in order to convince our people that the world is against us. But by now the fruits of this leadership are clear. They are graves, refugees, isolation, and bitterness against the whole world, which spurns us because of these very leaders.

I have been urged that this is not the time nor the place to speak this truth. We must wait, they say, until others also accept responsibility for their deeds. But I believe that there is no place and that there is no time where it is not appropriate to speak the truth. I believe that we must put our own house in order. Others will have to examine themselves and their own conduct. We must live in the world and not in a cave. The world is always imperfect and often unjust, but as long as we persevere and preserve our identity and our character, we have nothing to fear.

As for me, it is the members of this Trial Chamber that have been given the responsibility to judge. You must strive in your judgment to find whatever justice this world can offer, not only for me but also for the innocent victims of this war. I will, however, make one appeal, and that is to the Tribunal itself, the Judges, Prosecutors, investigators; that you do all within your power to bring justice to all sides. In doing this, you may be able to accomplish the mission for which this Tribunal has been created.

ANNEX II

CORRESPONDENCE ON AND FROM PLAVŠIĆ

In the following pages, I reproduce several letters written to me or to Biljana Plavšić that illustrate how some people regarded her. To protect their identity, I have anonymised the letters sent to Plavšić from those who requested interviews or asked for her signature.

11 August 2017
Email to Olivera Simić from Biljana Plavšić's priest Prota Vlada Rafailović
Translated into English from Serbian Cyrillic by the author

In the Serbian public today there is a divided opinion about Madam Biljana Plavšić. Some praise her as a Serbian hero, martyr and patriot, while others consider her a traitor.

It is my wish, as a man and a priest, to speak more about this spiritual figure and the Christian works of Madam Biljana Plavšić, of course, with her approval. It is not my intention to judge her or defend her. I want only to present impartially before the readers, based on what I have read or heard from her personally, who can then judge for themselves what kind of spiritual greatness and Christian personality she is. As she dealt with humanitarian aid, Ms Plavšić came several times during the war to the Serbian church of St Sava in Stockholm, where I was a parish priest, to collect humanitarian aid to the endangered Serbian people. She was particularly concerned for the Serbian wounded who were stationed in Slankamen.

I called Mrs Biljana Plavšić Mother Teresa because she managed to invite every Serb to help its people like Mother Teresa could. The priest receives the blessing of his bishop to work as a prison priest. I don't know what it's like in other countries, but a priest in Sweden is obliged to take courses to get permission to work as a prison priest. I took care of The Hague prisoners in Sweden, and as far as I know, the care of The Hague prisoners in the Netherlands was led by a respected priest, Dr Voja Bilbija.

In addition to Mrs Plavšić, I also took care of The Hague prisoners, Miroslav Deronjić and General Nebojša Pavković, who is still serving his sentence in Finland. I do not know that there was some kind of contract to be made but it was necessary for the prisoner to express his desire with the prison authorities to approve the visit of the priest (and the prison authorities probably sought approval from The Hague). When this request was granted, the priest could come to visit.

Just as the Lord Jesus Christ took upon Himself the sins of the whole world, so Mrs Biljana Plavšić took the sins of the entire Serbian people on her weak old shoulders. It just shows her greatness both as a woman and as a believer. Many times she asked the prison authorities for permission to visit her, and it was sometimes several times a month I would come to visit. I have to mention here that the prison is about 220 kilometres away from my home, so I usually had to book the whole day to visit Mrs Biljana Plavšić, counting the time it took me to get to the prison and back, as well as the time I spent with her. My book has not been translated into any other language. The book was not promoted either in Serbia or in Republika Srpska. My wish was

ANNEX II

to do so, wishing through these promotions to illuminate the character and work of Madam Biljana Plavšić and to introduce people to her human greatness.

However, Madam Biljana Plavšić did not have the strength to attend the promotions (which I fully understand after all the suffering she went through). For this reason, the book did not enter the wider circles of our society, which I am very sorry for. Working as an active priest in the parish of Saint Sava in Stockholm, I often received calls from our people who were serving sentences in prisons to visit them. I did it gladly whenever I had time. I came to Stockholm in 1981. In the first decades of my stay in Stockholm, I was the only priest for the Stockholm parish. During this period, the construction of the church in Stockholm began, so I was very busy. With the blessing of the bishop in 2003, I started working as a prison priest. Madam Biljana Plavšić is primarily a great woman, a great believer, a person of exceptional higher education. It is rare today to meet a person with such moral qualities as Madam Biljana Plavšić.

From my book you will best find out what the prison conditions are. Madam Biljana expressed the most about them, and what she did in certain places. Of course, she had a different status. She was treated according to the orders of The Hague. The letter about her treatment was given to her legal representative (the best lawyer in Sweden) who defended Madam Biljana Plavšić, where it was explained that she was under The Hague Tribunal jurisdiction. I did not personally write petitions for other convicts because I did not know them as I did Madam Biljana Plavšić, but I asked Patriarch Irinej, Metropolitan Amphilohije, and Bishop Lavrentije in writing to stand up for General Nebojša Pavković.

As I said before, Madam Biljana Plavšić is a woman of high quality. She did not approve of the fact that Serbian Orthodox priests left their homes and went abroad while their people died and suffered. Of course, the priests in question did not like her because she publicly criticised them, but that did not bother her at all. I personally think that the court [ICTY] is a political court. The conditions in prisons must be very bad but I think that's what the defendants themselves should be asked to reveal. When I met them, I met them in finely furnished rooms, drinking tea or coffee, and talking. What happened outside of those rooms only the prisoners can say.

Everything is difficult for them. Very often these people have higher education and were in significant state or military positions. They enjoyed the respect of their fellow citizens. They were surrounded by love from their family and friends. And then there's the fall. They lost the ground under their feet and became a rag on which everyone wipes their dirty shoes. Terrible. Isolated, worried for their children, grandchildren, wives, husbands. They want to breathe the air freely into their lungs.

The role of the Church is very important. Meeting a priest is the most beautiful thing that happened to them in those long and difficult years of imprisonment. I also enclose two letters from which you can conclude what the Serbian priest meant to The Hague prisoners and their families.

Letter to Serbian Patriarch Irinej from Biljana Plavšić following her release from prison

PATRIARCH OF SERBIA
MR IRINEJ

Our Holiness,

I remember the events during my prison sentence in Sweden, from mid-August 2003 to October 27, 2009, when on Holy Friday I was told 'you are free'. I will talk only about those events, which

ANNEX II

are relevant to the purpose of this letter. After the verdict of 11 years by The Hague Tribunal, I was transported to the Swedish prison of Hinsenberg. I found myself among women murderers, infanticides, drug addicts, prostitutes, etc. Among them, I got to know the darkest side of life. In prison one survives in a special way known to them and unthinkable to me.

In such a situation, God himself sent me Father Vladislav Rafailović, who helped me get out of that hell healthy and wise. Father Vlada used to visit me every Saturday or Sunday and helped me to cope with the conditions of prison life more easily. He also organised visits to our people from Sweden. He used to drive to Hinsenberg, which is far away (more than 200 km away) from Stockholm. To those who came from other countries like my nephew from Canada he offered hospitality and transportation to the prison. During the visits of the then prime minister of Republic of Srpska, he selflessly engaged himself with the organisation and transportation to the prison.

Word quickly spread that through Father Vlada, contact with me could be arranged. Serbs came from America, for example, Mihailo Djordjevic with his wife. All these visits helped me to endure the cruelty of everyday life more easily. There was a hope in me that I would endure what few believed I would be able to. In order to receive Communion twice a year, there was a great struggle at several levels of the state administration that banned the intake of alcohol. When they saw the quantity involved that can fit into a small spoon, the endless discussions around Communion stopped. This struggle was successfully fought by Father Vlada. I fasted during two Christian holidays and asked for the simplest fasting food so I could prepare myself. I was told by the prison administration that only Muslims fast and Christians do not. They didn't know the Christians fast too!!! I fought this fight on my own and I succeeded.

Father Rafailović, among other things, convinced the prison administration that in addition to Catholic and Islamic worship, an Orthodox Liturgy for Orthodox prisoners should also be held. At that time there were a small number of them, but equality was established when I was in Hinsenberg precisely thanks to Father Rafailović. I was the oldest prisoner in Sweden, and according to their regulations, there is a limitation in that sense that I had passed. Father Vlada hired a well-known Swedish lawyer, Dr Altina, who argued for my early release based on my age and prison conditions. The request was rejected because the Tribunal in The Hague has jurisdiction over it.

Archpriest Vladislav Rafailović wrote a book entitled *The Golgotha Road of Biljana Plavšić* (publisher, Nezavisne novine, Banja Luka, 2009).

Respectfully,

Biljana Plavšić

20 February 2004

An English-language invitation by the Academic Society of Lund University to Plavšić while she was serving her sentence in Sweden

INVITATION TO THE ACADEMIC SOCIETY OF LUND UNIVERSITY

Lund, 20 February 2004

Dear Madam,

The Academic Society of Lund is an non-profit organisation of students and teachers at Lund University, which was founded in

ANNEX II

1666. Lund University is the largest university in the Scandinavian countries, situated in the southernmost part of Sweden. The Academic Society hosts many cultural and social activities in Lund. These include lectures, theatrical performances, concerts and public debates.

Particularly well known are the Student Evening Sessions featuring prominent politicians, authors, musicians, scientists and other persons of interest to the student body. These evenings, which take place in our classic 19th century halls, were initiated in 1905.

Among our distinguished guests are Dag Hammarskjöld, Mahalia Jackson, Ingmar Bergman, Duke Ellington, Miriam Makeba, Richard Lester, Jimi Hendrix, Bobby Seale, Ella Fitzgerald, Olof Palme, Frank Zappa, Albert Speer, Kurt Vonnegut, Ray Charles, Georg Henrik von Wright, David Attenborough, Anton Corbijn, Hans Blix and Her Majesty Queen Silvia of Sweden.

The Academic Society of Lund would be honoured if you accept our invitation to attend a Student Evening Session in Lund during the semester of 2004.

Your Sincerely,

[redacted]

The Academic Society of Lund University

22 March 2004

Plavšić's reply to the above invitation, translated into English from Serbian Cyrillic. There was also a copy of the letter translated into Swedish. Plavšić believes the translation was

done by her priest Rafailović. Both letters were stuffed into one envelope.

Academic Society

Hinsenberg, 22 March 2004

REPLY TO INVITATION OF ACADEMIC SOCIETY— LUND UNIVERSITY

Thanks for your invitation.

I feel privileged by your invitation, but unfortunately I am not in the position to accept it.

As you probably know and understand, my current possibilities to decide something on my own are very limited due to strict regulations enforced by higher prison management for getting permission to leave the prison.

I am not in a position [to accept]. Since I have been here [I cannot] receive communion from my priest due to strict prison regulations that ban the intake of alcohol in prison, although in my case we are talking about a small amount of wine that equals a very small spoonful of liquid. I cannot even imagine how the prison administration would react if I would ask to leave the prison on your invitation due to strict security reasons.

But I have nothing against it—on the contrary—I would be delighted if someone on your behalf would negotiate with the prison administration. I would be honoured to attend one of the evenings that you organise.

Sincerely,

Biljana Plavšić

ANNEX II

8 June 2004

A second invitation sent to Plavšić by a student at Lund University, written in English (unedited below). Both invitations were sent to Plavšić as hard copy letters with the imprinted logo of Lund University on the envelopes.

Dear Biljana Plavšić,

My name is [redacted] and I am four years architect student at the Lund University in the south of Sweden. I am writing on Behalf of the Studentevening Council and the Academic Society of Lund. The Student evening Council is working with arranging lectures, debates etc for the students of the old well-known Lund University, founded in 1666.

Last year the Council celebrated its 100th anniversary as one of the leading platforms of its kind that offers interesting guests of a great variety. We are non-political and non-religious. Some of the people that visited us during the years are ....

The traditional Student Evening is held in the Academic Society in Lund ...You are a most fascinating person and I would love to have you as our guest.

The Academic Society would be honoured if you'd agreed on a visit. I have been in contact with the Head of Information at Hinseberg: [redacted] and she convinced me to contact you by this letter.

I look forward to hearing from you.

Sincerely yours,

[redacted]

Chairman Studentevening Council

28 August 2004

A sample letter to Plavšić from a journalist seeking an interview while she was imprisoned in Sweden

The letter was handwritten and included a copy of the journalist's Press permission with his photo on it. The permission was issued in August 1992 by the Ministry for Information, Republic Srpska, Sarajevo. On the front of the envelope was written 'Urgent and personal: Mrs Biljana Plavšić'. Plavšić handwrote 'Vatikan' below the letter and circled it. She gave me the letter in October 2017, which I typed up as written, preserving a few grammatical mistakes; the underlined text is original.

Rai vaticano (imprinted logo at the top of the letter)

Dear President Plavšić,

The staff of Director ... has told me the strong doubts that you feel about the interview. I understand that this would be the first time, since you are in Sweden, but as we know very well, <u>in our lives there is always 'a first time'</u>.

The enclosed photocopy will show the evidence of my past reporting, always on the rights side and proper time, with full honesty.

For this reason, I beg you to dedicate me <u>just 15 minutes</u> of your time, focusing on religious subjects or whatever You would like to be clarified in the world, considering that Italian and Vatican media have an excellent reputation, as far as their behaving policy is concerned. The recorded conversation will be conducted with full dignity and delicacy of the subject.

Now, I am completely in Your hands, hoping in a positive and partial change of Your doubts.

ANNEX II

Last alternative (and this would be for me a great privilege anyway) could be the opportunity to just meeting You for few minutes, kissing a gentle lady hand Italian style and going back to Roma just with a historical picture together.

Anxiously awaiting Your kind reply this morning (since I will leave Hinsenberg this afternoon). I heartly thank you and I apologise for my hand writing, but there was no typing machine available.

Very devoutly Yours

[redacted]

31 August 2017

A sample letter from a man asking for Plavšić's signature

Translated into English by the author.

He wrote his full name, address, email address and phone number on the front top corner of the letter. This letter was sent to Plavšić's ('Respected Madam') home address in Belgrade. Plavšić could not explain how the author of the letter knew her home address. In the envelope was a handwritten letter, his photograph, a postcard from his hometown, the first page from her book, and a photo collage of her second memoir *Svedočim*. A return envelope with author's name, full address and a pre-paid stamp was also included. There was a small pink notepad pasted to the copy of the first page of her book with writing in the Serbian/Bosnian/Croatian language although the author is not from the former Yugoslavia but one of its neighbouring countries. It says, 'Would you mind signing this page from your book for me? And can you send it back via mail to me? I would return that page back to the book. Thank you a lot.' The letter was written in Serbian/Croatian/Bosnian too.

Dear Madam Biljana Plavšić,

My name is [redacted] (37 years old) and I live in [redacted]. I work as a teacher of German language and geography in a Grammar school. Three weeks ago I visited Belgrade and wanted to meet with you personally. I have your book *Svedočim* and I wanted to ask you to sign it for me but it was not possible to meet with you and I understand that. Because of that I am sending you my photo so you can see who is writing to you and I am sending you one page from your book.

Since I respect you and admire your work, I would like to ask you, if you could sign the page from your book for me. You are huge authority, and it would be my great honour if you could respond to me.

I admire and honour you and your work for your country. I know it was not easy for you. I respect you so much. I have a special sympathy for Slavic people and I think that ... has a good and friendly relationship with other Slavic people so I would like to stay in contact with you and find out more about you and your life.

I want to thank you on your time and goodwill. I wish you lots of luck and plenty of sunny days.

Sincere greetings from [redacted]

ANNEX II

A sample letter in English from an academic seeking an interview with Plavšić

Dear Madam Plavšić,

I am writing to you in the hope that your response to my proposal will be positive. I specialise in the political and cultural history of the South Slavs at the University ... with a special emphasis on the issue of nation, nationalism, and the construction of identity. I have devoted the last ten years to work on the issue of the disintegration of the former SFR Yugoslavia. I am currently working on a research project on the initiation of the reconciliation process in the former Yugoslavia. The reason for this letter is, in fact, an integral part of my reconciliation project.

Namely, I would like to hold a series of talks with you on the subject of the dissolution of the former SFRY and the events in Bosnia and Herzegovina during the last fifteen years. Simply put, my intention is to give you the opportunity to tell your life story with all the elements of politics, ideology, history, culture and patriotism, which always accompany memories of the past. My 'questions' would, in fact, be suggestions for topics to discuss. Of course, you have the freedom to choose topics for conversation. My goal is to, without any interference and desire to valorise your analysis, provide you with a platform for your interpretation of events and analysis of the reasons and consequences of those events. I would then translate the text into English and send you the translation and the original for authorisation.

This series of conversations would then, in cooperation with my colleague [redacted] be published as an academically formatted book—a primary source in researching the history, culture and politics of the former Yugoslavia and the Balkans. Practical details regarding the publication, as well as issues of the publisher's obligations to the author, would be agreed later. I am ready to come to Sweden and spend a few weeks there in order to complement this series of talks. I think that three weeks of conversations would have produced more than a hundred pages of very interesting text. As a direct participant in many events in our area, your analysis carries inestimable values. I think that such an analysis was an indispensable primary source for all those who deal with the modern history of the Balkans.

I hope that my proposal is acceptable to you, and that you will respond to this letter. My address, phone numbers, and e-mail are in the header of this letter.

Best Regards,

[redacted]

NOTES

INTRODUCTION

1. Another woman, Pauline Nyimarasuhuko, was charged with crimes against humanity, war crimes and genocide by the International Criminal Tribunal for Rwanda (ICTR). She was sentenced to life in prison on 24 June 2011. See, *Prosecutor v Pauline Nyriamasuhuko, Arsène Shalom Ntahobali, Sylvain Nsabimana, Alphonse Nteziryayo, Joseph Kanyabashi, and Élie Ndayambaje* (International Criminal Tribunal for Rwanda, Trial Chamber II, Case No. ICTR-98-42-T, 24 June 2011).
2. The vast majority of ICTY offenders have been released early i.e., after serving only two thirds of their sentences. As of 31 May 2017, Momčilo Krajišnik and Plavšić were among fifty-seven individuals (70% of those convicted) who have been released early. See, Barbora Hola and Joris van Wijk, 'Does Remorse Count? ICTY Convicts' Reflections on Their Crimes in Early Release Decisions', *International Criminal Justice Review* 28 (4) 2018.
3. See, Zygmunt Bauman, *Modernity and the Holocaust* (Cambridge, 1989) and Alette Smeulers, *Perpetrators of Mass Attrocity: Terribly and Terrifyingly Normal?* (Routledge, 2024), 3.
4. See for example, Hans-Christian Jasch and Christoph Kreutzmuller, *The Participants: The Men of the Wannssee Conference* (Berghann Press, 2017). The book presents fascinating profiles of the men who implemented some of the most inhumane acts in history. The Wannsee Conference is today understood as a signal episode in

the history of the Holocaust, exemplifying the labour division and bureaucratisation that made the 'Final Solution' possible. Ten of the fifteen participants had been to university. Eight of them had been awarded doctorates, and another eight had studied law.

5. See, Vladimir Petrović, *Etničko čišćenje: geneza koncepta* (Arhipelag, 2019). About lack of clarity and its euphemism for the most serious violations of human rights, see, for example, Andrew Bell-Fiakoff, *Ethnic Cleansing* (St Martin's Press, 1996); Michael Mann, *The Dark Side of Democracy: Explaining Ethnic Cleansing* (Harvard University Press, 2005); Norman Naimark, *Fires of Hatred: Ethnic Cleansing in Twentieth-century Europe* (Harvard University Press, 2001).
6. Julian Borger, *The Butcher's Trial: How the Search for Balkan War Criminals Became the World's Most Successful Manhunt* (Other Press, 2016), 15.
7. Alette Smeulers, above n 3, 89.
8. Ethnic purity means an ethnic group that contains no genetic material from a different ethnic group. This was the ideology for which Plavšić advocated, on behalf of the Serbs.
9. Katerina Krulišova, 'Biljana Plavšić at the ICTY: Feminist Analysis of Representations of the Self' 3(1) (2020) *Journal of Perpetrator Research*, 12.
10. On the denial of Srebrenica genocide by the Serb government and population, see Olivera Simić, '"Celebrating" Srebrenica Genocide: Impunity and Indoctrination as Contributing Factors to the Glorification of Mass Atrocities', *Journal of Genocide Research* (2024), 1–19.
11. The United Nations Protection Force was the first United Nations peacekeeping force in Croatia and Bosnia and Herzegovina during the Yugoslav Wars. The force was formed in February 1992, and its mandate ended in March 1995.
12. Biljana Plavšić, *Svedočim I: Knjiga pisana u zatvoru* (I testify: the diary written in prison) and *Svedočim II: Knjiga pisana u zatvoru* (Trioprint, Banjaluka, 2005).
13. See, T.D. Jick, 'Mixing qualitative and quantative methods: Triangulation in action', *Administrative Science Quarterly* 24, 1979;

Veronica A. Thurmond, 'The Point of Triangulation', *Journal of Nursing Scholarship*, 33 (3) (2001).
14. Gitta Sereny, *Albert Speer: His Battle with Truth* (Vintage, 1996).
15. Gitta Sereny, *Into That Darkness: An Examination of Conscience* (Vintage, 1993).
16. See, for example, Alette Smeulers, above n 3; Uğur Ümit Üngör, 'Studying Mass Violence: Pitfalls, Problems, and Promises,' *Genocide Studies and Prevention: An International Journal* 7 (1) (2012).
17. James Waller, *Becoming Evil: How Ordinary People Commit Genocide and Mass Killing* (University Press Oxford, 2002); Donald G. Dutton, *The Psychology of Genocide, Massacres, and Extreme Violence: Why Normal People Come to Commit Atrocities* (Bloomsbury, 2007).
18. Uğur Ümit Üngör, above n 17.
19. Kjell Anderson and Erin Jessee (eds.), *Researching Perpetrators of Genocide* (University of Wisconsin Press, 2020).
20. Jessica Stern, *My War Criminal: Personal Encounters with an Architect of Genocide* (Harper Collins Publishers, 2020).
21 Janine di Giovanni, 'I can never forget the Bosnian genocide. But others are trying to rewrite history', *The Washington Post*, 3 February 2020. See https://www.washingtonpost.com/opinions/2020/02/03/i-can-never-forget-bosnian-genocide-others-are-trying-rewrite-history/.
22. Rafia Zakaria, 'Empathy for the Devil', https://thebaffler.com/latest/empathy-for-the-devil-zakaria.
23. Emina Melonic, 'Jessica Stern's denial of evil', *The Spectator*, 4 February 2020, https://thespectator.com/book-and-art/jessica-stern-denial-evil-war-criminal-architect-genocide/.
24. 'Jessica Stern on Interviewing Perpetrators' in *Terribly and Terrifyingly Normal?* podcast episode, 29 November 2023.
25. Kjell Andreson and Erin Jessee (eds.), above n 20, 7.
26. In my series of interviews with Esad Landzo, perpetrator and convicted war criminal, this is precisely what he also asked himself, and he told me he 'simply cannot answer this question'. Olivera Simić, 'Traumatized War Criminal: Documenting the Case of Esad Landzo', *International Criminal Justice Review* 34 (4) (2020).
27. Elliot Aronson, *The Social Animal* (Worth Publishers, 2003).

28. Ethan Hollander, 'Interview with a Nazi War Criminal', https://www.storycollider.org/singles/2020/10/2/ethan-hollander-interview-with-a-nazi-war-criminal.
29. See, for example, Olivera Simic, 'Drinking coffee in Bosnia: Listening to Stories of Wartime Violence and Rape,' *Journal of International Women's Studies* 18 (4) (2016); Olivera Simic, 'A Tour to a Site of Genocide: Mothers, Bones and Borders' *Journal of International Women's Studies*: 9 (3) (2013); Olivera Simic, 'Memorial Culture in the Former Yugoslavia: Mothers of Srebrenica and the Destruction of Artefacts by the ICTY' in Peter Rush and Olivera Simic (eds.), *The Arts of Transitional Justice: Culture, Activism, and Memory After Atrocity* (Springer, 2014); Olivera Simic, *Silenced Victims of Wartime Sexual Violence* (Routledge, 2017); Olivera Simic, *Lola's War: Rape Without Punishment* (MacMillan, 2023).
30. Lisa Davis, 'Dusting Off the Law Books: Recognizing Gender Persecution in Conflicts and Atrocities', *Northwestern Journal of Human Rights* 20 (1) (2021), 4.
31. Janine Natalya Clark, 'Genocide, War Crimes and Conflict in Bosnia: Understanding the Perpetrators', *Journal of Genocide Research* (4) (2009).
32. Douglas M. Kelly, *22 Cells in Nuremberg: A Psychiatrist Examines the Nazi Criminals* (Greenberg Publisher, 1947), 237.
33. Christopher Browning, *Ordinary Men: Reserve Police Battalion 101* (Penguin Press, 2001).
34. Timothy Williams and Susanne Buckley-Ziestel, 'Perpetrators and Perpetration of Mass Violence: an introduction' in Timothy Williams and Susanne Buckley-Ziestel (ed.), *Perpetrators and Perpetration of Mass Violence: Actions, Motivations and Dynamics*, 1.
35. Browning, above n 34, xviii.
36. Kjell Anderson and Erin Jessee, above n 20, 3.
37. Frédéric Mégret, 'Bring Forth the Accused: Defendant Attitudes and the Intimate Legitimacy of the International Criminal Trial', *Arizona Journal of International and Comparative Law* 36 (3) (2019).
38. Kjell Anderson and Erin Jessee, above n 20, 3.
39. For some notable exceptions, see Mark Drumbl and Solange Mouthaan, 'A Hussy Who Rode on Horseback in Sexy Underwear

in Front of the Prisoners: The Trials of Buchenwald's Ilse Koch', *International Criminal Law Review* 280 (2021); Mark Drumbl, 'She Makes Me Ashamed to Be a Woman: The Genocide Conviction of Pauline Nyiramasuhuko, 2011', *Michigan Journal of International Law* 34 (3) (2013); Alette Smeulers and Olivera Simić, 'Female war crime perpetrators in Bosnia and Herzegovina' in Solange Mouthaan and Olga Jurasz (eds.) *Gender and War: International and Transitional Justice Perspectives* (Cambridge, 2019); Laura Sjoberg, *Women as Wartime Rapists: Beyond Sensation and Stereotyping* (New York University Press, 2016); Izabela Stefija and Jessica Trisko Darden, *Women as War Criminals: Gender, Agency* (Stanford Briefs, 2020); Sarah Helm, *If This Is A Woman: Inside Ravensbruck, Hitler's Concentration Camp For Women* (Little Brown, 2015). Sheri Labenski, *Women Defendants and International Law: Feminist Dialogues* (Routledge, 2024); Wendy Adele-Marie, *Women as Nazis: Female Perpetrators of the Holocaust* (Independently Published, 2019).

40. J. Ann Tickner, *Gendering World Politics* (Columbia University Press), 59.
41. Sara E. Brown, *Gender and the Genocide in Rwanda: Women as Rescuers and Perpetrators* (Routledge, 2017).
42. Ibid.
43. Reva N. Adller, Cyanne E. Loyle, and Judith Globerman, 'A Calamity in the Neighbourhood: Women's Participation in Rwanda's Genocide', *Genocide Studies and Prevention* 2(3) (2007), 211.
44. Laura Sjoberg and Caron E. Gentry, *Mothers, Monsters, Whores: Women's Violence in Global Politics* (London: Zed Books, 2007).
45. The recently published monograph by Tomaz Jardim *Ilse Koch on Trial: Making the Bitch of Buchenwald* (Harvard University Press, 2023) is based on archival research.
46. See, Scott Straus, 'Studying Perpetrators: A Reflection' *Journal of Perpetrator Research* 1(1) (2017), 1.
47. Joel E. Dimsdale, 'Use of Rorschach Tests at the Nuremberg War Crimes Trial: A Forgotten Chapter in History of Medicine', *Journal of Psychosomatic Research* 78 (2015), 528.
48. See, Scott Straus, 'Is a comparative theory of perpetrators possible?'

in Timothy Williams and Susanne Buckley-Zistel, *Perpetrators and Perpetration of Mass Violence* (Routledge, 2018).

49. Eric Staub, *The Roots of Evil: The Origins of Genocide and Other Group Violence* (Cambridge, 1989); Browning above n. 34; Pumla Gobodo Madikizela, *A Human Being Died That Night: Forgiving Apartheid's Chief Killer* (Granta Books, 2013).
50. James Waller, above n 18, 18.
51. Alette Smeulers et al., *Perpetrators of International Crimes: Theories, Methods, and Evidence* (Oxford, 2019), 2.

1. MEETING BILJANA PLAVŠIĆ

1. Between approximately 1,000 and 1,500 euros.
2. Martin Mutschlechner, 'The Bosnians in the Habsburg Monarchy', *Habsburget.net* https://ww1.habsburger.net/en/chapters/bosnians-habsburg-monarchy.
3. Dejan Jovic, *Yugoslavia: A State that Withered Away* (Purdue University Press, 2009); Pål Kolstø, *Strategies of Symbolic Nation-building in South Eastern Europe* (Routledge, 2014).
4. Sabrina P. Ramet and Marko Valenta (eds.), *Ethnic Minorities and Politics in Post-Socialist Southeastern Europe* (Cambridge, 2016).
5. Kenneth Morrison and Paul Lowe, *Reporting the Siege of Sarajevo* (Bloomsbury, 2022).
6. See, Barbora Hola and Olivera Simić, 'ICTY Celebrities, War Criminals Coming Home', *International Criminal Justice Review* 28 (4) (2018).
7. John C. Kornblum served as the US ambassador to Germany from 1997 to 2001.
8. Biljana Plavšić, *Svedočim I: Knjiga pisana u zatvoru* (Trioprint, Banjaluka, 2005), 319.
9. Marcus Tanner, 'Foreign Office to welcome Serbian "Nazi"', *The Independent*, 28 June 1997.
10. I also found Plavšić's story about meeting with Carla del Ponte and smoking cigarettes with her in Del Ponte's book *Madame Prosecutor: Confrontation's with Humanity's Worst Criminals and the Culture of Impunity* (Other Press, 2011).

11. Elizabeth Rubin, 'The Enemy of Our Enemy', *The New York Times Magazine*, 14 September 1997, http://www.nytimes.com/1997/09/14/magazine/the-enemy-of-our-enemy.html.
12. See, *Prosecutor v Zdravko Tolimir* (ICTY, Case No. IT-05-88/2-T, 12 December 2012).
13. AFP/The Hague, 'Mladic's former right-hand man dies in UN prison', *Gulf Times*, 9 Februry 2016, https://www.gulf-times.com/story/479406/mladics-former-right-hand-man-dies-in-un-prison.
14. Ustaša, also spelled Ustasha (plural Ustaše), was a Croatian fascist movement that nominally ruled the Independent State of Croatia during World War II.
15. Samples of such letters are in Annex II.

2. PERSONAL AND PROFESSIONAL LIFE

1. In 1929 the Kingdom of Serbs, Croats and Slovenes adopted the name Yugoslavia. The state has changed names several times throughout the twentieth century.
2. Elizabeth Rubin, 'The Enemy of Our Enemy', *The New York Times Magazine*, 14 September 1997, https://www.nytimes.com/1997/09/14/magazine/the-enemy-of-our-enemy.html.
3. Darko Periša, 'Mihovil Mandić kao Arheolog', *Arheološki Radovi i Rasprave* (15) (2007), 249.
4. Svetislav Plavšić, 'Zur Kenntnis der Standorte von Picea Omorica', *Österreichische Botanische Zeitschrift 303* 85(4) (1936).
5. Steven Rathgeb Smith, 'Religion under Communism: State Regulation, Atheist Competition, and the Dynamics of Supply and Demand' in Rachel M. McCleary (ed), *The Oxford Handbook of the Economics of Religion* (Oxford, 2011), 235.
6. Udbaši were members of the State Security Administration/Service (UDBA), which was the secret police organisation in Yugoslavia. They were responsible for the 'eliminations' of dozens of enemies of the state.
7. Its members murdered hundreds of thousands of Serbs, Jews and Roma, as well as political dissidents in Yugoslavia during World War II. See, Ivo Goldstein, *Croatia: A History* (C. Hurst and Co, 2001);

Jozo Tomasevich, *War and Revolution in Yugoslavia, 1941–1945: Occupation and Collaboration* (Stanford University Press, 2001). During World War II, there were numerous concentration camps in the Independent State of Croatia. Most were operated by the Croatian Ustaša authorities, and some by Nazi Germany and Fascist Italy. See, for example, Raphael Israeli, *The Death Camps of Croatia: Visions and Revisions, 1941–1945* (Transaction Publishers, 2013); Rory Yeomans, *The Utopia of Terror: Life and Death in Wartime Croatia* (Boydell and Brewer, 2015).

8. The Independent State of Croatia was a WWII-era puppet state of Nazi Germany and Fascist Italy. It was established in parts of occupied Yugoslavia on 10 April 1941, after the invasion by the Axis powers.
9. Jovanka Simić, 'Tajni nemački dosije: i nacisti se zgražavali and ustaškim zverstvima', *Veritas* (online, 12 August 2019), http://www.veritas.org.rs/vecernje-novosti-11-08-2019-tajni-nemacki-dosije-i-nacisti-se-zgrazavali-nad-ustaskim-zverstvima/.
10. The Chetniks were members of a Yugoslav royalist and Serbian nationalist movement and guerrilla force in Axis-occupied Yugoslavia.
11. One of Niko's grandsons lives in Canada and another in Serbia. See M. Milojković, 'Gavrilo ovo ne bi mogao ni da zamisli: potomak Principa posle rukovanja sa praunukom Ferdinanda otkriva tajnu pomirenja staru gotovo čitav vek', *Blic* (online, 13 November 2018), https://www.blic.rs/vesti/politika/gavrilo-ovo-ne-bi-mogao-da-zamisli-potomak-principa-posle-rukovanja-sa-praunukom/jqzr5ky.
12. In the Serbian language, 'a big Serb' is used to describe someone who is a radical nationalist.
13. Milan Stojadinović was the prime minister of the Kingdom of Yugoslavia from 1935 to 1939.
14. After his death, Nikola's whole family moved to Sarajevo. See, 'Potomak Gavrila Principa: Gavrilovog brata Nikolu ubile su ustaše', *Kurir* (online, 15 November 2018), https://www.kurir.rs/vesti/drustvo/2808115/potomak-gavrila-principa-gavrilovog-brata-nikolu-ubile-su-ustase.
15. Benjamin Beasley-Murray, 'Gavrilo Princip's Legacy Still Contested', *Institute for War and Peace Reporting: Global Voices* (online, 26 June

2014), https://iwpr.net/global-voices/gavrilo-princips-legacy-still-contested.
16. After World War I, it was rebuilt as a museum in the Kingdom of Yugoslavia. The Ustaša destroyed the house again. After the establishment of Communist Yugoslavia in 1944, the house of Gavrilo Princip became a museum again, and there was another museum dedicated to him in the city of Sarajevo. During the Yugoslav wars of the 1990s, the house of Gavrilo Princip was destroyed and then rebuilt for the third time in 2015.
17. Baščaršija is the historical and cultural centre of Sarajevo. The Old Orthodox Church was built during the sixteenth century.
18. From 1941 to 1945, Livno was part of the Axis Independent State of Croatia, and was labelled as a pro-Ustaša region. Plavšić's mother Živana was born in Livno and lived there until she married and moved to Sarajevo. Her whole family stayed in Livno during World War II. In July 1941 the Ustaša killed more than 1,600 Serbs in Livno and the area. Livno and other villages were emptied and some families exterminated.
19. Biljana Plavšić, *Svedočim I: Knjiga pisana u zatvoru* (Trioprint, Banjaluka, 2005), 21.
20. Tito's Yugoslavia refers to the Socialist Federative Republic of Yugoslavia, which was created in 1945 after World War II. Tito was its lifelong president until he died in 1980. During his presidency, practising religion was controlled and limited.
21. See, Olivera Simić, *Surviving Peace* (Spinifex, 2014).
22. Plavšić, above n 19, 19.
23. Paul Mojzes, 'Religious Liberty in Yugoslavia: A Study in Ambiguity', *Occasional Papers on Religion in Eastern Europe* 6(2) (1986), 23, 28. Mojzes writes that it was 'quite impossible for an explicitly religious person to attain higher ranks in government, education, the army, or economic management'. See also Plavšić, above n 19, 28.
24. Iva Dujmović, 'Radnice u Jugoslaviji 1960-1980; Uloga i položaj u industriji i društvu', Diplomski rad, Master's thesis, 2016, https://core.ac.uk/download/pdf/197683723.pdf.
25. Adila Pašalić-Kreso, 'Obrazovanost stanovništva u Bosni i Hercegovini:

Bosna i Hercegovina izmedju najviše stope nepismenosti i najnižeg nivoa obrazovanosti', conference paper 2017, 102.

26. Rose M. Somerville, 'The Family in Yugoslavia', *Journal of Marriage and Family* 27/3 (1965), National Council on Family Relations, 350–62.
27. 'Assistant' is an entry-level academic role.
28. See, 'Humboldt Research Fellowship for postdoctoral and experienced researchers', *Alexander von Humboldt Foundation*, https://www.humboldt-foundation.de/web/humboldt-fellowship-postdoc.html.
29. Plavšić, above n 19, 13.
30. Ibid.
31. Karl Maramorosch, *The Thorny Road to Success: A Memoir* (Universe, 2015).
32. Ibid.
33. She obtained funds to go there through an FAO organisation that sent scientists to assist other scientists with their expertise and advice. See Food and Agriculture Organization of the United Nations, 'Scientific Advisory Group', *Globally Important Agricultural Heritage Systems*, http://www.fao.org/giahs/become-a-giahs/scientific-advisory-group/en/.
34. I found four of her co-authored papers with Maramorosch and other scholars on Google Scholar. I also found seventy-five publications citing her single authored or co-authored works. The latest citation of her work was in October 2016.
35. See, Izabela Stefija and Jessica Trisko Darden, *Women as War Criminals* (Stanford University Press, 2020).
36. They were both arrested in Sarajevo. In 1983, Krajišnik was convicted and served eight months in jail. In 1985, Karadžić was sentenced to three years in jail. He served only one year. See, Tim Judah, *The Serbs: History, Myth and the Destruction of Yugoslavia* (Yale University Press, 1997); 'Karadžić's right-hand man', *BBC News* (online, 3 April 2000), http://news.bbc.co.uk/2/hi/europe/699795.stm.
37. The process of nationalisation by the Communist Party took place after World War II. See Uroš Komljenović, 'Varanje crkve', *Politika* (online, 9 January 1999), https://www.vreme.com/arhiva_html/429/3.html. Plavšić said that just days before she met him for

38. Plavšić, above n 19, 39.
39. Jelena Gruba Kotromanić was the only female head of state in the history of Bosnia and Herzegovina. She ruled the Kingdom of Bosnia from September 1395 until early May 1398. See Nenad Kecmanović and Čedomir Antić, *Istorija Republike Srpske* (Nedeljnik, 2016), 345.
40. A well-known Croatian feminist, journalist, novelist and essayist.
41. Slavenka Drakulić, *They Would Never Hurt a Fly: War Criminals on Trial in the Hague* (Little Brown, 2003), 116.
42. The Patriotic League (Patriotska Liga) was the first paramilitary unit of the Territorial Defence Force of the Republic of BiH. In December 1990, the Party of Democratic Action discussed forming an independent paramilitary unit separate from the Yugoslav Peoples' Army. The Patriotic League would later become the army of BiH. See John Schindler, *Unholy Terror* (Motorbooks International, 2007), 70.
43. Haris Rovcanin, 'Controversial Report Highlights Serb victims in Wartime Sarajevo' *Balkan Insight* (online, 13 April 2021), https://balkaninsight.com/2021/04/13/controversial-report-highlights-serb-victims-in-wartime-sarajevo/; 'Slobo: Serbs Were Real Victims' *CBS News* (online, 2 September 2004), https://www.cbsnews.com/news/slobo-serbs-were-real-victims/; 'Serbs the real victims, claims Milosevic', *The Guardian* (online, 1 September 2004), https://www.theguardian.com/world/2004/aug/31/balkans.warcrimes; Dobrica Cosic, *Bosanski rat* (Sluzbeni glasnik, Beograd, 2012).
44. The Yugoslav People's Army, also called the Yugoslav National Army, was the army of Yugoslavia from 1945 to 1992 and the primary part of Yugoslavia's armed forces. The main task of the Yugoslav People's Army was to protect the independence, sovereignty, territorial integrity and social organisation of the Socialist Federal Republic of Yugoslavia (SFRY). Under the constitution and laws of the SFRY, the Yugoslav People's Army was a part of the armed forces with the Territorial Defence as the joint armed forces of all working people and citizens of Yugoslavia. The Yugoslav People's Army officially withdrew from Bosnia and Herzegovina in May 1992.
45. See Denis Džidić, 'Sijekovac Killings "Happened Before Bosnian War

Started'" *Balkan Transitional Justice* (online, 11 December 2013), https://balkaninsight.com/2013/12/11/bosnian-expert-claims-sijekovac-killings-occurred-before-war/; Vladimir Susak, 'Forgotten Victims: Serbs Targeted in Bosnia-Croatia Border Village Killings' *Balkan Transitional Justice* (online, 12 August 2020), https://balkaninsight.com/2020/08/12/forgotten-victims-serbs-targeted-in-bosnia-croatia-border-village-killings/.

46. 'Bosnian Fighter's Sijekovac Killings Conviction Upheld', *Balkan Transitional Justice* (online, 27 May 2015), https://balkaninsight.com/2015/05/27/verdict-against-zemir-kovacevic-confirmed/.
47. 'Željko Ražnatović "Arkan"' *United Nations International Criminal Tribunal for the former Yugoslavia* (Case Information sheet), https://www.icty.org/x/cases/zeljko_raznjatovic/cis/en/cis_arkan_en.pdf.
48. Milica Stojanovic, 'Arkan's "Tigers" Unpunished 20 Years after Leader's Death' *Balkan Insight* (online, 15 January 2020), https://balkaninsight.com/2020/01/15/arkans-tigers-unprosecuted-20-years-after-leaders-death/.
49. Denis Džidić et al., 'Arkan's Paramilitaries: Tigers Who Escaped Justice', *Balkan Transitional Justice* (online 8 December 2014), https://balkaninsight.com/2014/12/08/arkan-s-paramilitaries-tigers-who-escaped-justice/.
50. Milica Stojanovic, above n 48.
51. For an in-depth analysis of the role Serbian paramilitaries, please see Iva Vukušić, *Serbian Paramilitaries and the Breakup of Yugoslavia: State Connections and Patterns of Violence* (Routledge, 2022).
52. She writes in detail about this in her memoir above n. 19, 166.
53. Plavšić, above n 19, 138.
54. After the war, he was a politician, and during Plavšić's presidency, he was appointed as a police chief in Bijeljina. Savić was the victim of repeated assassination attempts due to his fight against corruption. He was assassinated in his vehicle near a railway station on 7 June 2000.
55. For an in-depth overview of detention facilities in BiH, see, Hikmet Karcic, *Torture, Humilate, Kill: Inside the Bosnian Serb Camp System* (University of Michigan Press, 2022).

56. Emir Suljagic, 'Kisses as Bosnian War Kicked Off', *IWPR*, 30 April 2005, https://iwpr.net/global-voices/kisses-bosnian-war-kicked.
57. 'Dan kada je Arkan "oslobodio" Bijeljinu od Bosnjaka: Lesevi su danima lezali po ulici', *Faktor.ba*, 1 Paril 2021, http://www.istocnabosna.com/dnews/index.php/vijesti/istocna-bosna/item/11010-dan-kada-je-arkan-oslobodio-bijeljinu-od-bosnjaka-lesevi-su-danima-lezali-po-ulicama.
58. Bajram, known as Eid al-Adha, is the Feast of the Sacrifice, honouring the willingness of Abraham to sacrifice his own son Ishmael, according to the Muslim tradition. In Bosnia and Herzegovina, Bajram is mainly a day to spend with family and friends.
59. Vladimir Petrović, 'Power(lessness) of Atrocity Images: Bijeljina Photos between Perpetration and Prosecution of War Crimes in the Former Yugoslavia', *International Journal of Transitional Justice* 9 (3) (2015).
60. Rachel Irwin, 'Karadžić Talks of "Highway to Hell": Court views footage of defendant addressing Bosnian assembly several months before the outbreak of war' *IWPR* (online, 4 June 2010), https://iwpr.net/global-voices/karadzic-talks-highway-hell.
61. 'Kada i kako je nastala Republika Srpska' *Al Jazeera* (online, 23 November 2016), https://balkans.aljazeera.net/news/balkan/2016/9/25/kada-i-kako-je-nastala-republika-srpska.
62. Tracy Wilkinson, 'Alija Izetbegovic, 78; Led Bosnia Through War', *Los Angeles Times* (online, 20 October 2003), https://www.latimes.com/archives/la-xpm-2003-oct-20-me-izetbegovic20-story.html.
63. 'Raja' in Turkish means shepherd, which alludes to the position of Serbs during the Ottoman Empire when they were controlled by the Turks and treated as second-class citizens.
64. Kenneth Morrison and Paul Lowe, *Reporting the Siege of Sarajevo* (Bloomsbury, 2022).
65. 'Baba' means grandmother in Serbian, but here it was used to ridicule Plavšić due to her age.
66. Mirjana Mira Marković was a Serbian politician, an academic and the wife of Slobodan Milošević (see Characters and Places).
67. ICTY, Case No. IT-95-14/2-A, 17 December 2004) [1087]; See also, Florian Jeßberger and Julia Geneuss (eds) *Why Punish Perpetrators of*

Mass Atrocities? (Cambridge, 2022); Jessica Wolfendale and Mathew Talbert, *War Crimes, Causes, Excuses and Blames* (Oxford, 2019).
68. Cited from Jelena Subotic, 'The Cruelty of False Remorse: Biljana Plavšić at the Hague' *Southeastern Europe* 36 (1) (2012).
69. Biljana Plavšić statement in *Svet* (Belgrade, 6 September 1993).
70. Plavšić, above n 19, *Svedočim II*.
71. Dayton Accords is a peace agreement reached on 21 November 1995 by the presidents of BiH, Croatia and Serbia, ending the war in Bosnia and outlining a General Framework Agreement for Peace in Bosnia and Herzegovina. It preserved Bosnia as a single state made up of two parts, the Bosniak-Croat Federation and the Bosnian Serb Republic, with Sarajevo remaining as the undivided capital city. For the full text see, General Framework Agreement for Peace in Bosnia and Herzegovina UN SCOR, 50th sess., Agenda Item 28, UN Doc A/50/790 S/1995/999 (signed 14 December 1995).
72. See, 'Biljana Plavšić otkrila zašto je udarila Radovana Karadžića', *ATV* (online, 8 December 2021). https://www.atvbl.rs/magazin/zanimljivosti/biljana-plavsic-otkrila-zasto-je-udarila-radovana-karadzica-8-12-2021; Plavšić, above n 19, *Svedočim II*.
73. Edward Cody, 'Serb President Gains Support At Cost To Karadzic', *The Washington Post* (online, 28 August 1997), https://www.washingtonpost.com/archive/politics/1997/08/28/serb-president-gains-support-at-cost-to-karadzic/c5499385-c447-49c6-995b-f08a174c4105/; Lee Hockstader, 'Bosnian Serb Elections Appear To Deal Setback To Hard-Line Nationalists', *The Washington Post* (online 2 December 1997), https://www.washingtonpost.com/archive/politics/1997/12/02/bosnian-serb-elections-appear-to-deal-setback-to-hard-line-nationalists/8fb95357-1abd-4daf-b8fb-6f7c241b318e/.
74. The Stabilisation Force (SFOR) was a NATO-led multinational peacekeeping force deployed to Bosnia and Herzegovina after the Bosnian War.
75. Robert Thomas, *Serbia under Milosevic: Politics in the 1990s* (Hurst, 1999), 358.
76. Ibid.

77. Madeleine Albright, *Madam Secretary: A Memoir* (Hyperion, 2003), 342.
78. Ibid., 343
79. 'Karadžić, Radovan (MICT-13-55-ES)', *United Nations: International Residual Mechanism for Criminal Tribunals*, https://www.irmct.org/en/cases/mict-13-55.
80. Mladić was indicted on the same day as Karadžić, 24 July 1995. He was charged before the ICTY with two counts of genocide, five counts of crimes against humanity and four counts of violations of the laws or customs of war committed by Serb forces during the armed conflict in BiH from 1992 until 1995: 'Mladić, Ratko (MICT-13-56)', *United Nations: International Residual Mechanism for Criminal Tribunals,* https://www.irmct.org/en/cases/mict-13-56.
81. Plavšić, above n 19, *Svedočim II*, 248.
82. Ibid., II, 244.
83. 'Failure to Arrest Radovan Karadzic Gravely Undermines Municipal Elections', *Human Rights Watch* (article, 12 September 1997), https://www.hrw.org/news/1997/09/12/failure-arrest-radovan-karadzic-gravely-undermines-municipal-elections.
84. Ibid.

3. INDICTMENT AND DETENTION

1. Edina Bećirević, 'Žene su za kuhanje i pečenje, a ne genocide?!' *Dani Magazin*, no 641 (Sarajevo, 25 September 2009).
2. Stanislav Čađo was the Minister of the Interior in Bosnia at that time. Zdravko Tolimir was a Bosnian Serb military commander and war criminal convicted of genocide, conspiracy to commit genocide, extermination, murder, persecution on ethnic grounds and forced transfer. Tolimir was a commander of the army of Republika Srpska during the Bosnian War.
3. Baščaršija is Sarajevo's old bazaar and the historical and cultural centre of the city.
4. Mladen Ivanić is a Bosnian Serb politician who served as the sixth Serb member of the Presidency of Bosnia and Herzegovina from

17 November 2014 until 20 November 2018. He is the founder and former president of the Party of Democratic Progress.

5. In our conversations, Plavšić admitted to me that the man who offered to hide her was sent by the then government of Republika Srpska. She never mentioned his name.

6. Plavšić was referring to house searches that members of NATO and SFOR had been conducting under the pretext of looking for war criminals. They would do these sometimes in the middle of the night, other times during the day, but their actions were often violent and would sometimes occur in front of women and children. Perhaps the most notorious case was a search in the middle of the night, under the pretext of looking for Karadžić, of the home of a Serb priest from Bosnia named Jeremija Starovlah. On the night between 31 March and 1 April 2004, the SFOR and NATO special units violently entered his house and severely beat him and his son Aleksandar. They used explosives to remove the house entrance door, locked Starovlah's wife in one room, and then beat him for over an hour. Starovlah suffered from the consequences of this beating for the rest of his life while his son Aleksandar became disabled. No one was ever held accountable for this attack. See, Nikola Vidackovic, 'Jeremija i Aleksandar Starovlah: Na pravdu čekaju dugih 12 godina', *Nezavisne Novine* (online, 6 July 2016), https://www.nezavisne.com/novosti/drustvo/Jeremija-i-Aleksandar-Starovlah-Na-pravdu-cekaju-dugih-12-godina/377714.

7. *Prosecutor v. Krajišnik* (Consolidated Indictment) (ICTY, Case Nos IT-00-39 & 40-PT, 9 March 2001); *Prosecutor v. Krajišnik* (Amended Consolidated Indictment) ICTY, Case Nos IT-00-39 & 40-PT, 7 March 2002).

8. Plavšić here refers to some of the Stabilisation Force in Bosnia and Herzegovina (SFOR) arrests of indicted war criminals in Bosnia and Herzegovina. See 'Statement concerning detained indicted war criminal' *Nato.int* (web page), https://www.nato.int/sfor/trans/1997/t970710b.htm; 'Bosnia War Crimes Suspect Blows Himself Up' *ABC News* (online), https://abcnews.go.com/International/story?id=82397&page=1; Julian Borger, *The Butcher's Trial: How the*

Search for Balkan War Criminals Became the World's Most Successful Manhunt (Other Press, 2016).

9. The United Nations Detention Unit was a UN-administered jail. It was part of The Hague Penitentiary Institution's Scheveningen location, more popularly known as Scheveningen Prison.
10 This is a three-handed Theotokos (Virgin Mary), a famous icon in the Serbian Orthodox monastery of Hilandar on Mount Athos in Greece.
11. Plavšić here refers to the terminology that Carla Del Ponte used in her book, *The Hunt: Me and the War Criminals*, which she read a several times. The book was published in 2008 while Plavšić was still in prison. Del Ponte served as a prosecutor of the ICTY from 1999 to 2007.
12. Carla Del Ponte (and Chuck Sudetic), *Madam Prosecutor: Confrontations with Humanity's Worst Criminals and the Culture of Impunity* (Other Press, 2009).
13. See, *Prosecutor v. Kvocka* (Judgement) (ICTY, Trial Chamber, Case No IY-98-30/1-T, 2 November 2001). Prcać was released on 4 March 2005, having served his sentence in full. Plavšić told me that Prcać was accused 'just because some Muslims saw him going into one of those buildings to his work every morning'. According to Plavšić, he was not guilty of anything. His case influenced her decision to plead guilty and not subject herself to the full-on trial.
14. The Drina Corps, a sub-unit of the Army of Republika Srpska (VRS) was responsible for the Srebrenica genocide where more than 7,000 Bosniaks from Srebrenica were murdered in July 1995. Krstić's judgement authenticates that genocide was in fact perpetrated against the Bosnian Muslims of Srebrenica. Srebrenica is the only incidence of genocide that the ICTY found amidst the pervasive violence incited in the former Yugoslavia. See, Mark Drumbl, 'Prosecutor v. Radislav Krstić: ICTY authenticates genocide at Srebrenica and convicts for aiding and abetting', *Melbourne Journal of International Law* 5(2) (2004), 434; *Prosecutor v. Krstić* (Judgement) (International Criminal Tribunal for the Former Yugoslavia, Appeals Chamber, Case No IT-98-33-A, 19 April 2004). Krstić filed many requests for early release but they were all rejected by the Mechanism for

International Criminal Tribunals in The Hague. He is serving his sentence in Poland.

15. Naser Orić, the ex-military leader, and his co-defendant Sabahudin Muhić, were charged with killing Serb prisoners in villages around Srebrenica in 1992. He was acquitted of war crime charges in 2018. See *Prosecutor v. Naser Orić (Judgement)* International Criminal Tribunal for the Former Yugoslavia, Trial Chamber II, Case No. IT-03-68-T, 30 June 2006); see also Darko Janjevic, 'Defender of Srebrenica' acquitted of war crimes' *DW* (online, 30 November 2018), https://www.dw.com/en/defender-of-srebrenica-naser-oric-acquitted-of-war-crimes/a-46517517.

16. Goran Jelisić was a former Bosnian Serb police officer who was found guilty of having committed crimes against humanity and violating the customs of war at the Luka camp in Brčko during the Bosnian War. Those detained were subjected to inhumane conditions, killings and mistreatment. Jelisić regularly entered the Luka camp and beat, mistreated and often killed the detainees. In 2001, Jelisić was sentenced to forty years imprisonment.

17. Mujahideen, in the broadest sense of the term, refers to Muslims who fight on behalf of their faith or the Muslim community.

18. Amir Kubura was a former Bosnian commander of the army of the Republic of BiH and an officer of the Yugoslav People's Army. He was sentenced to two years imprisonment for 'plunder of public or private property'. In 1993, he was assigned as acting commander of the 7th Muslim Mountain Brigade, and during this period, under his command, there was a notable number of foreign mujahideen from Islamic countries fighting for the Bosnian Muslims.

19. Plavšić told me in one of our last conversations in February 2024 that Jelisić called her several times from the Italian prison where he served his sentence at the time to tell her that 'they will drink coffee one day again'. She asked about his son, who had visited him while he was in detention in The Hague, and he said, 'I have two more kids now. My wife is my lawyer'. Jelisić was transferred back to The Hague from Italy where he was serving his 40-year imprisonment for crimes against humanity and violations of the laws or customs of war. His plea for early release from prison was rejected, and in March

2023 he returned to the Dutch prison in Scheveningen as the Italian authorities did not want to keep him in their facilities anymore. https://www.novosti.rs/hronika/sudjenja/1214962/nece-vise-srbina-drze-zatvoru-goran-jelisic-italijanskim-zakonima-izdrzao-kaznu-prebacen-sheveningen.

20. 'Goran Čengić was killed for trying to protect his Muslim neighbour from the so-called "Monster of Grbavica"', https://en.gariwo.net/righteous/ethnic-cleansing-and-genocide-in-the-balkans/goran-cengi-23956.html.
21. Plavšić stayed friends with her after she was released from prison.
22. This was probably due to the fact that the ICTY was established by Kofi Annan, who was Secretary-General of the United Nations at the time of the ICTY's establishment in 1993.
23. Esad Landžo was a former Bosnian camp guard who worked at the Čelebići camp during the Bosnian War from May 1992 until December 1992 when it ceased operations. On 16 November 1998, Landžo was found guilty of violations of the laws and customs of war, and grave breaches of the Geneva Convention, and sentenced to fifteen years in prison. Landžo was granted early release on 13 April 2006 after serving nearly eight years of his sentence. I undertook a series of interviews with him. See Olivera Simić, 'Traumatized War Criminal? Documenting the Case of Esad Landžo', *International Criminal Justice Review* 32(4) (2020), 357; Olivera Simić and Barbara Holá, 'A War Criminal's Remorse: the Case of Landžo and Plavšić', *Human Rights Review* 21 (2020), 267. While Landžo seems truly remorseful for his deeds, Plavšić remains unrepentant. This is a difference between these two war criminals. Landžo even personally apologised to his victims after serving his sentence. See documentary film, 'The Unforgiven, A War's Criminal Remorse' (2017), https://www.youtube.com/watch?v=xSc3JbC7B88; Olivera Simić, 'The Remorseful War Criminal: How a Bosnian Convict's Apologies Were Ignored', 14 September 2023, *BalkanInsight*, https://balkaninsight.com/2023/09/14/the-remorseful-war-criminal-how-a-bosnian-convicts-apologies-were-ignored/.
24. Natalia Vdovychenko, 'Reusing Churches in the Netherlands', *Diggit*

Magazine (online, 28 June 2019), https://www.diggitmagazine.com/articles/church-buildings-reused.

25. 'Sloba' was the nickname for Slobodan Milošević (see Characters and Places). His five-year trial ended without a verdict. On 11 March 2006, Milošević was found dead in his prison cell in The Hague's detention centre. He died from a heart attack, unpunished.
26. Aleksandar Tijanić, a well-known Serbian journalist, once described Milošević as the 'Bengal Tiger' of Serbian politics, so powerful that the opposition could 'not even step on his tail'. Milojko Pantić, 'Srbija stvorena za "Udbinu decu"', *Danas* (online, 22 January 2021), https://www.danas.rs/dijalog/licni-stavovi/srbija-stvorena-za-udbinu-decu/.
27. The prosecutor was referring to Plavšić's infamous statement that 'all Muslims should be evicted from Eastern Bosnia'.
28. As previously mentioned, the crime happened on 1 March 1992 during a Serbian wedding at the Orthodox Church in Baščaršija, Sarajevo, when the pre-war criminal and member of the Muslim paramilitary unit called the Green Berets, Ramiz Delalić aka Ćelo, shot dead the groom's father, Nikola Gardović, and wounded a priest of the Serbian Orthodox Church, Radenko Miković. This was one of the events that triggered the outbreak of war in BiH.
29. On 3 April 1992, members of the Croatian forces of Croatian Defence Council (HVO) and Croatian Defence Forces (HOS) entered Serbian villages in Kupres and killed some Serbian civilians, burning Serbian houses and business premises.
30. I found something along these lines in Carla Del Ponte's (and Chuck Sudetic's) book, above n 12, Chapter 6.
31. Larry Hollingworth, Head of Office for the United Nations High Commissioner for Refugees (UNHCR), was in Bosnia during the war and filed a statement on behalf of Plavšić, confirming that Plavšić co-operated with the UN and helped with making sure that humanitarian convoys could pass through Serbian territory and reach Muslim villages.
32. *NIN* (Serbian Cyrillic: НИН) is a weekly news magazine published in Belgrade. Its name is an acronym for Nedeljne informativne novine (Serbian Cyrillic: Недељне информативне новине), which roughly

translates into *Weekly Information Newspaper*. NIN was originally started in 1935 and has an esteemed reputation due to its long tradition.
33. Pavle was the patriarch of the Serbian Orthodox Church from 1990 until his death in 2009. His full title was His Holiness the Archibishop of Peć, Metropolitan of Belgrade and Karlovci. Before his death, Pavle was the oldest living leader of an Eastern Orthodox church. Plavšić had a sacred admiration for him.
34. Transcript of Proceedings, *Prosecutor v. Biljana Plavšić* (International Criminal Tribunal for the former Yugoslavia, Case Nos IT-00-39 & IT-00-40/1, Sentencing Hearing Transcript, 18 December 2002), 609: 11–14: *ICTY.org*, https://www.icty.org/x/cases/plavsic/trans/en/021218IT.htm.
35. *Prosecutor v. Biljana Plavšić*, (ICTY, Case Nos IT-00-39 & IT-00-40/1, (Indictment) 9 March 2001).
36. The entirety of the persecution counts were laid out in Plavšić's joint indictment with her co-president, Krajišnik. Not all of these counts were articulated in Plavšić's plea bargain, but only some elements of 'persecutions', such as the existence of an armed conflict, the existence of a widespread or systematic attack against the civilian population and that the accused's conduct was committed with the intent to discriminate. For the full counts, see *Prosecutor v. Biljana Plavšić*, (Case Nos IT 00-39 &. IT-00-40/1-S (Plea Agreement of Biljana Plavšić), 30 September, 2002).
37. Carla Del Ponte (and Chuck Sudetic), above n 12.
38. Ibid.
39. Theodor Meron was elected president of the ICTY by his fellow judges on 19 October 2011, and again on 1 October 2013. *Prosecutor v. Biljana Plavsic* (Sentencing Judgement) (International Criminal Tribunal for the former Yugoslavia, Trial Chamber, Case No. IT-00-39 & 40/1, 27 February 2003).
40. Carla Del Ponte wrote about this meeting with Plavšić in her book, above n 12.
41. Sadako Ogata was the UN High Commissioner for Refugees in Bosnia and Herzegovina during the Bosnian War.
42. Plavšić said the same in her interview with the OTP. See, Transcript,

OTP Interview with Biljana Plavšić, 12 February 2004, IT-00-39&40/1-S, 498.
43. Pale is a small town in eastern Bosnia and Herzegovina where the Serb leadership had its headquarters during the Bosnian War.
44. She wrote something similar in 2005 in her memoir *Svedočim II*, above Biljana Plavšić, *Svedočim II* (Trioprint, Banjaluka, 2005), 147.
45. I found the reference to Pale in the Office of Trial Prosecutor (OTP) Interview of Biljana Plavsic, 10 February 2004, IT-00-39&40/1-S, p.518. She wrote similarly about Muslims 'voluntarily' leaving Bijeljina in her memoirs, *Svedočim I*.
46. She also talks about this is *Svedočim I*.
47. *Prosecutor v. Ratko Mladic*, IT-09-92-T, Judgement, 24 November 2020.
48. *Prosecutor v. Momcilo Krajisnik*, IT-00-39-T, Judgement, 27 September 2006.; *Prosecutor v. Radovan Karadzic* IT-95-5/18-T, Judgement, 24 March 2016.
49. 'Reakcije na smrt zločinca Brđanina u Republici Srpskoj bez empatije za žrtve', *Fokus.ba*, https://www.fokus.ba/vijesti/bih/reakcije-na-smrt-zlocinca-brdjanina-u-republici-srpskoj-bez-empatije-za-zrtve/2395507/; 'Emotivan oprostaj od Brdjanina', *Novosti*, 7 September 2022, https://www.novosti.rs/republika-srpska/vesti/1151957/radoslav-brdjanin-smrt-banjaluka-milorad-dodik-republika-srpska-zeljka-cvijanovic-radovan-viskovic-bih-bosna-sef-kriznog-staba-krajina-saucesce-najnovije-vesti-2022-sud-kazna-hag.
50. Anto Orlovac, 'Gubici Banjalucke biskupije u ratu 1992–1995' (Banjaluka, 2018). Human Rights, Watch, 'War Crimes in Bosnia-Hercegovina: U.N. Cease-Fire Won't Help Banja Luka' 6) (8) (1994); Chuck Sudetic, 'U.N. Says "Ethnic Cleansing" by Serbs Intensifies,' *The New York Times*, 30 January 1994.
51. *Prosecutor v. Enver Hadizhasanovic and Amir Kubura*, ICTY, IT-01-47-T, Judgement, 15 March 2006.
52. Ibid.
53. *Prosecutor v. Delalic et al.*, IT-96-21-T, Judgement, 16 November 1998.
54. See Annex I for excerpts from Sentencing Hearing on 16 December 2002 and her Guilty Plea Statement.

55. 'Former Bosnian Serb leader pleads guilty', *BBC News* (online, 2 October 2002), http://news.bbc.co.uk/1/hi/world/europe/2293037.stm; Daniel Simpson, 'U.N. Tribunal, With Surprise Guilty Plea, Rivets Bosnians', *The New York Times* (online, 4 October 2002), https://www.nytimes.com/2002/10/04/world/un-tribunal-with-surprise-guilty-plea-rivets-bosnians.html; Kerstin Bree Carlson, 'Failures in Reconciliation: The Lost Opportunity of Milan Babić, "Reformed Nationalist"' in Kerstin Bree Carlson (ed), *Model(ing) Justice Perfecting the Promise of International Criminal Law* (Cambridge, 2018), 155.

4. IN JAIL

1. The ICTY entered into bilateral agreements with a number of Western European countries on the execution of sentences. See, for example, Stephen Farrall et al., *Escape Routes: Contemporary Perspectives on Life After Punishment* (Routledge, 2011); Richard H. Steinberg (ed), *Assessing the Legacy of the ICTY* (Martinus Nijhoff Publishers, 2011). For a full list of countries, see, United Nations ICTY, 'Member States Cooperation: Agreements on the Enforcement of Sentences', *United Nations International Criminal Tribunal for the former Yugoslavia*, https://www.icty.org/en/documents/member-states-cooperation.
2. Eric Stover, *The Witnesses: War Crimes and the Promise of Justice in The Hague* (University of Pennsylvania, 2006), 142.
3. 'Bosnia's "Iron Lady" in hospital', *BBC News* (online, 16 September 2003), http://news.bbc.co.uk/2/hi/europe/3114046.stm.
4. 'Luxury prison for Bosnia's Iron Lady', *The Telegraph Online* (online, 7 June 2003), https://www.telegraphindia.com/world/luxury-prison-for-bosnia-s-iron-lady/cid/1569088.
5. In this context, *naša* means someone from Bosnia and Herzegovina.
6. Albert Speer, *Inside the Third Reich* (Ishi Press, 2010).
7. Philippe Sands, *38 Londres Street: On Impunity, Pinochet in England and a Nazi in Patagonia* (Weidenfeld & Nicolson, 2025), 105.
8. She said that someone told her while still in prison that the Serbian media published some paragraphs from this letter. She does not know how the media got possession of it.
9. The Serbian Unity Congress was formed in 1990 in Cleveland, Ohio,

as a not-for-profit organisation. In 1998, Michael Djordjevich was established internationally and became the first president of the Council for Democratic Changes in Serbia. Its aim was to support transition to democracy in Yugoslavia and peace and stability in the Balkans. See Maciej Siekierski, 'A Decade of Illusions: Miroslav Michael Djordjevich's Papers On The Disintegration Of Yugoslavia Donated To Hoover', *Hoover Institution* (news article, 19 June 2018), https://www.hoover.org/news/decade-illusions-miroslav-michael-djordjevichs-papers-disintegration-yugoslavia-donated-hoover.

10. Vladeta Jerotić, *Duhovni razgovori* [English trans: *Spiritual conversations*], (Partenon, 2017).
11. Plavšić is referring to Albert Speer's book, *Spandau: The Secret Diaries* (Ishi Press, 2010).
12. Plavšić makes reference to Spandau prison, which after 1946 housed Nazi war criminals sentenced by the Allies. The prison was demolished following the death of the last inmate, Rudolf Hess, one of Adolf Hitler's longest-serving allies, in 1987.
13. A small town in Bosnia and Herzegovina.
14. The term 'our' people was used to refer to people from ex-Yugoslavia, but in this context, it meant 'Serb'.
15. Haile Selassie was Crown Prince and Regent of the Ethiopian Empire from 1916 to 1928, and then King and Regent from 1928 to 1930, and finally Emperor from 1930 to 1974.
16. See Annex II.
17. Slavenka Drakulić, *They Would Never Hurt a Fly* (Little Brown, 2003).
18. Margaret Nordgren published that interview in the Swedish newspaper *Vi*.
19. 'Bosnian war criminal: "I did nothing wrong"', *The Local* (online, 26 January 2009), https://www.thelocal.se/20090126/17162/.
20. Jelena Subotić, 'The Cruelty of False Remorse: Biljana Plavšić at The Hague', *Southeastern Europe* 36(1) (2012), 39.
21. Edina Bećirević, 'Bosnian Court Should Try Plavšić', *IWPR* (online, 28 July 2008) [45], https://iwpr.net/global-voices/bosnian-court-should-try-plavsic.

22. See, Carla Del Ponte, *Madame Prosecutor: Confrontations with Humanity's Worst Criminals and the Culture of Impunity*, (Other Press, 2009).
23. Ibid., 150.
24. Miroslav Lazanski—Aktuelnosti, članci, arhiva, 'Miroslav Lazanski:u poseti Biljani Plavšić u zatvoru u Švedskoj. objavljeno:Politika-21/03/2009', Facebook (Facebook post, 26 October 2013, 2.03 pm AEST), https://www.facebook.com/545449432198096/posts/546425948767111/.
25. One of the oldest and most well-known daily newspapers printed and published in Belgrade.
26. Plavšić probably knew that some judges in the international courts do not have a law background but are laypersons and diplomats. They may come from countries that do not require legal training for judges. Still, it would be expected that they were trained in The Hague when they accepted the post. However, sometimes no training was provided.
27. *The President of the International Tribunal (Decision of the President on the Application for Pardon or Commutation of Sentence of Mrs. Biljana Plavšić)* (International Tribunal for the Prosecution of Persons Responsible for Serious Violations of International Humanitarian Law Committed in the Territory of the Former Yugoslavia since 1991, Case No. IT-OO-39 & 40/l-ES, 14 September 2009).
28. Ibid.
29. Kerstin Carlson, 'Model(ing) Law: The ICTY, the International Criminal Justice Template, and Reconciliation in the Former Yugoslavia' (PhD dissertation, University of California, Berkley, 2013), 182.
30. 'Bosnian Muslims Protest Against UN Tribunal Rulling', 16 September 2009, *Radio Free Europe*, https://www.rferl.org/a/Bosnian_Muslims_Protest_Against_UN_Tribunal_Ruling/1824263.html.

5. OUT OF JAIL

1. Z J, T M D and N T, 'Biljana Plavšić zaplakala je kad je sletela u Beograd', *Blic* (online, 28 October 2009), https://www.blic.rs/vesti/tema-dana/biljana-plavsic-zaplakala-kad-je-sletela-u-beograd/lhcr46d.

2. 'Plavšić u Beogradu', *Radio Slobodna Evropa* (online, 27 October 2009), https://www.slobodnaevropa.org/a/plavsic/1861917.html.
3. Cirilica TV Happy, 'Cirlica—Biljana Plavsic—(TV Happy 2014)', YouTube (online, 28 May 2015), https://www.youtube.com/watch?v=zs17IqwwTDo.
4. Josip Broz Tito was a Yugoslav communist revolutionary and politician who served in various positions of national leadership from 1943. He served as the president of the Socialist Federal Republic of Yugoslavia from 14 January 1953 until his death on 4 May 1980.
5. 'As-salamu alaykum' is a greeting in Arabic that means 'Peace be upon you'. Greeting a Serb in such fashion is a mockery.
6. '*Lijepa naša domovino*' ['Our Beautiful Homeland'] is the national anthem of Croatia. It is often referred to as '*Lijepa naša*' for short.
7. Jasenovac was a concentration and extermination camp established in the village of the same name by the authorities of the Independent State of Croatia.
8. She stated the same for BALKAN INFO—Zvanični kanal, 'INTERVJU: Biljana Plavšić—Ovo je moje poslednje obracanje srpskom narodu', YouTube (online, 6 October 2018), https://www.youtube.com/watch?v=cYBc1gteoMs.
9. See Slavko Goldstein, *1941: The Year That Keeps Returning* (New York Review Books, 2013).
10. 'Reakcije posle presude Karadzicu: Ako je genocid, onda ubijaju zene i decu, a ja sam videla da ih spasavaju', *Novosti* (online, 24 March 2016), http://www.novosti.rs/vesti/naslovna/dosije/aktuelno.292.html:597162-REAKCIJE-POSLE-PRESUDE-KARADzICU-Biljana-Plavsic-Ako-je-genocid-onda-ubijaju-zene-i-decu-a-ja-sam-videla-da-ih-spasavaju.
11. Marcus Tanner, 'Foreign Office to welcome Serbian 'Nazi'', *The Independent*, 28 June 1997.

EPILOGUE

1. A well-established Serbian journalist and writer who runs his own weekly panel and one-on-one shows on a local Belgrade TV station.

2. See, Elif Shafak, *There Are Rivers in the Sky* (Penguin Random House, 2024), 364.
3. Philippe Sands, *The Ratline: Love, Lies and Justice on the Trail of a Nazi Fugitive* (Weidenfeld and Nicolson, 2020), 330.
4. Philippe Sands, *38 Londres Street: On Impunity, Pinochet in England and a Nazi in Patagonia* (Weidenfeld and Nicolson, 2025), 15.
5. 'Trump's plan for "ethnic cleansing" in Gaza is illegal, say UN investigator', *Politico*, https://www.politico.eu/article/trumps-plan-to-ethnically-cleanse-gaza-is-illegal-says-un-backed-judge/; Shweta Sharma and Tom Watling, 'Arab world rejects Trump's plan for US to "take over" Gaza and relocate Palestinians', *The Independent*, 5 February 2025, https://www.independent.co.uk/news/world/middle-east/trump-gaza-palestinians-saudi-arabia-egypt-jordan-b2692520.html.
6. 'Italy's far-right leader Giorgia Meloni forms new government', *NBC News*, 22 October 2022, https://www.nbcnews.com/news/world/italy-far-right-leader-giorgia-meloni-new-government-fascist-roots-rcna53453.
7. See Eviane Leidig, *The Women of the Far Right: Social Media Influencers and Online Radicalization* (Columbia University Press, 2023); Tim Hume and Isa Tejera, "Are Women the Far-Right's Trump Card?", *Vice*, 12 December 2022, https://www.vice.com/en/article/far-right-women-giorgia-meloni-marine-le-pen/.
8. See Olivera Simić, 'A War Criminal's Remorse: The Case of Landžo and Plavšić', *Human Rights Review* 21 (2020); Olivera Simić, 'Traumatised War Criminal? Documenting the Case of Esad Landžo', *International Criminal Justice Review* 32 (4) (2020).
9. Kjell Anderson, '"Who Was I to Stop the Killing?" Moral Neutralization among Rwadan Genocide Perpetrators', *Journal of Perpetrator Research* 1 (1) (2017).
10. Sarah Lyall, 'Murder, She Wrote', *The New York Times*, https://fpp.co.uk/Legal/Observer/Sereny/OOFAge220898.html.
11. Will Self, 'A Life of Crime: Interview', *The Independent*, 8 May 1999.
12. 'Dogged determination to understand evil', *The Sydney Morning Herald*, 20 June 2012.

13. Emina Melonic, 'Jessica Stern's denial of evil', *The Spectator*, 4 February 2020.
14. Pumla Gobodo-Madikizela, *A Human Being Died That Night: A Story of Forgivness* (Houghton Mifflin, 2003), 122.
15. Ibid., 123.
16. Emilie A. Caspar, 'Understanding Individual Motivations and Desistance: Interviews with Genocide Perpetrators from Rwanda and Cambodia', *Journal of Perpetrator Research* 6 (2) (2024).
17. See Slavenka Drakulić, *They Would Never Hurt a Fly* (Little Brown, 2003).
18. Uğur Ümit Üngör, 'Studying Mass Violence: Pitfalls, Problems, and Promises', *Genocide Studies and Prevention: An International Journal* (7) 1 (2012), 69.
19. Ibid., 71.

INDEX

Abdić, Fikret, 71
Aegon Insurance Building, 101
Al Fateh University, 61
Albanian Catholic, 128
Albright, Madeleine, 85, 89–90
Annan, Kofi, 110
Arendt, Hannah, 180, 190
Arkan, 69–70, 72
'Arkan's Tigers', 70–1
Arsić, Boban, 69
Ashkali, 21
Australia, 31, 33, 41, 58
Austria, 47–8
Austro-Hungarian Empires, 20
Axis powers, 50
Azra, 128

Balkan style, 33, 35
Banjac, Žarko, 61–2, 96, 120
Banjaluka, 14, 20, 23, 90, 98
Bari, 57
Baščaršija, 53, 93
Belgrade, 4, 5, 20, 24, 27, 30, 34, 41, 42, 43, 61, 71, 96, 113, 115, 119
'Bengal tiger', 112
Bijeljina, 69, 71–2
Bildt, Carl, 82, 145
'Biljana', 33
Biserko, Sonja, 27
Borger, Julian, 3
Bosanski Brod, 68
Bosnia and Herzegovina (BiH), 1, 2, 3, 8, 20–2, 41–2, 45, 57, 60, 64, 66, 71, 73–5, 85, 88–9, 92, 106, 127
Bosniaks (Bosnian Muslims), 20, 22, 55, 66, 81, 109, 116, 128
Bosnian Serb army, 37–8
Bosnian War (1992 to 1995), 1, 2, 6, 17, 21–2, 24, 30, 41, 46, 115
  Plavšić life during, 66–83
Boyce Thompson Institute for Plant Research, 57
Brčko, 22, 72

INDEX

Brđanin, 128–9
Brisbane, 25
Brown, Sara E., 16
Browning, Christopher, 15
Bugojno, 129

Čađo, Stanislav, 92
Canada, 46
Čapljina, 53, 66
Čengić, Goran, 109
Ćerimagić, Husnija, 109
Čerkez, Mario, 110–11
Chetniks, 51
Čivljak, Skender, 127–8
Communist Party of Yugoslavia, 49
Communist Party, 21, 48–9, 58–9, 165, 166
Cornell University, 2
COVID-19 pandemic, 12, 41
Croatia, 69
Croatian Democratic Party (HDZ), 63
Croats (Catholic Christians), 20, 22, 46, 51, 66, 73, 82, 116, 122
Czechoslovakia, 52

Davis, Lisa, 14–15
Dayton Peace Agreement, 21, 82, 84, 87, 88, 177, 179
Dayton, 80
de Kock, Eugene, 188
Del Ponte, Carla, 103–5, 122–3, 151–2
Dimsdale, Joel E., 17
Dionisije, 47–8

Djordjevich, Miroslav Michael, 134–5, 153
Dodik, Milorad, 88, 98–9, 129, 157, 159, 160
Drakulić, Slavenka, 65–6
Drina Corps, 106
Drina River valley, 47
Duga (tabloid), 63
Duhovni razgovori (Jerotić), 141
Dutch guard, 111–12

Eastern Bosnia, 114
Eastern Orthodox Christian churches, 48
Egyptians, 21
Electronic Microscopic Association of Yugoslavia, 60
Europe, 20, 21

Faculty of Natural Sciences and Mathematics, 57
Federal People's Republic of Yugoslavia, 48
Ferdinand, Archduke Franz, 52
Fulbright Fellowship, 57

Gavrilo, 53
Geneva Conventions (1949), 70
Germany, 47–8
Gobodo-Madikizela, Pumla, 187–8

The Hague, 1, 5, 34, 37, 46, 62, 72, 96, 98, 114–15, 127, 130
Half smiling, 109–10
Harman, Mark, 123

INDEX

Herzegovina, 50–1, 66
Hinseberg Prison, 130, 131
    facilities, 131
Hitler, Adolf, 7
Hollander, Ethan, 12
Hollis, Prosecutor Brenda, 96–7, 99
Human Rights Watch, 72, 87
Hungarians, 21

Independent State of Croatia (NDH), 21
International Committee of the Red Cross (ICRC), 5
International Criminal Tribunal for the former Yugoslavia (ICTY), 1, 4–5, 11, 13–14, 19, 24, 32, 34, 37, 69, 73–4, 81, 85, 122–3, 130
'Iron Lady', 24, 39
Ivanić, Mladen, 93
Izetbegović, Alija, 64, 179

Jahorina, 79
Jelisić, 114
Jews, 3, 21
Jovan, 52

Karadžić, Dr Radovan, 2–3, 9, 46, 82, 73–5, 84–6, 95–6, 116–17, 162, 165, 173, 187
Kelly, Douglas, 15
Klein, General Jacques Paul, 88–9, 98
Kljujić, Stjepan, 92–3
Koljević, Dr Nikola, 3, 63, 117

Konjic, 129
Kordić, Dario, 81–3
Kovačević, Zemir, 68
Krajišnik, Momčilo, 1, 3, 63, 97, 116–17
Krstić, General Radislav, 106

Landžo, Esad, 111, 183
Lazanski, Miroslav, 152
Leovac, Prof. Slavko, 63
Libya, 61
Livno, 50–1
Lokteff, Lana, 182
London, 57

Magrabija Street, 49
Mahovljani Airport, 98
Mahovljani, 99
Maramorosch, Karl, 51, 61
Marić, Milorad, 178
Marijin Dvor, 49–50
Marlboro, 34
'Mauzer', 71–2
McCarthy, Tara, 182
Meloni, Giorgia, 182
Mihajlović, Svetozar, 99
Miller, Thomas, 91–2
Milošević, Slobodan, 64, 79–80, 95–6, 112–14, 116–17
Mina, 55–6
Ministry of Justice of Sweden, 134
Mirjana, Aunt, 52
mixed marriages, 165–6
Mladić, Ratko, 82, 116–17, 127, 162–3, 165

INDEX

'Monster of Grbavica', 109
Muslims, 46, 64, 73, 81–2, 114, 122
My War Criminal: Personal Encounters with an Architect of Genocide (Stern), 9

Nazi Independent State of Croatia (NDH), 50
Nazis, 133, 143
Netherlands, 99
New York, 2, 57
Nice, Geoffrey, 113–14
Nikola (Niko), 52–3
NIN (weekly magazine), 119
Nordgren, Margaretha, 150, 151, 155–6
Nuremberg, 1, 117

Office of the Prosecutor (OTP), 5
Old Orthodox Church, 53
Omarska prison camp, 106
Ordinary Men (Browning), 15
Örebro, 46
Orić, Naser, 107, 170
Orthodox and Catholic Easter, 111
Orthodox Church of Saint Sava, 162
Ottoman Empires, 20, 53

Pančićeva omorika [Serbian spruce], 47
Party of Democratic Action (SDA), 63
Patriach Pavle, 122
Patriarch Pavle of Serbia, 145

Patriotic League, 66–7
Pavich, Bob, 169
Petrović, Vladimir, 3
Pinochet, Augusto, 134
Plavšić, Biljana, 1–18, 91–2, 114–15
  academic career, 56–62
  Bosnian War, during, 66–83
  detention, 105–15
  early stage, 22–3
  family, 47–56
  guilty, 120–30
  Indictment, responding to, 115–20
  meetings with, 30–41
  political career, 62–6
  President, becoming, 83–90
  tribunal, 91–8
  See also Bosnia and Herzegovina (BiH); The Hague; Serbs (Orthodox Christians)
Plavšić, Biljana, in Hinseberg prison
  Belgrade apartment, 132
  book reading, 140–2
  descriptions of her jail environment, 132–3
  early release, 156–7
  Holy Communion request, 144
  interview with Nordgren, 155–6
  interview, 150–1
  journalists visits, 152–5
  Lazanski visit, 152
  left her prison cell, 159

letter to Ministry of Justice of
   Sweden, 134, 135–40
mentioned Speer, 142, 143
plea agreement, 152
positivity, 149–50
prison management, 133–4
on prison population, 132–3
requests for signature, 145–7
Swedish prison management,
   143–4, 149
visitors, 145
Plavšić, Biljana, out of jail
   Banjaluka visit (2010), 164
   on Bosnian Muslim
      population, 165–6
   daily routine, 162, 163
   diagnosed with COVID-19,
      164
   illegality of the Tribunal,
      169–71
   intention to write a third book,
      171–2
   interviews, 164–5
   invitations for interviews, 178
   on Karadžić's judgement, 173,
      177–8
   on Mladić, 162–3
   on ethnic cleansing, 168–9
   in people minds, 176–7
   on political re-entry, 167
   racial view of Bosnian
      Muslims, 173
   reconciliation possibility,
      Serbs-Croats-Bosniaks,
      177
   release of, 159–60

on remorse for policies and
   actions, 178–9
respect and admiration for,
   163–4
Serbian police protection,
   161–2
settled in Belgrade, 160–1
statement to journalists, 160
Ponte, Carla Del, 34
Pozderac, Hamdija, 60
Prague, 57
Prcać, Drago, 113, 114
Prcać, Dragoljub, 106, 110
Predrag, 168
Prica, Miloš, 134, 135
Princip, Gavrilo, 52–3
proto-clerical fascism, 180

Rafailović (priest), 145
Rašković, Dr Jovan, 63
Ražnatović, Željko, 69
Red Cross, 142
Republic of Yugoslavia, 21
Republika Srpska, 1, 3, 6, 19–20,
   26, 38, 65, 73, 78, 81, 86
Roma, 21
Royal Swedish Academy of
   Science, 147

Sands, Philippe, 180
Sarajevo High School, 45
Sarajevo Museum, 47
Sarajevo, 20, 24, 36, 45, 51, 53,
   56, 61, 91
   Bosnian War, Plavšić life
      during, 66–83

INDEX

Savić, Ljubiša, 71
Scheveningen Prison, 99, 105
Scheveningen, 1, 101, 111
Secretary-General of the United Nations, 110
Serb Democratic Party (SDS), 63, 83
Serb People's Alliance Party, 86
Serbia, 4, 5, 22, 49–51, 87
'Serbian Iron Lady', 3, 26
Serbian Orthodox Church, 48
Serbian Volunteer Guard, 69, 70–1
Serbs (Orthodox Christians), 20, 22, 64, 66, 73, 82
   committed crimes, 175–6
   crimes against, 175
Sereny, Gitta, 186, 187
Shakespeare, Yugoslav, 3
Sijekovac, 68
Simić, Krstan, 96, 99, 103
Skenderija Cultural and Sports Centre, 63
Slankamen, 79
Slavonska Požega detention camp, 50
Smeulers, Alette, 3
Socialist Federative Republic of Yugoslavia (SFRY), 21
Sophie Duchess von Hohenberg, 52
Southern, Lauren, 182
Speer, Albert, 7, 142, 143, 187
Srebrenica, 9
Stabilisation Force (SFOR), 84
Stangl, Franz, 7

Stern, Jessica, 9, 187
Stover, Eric, 131
Svetislav, 45, 47–8
Sweden, 6, 24, 40, 46, 130

Terezín fortress, 52
Thatcher, Margaret, 2
Tiger, Alan, 123
'Tigers', 69
Tijanić, Aleksandar, 112
Tito, 55–6, 165
Tokyo, 1, 117
Tolimir, General Zdravko, 37–8, 92
Treblinka, 7
Tripoli, 61
Trojeručica, Bogorodica, 102–3
Trump, Donald, 181
Tuzla, 45

Üngör, Uğur Ümit, 191
United Nations Protection Force (UNPROFOR), 5, 92–3, 98
University of Sarajevo, 2, 56, 59, 63–4, 190
USA (United States), 51, 57, 63
Ustaša, 40, 50–4

Vi (magazine), 150
Vienna, 47
Vladika, Bishop, 145
Vlahović, Veselin, 109

Waller, James, 18
Westendorp, Carlos, 89

INDEX

Witness, The (Stover), 131
World War I, 51–2
World War II, 1, 21, 40, 49, 51, 53, 56, 64, 167, 168, 173, 175

Young Bosnia Movement, 52
Yugoslav People's Army, 66, 92

Yugoslavia, 10, 20, 25, 45, 48, 55–7, 63, 66, 73–4, 109

Zagreb, 36, 56, 61
Zdravko, 45
Zenica, 129
Živana, 45–6